Massacre at Passchendaele

The New Zealand Story

Massacre at Passchendaele

The New Zealand Story

Foreword by the Governor General,
Sir Michael Hardie Boys

FIRESTEP
Books

To the New Zealand soldiers of 1917 who remain
in the Ypres Salient.
Not Forgotten

First published in hardback 2000
Paperback edition first published 2000
2nd Revised Edition 2011

Published by FireStep Books, an imprint
of FireStep Publishing in 2011

Set in 11pt Sabon
ISBN is 978-1-908487-03-2

CONTENTS

Acknowledgements

My first thanks go to my daughters, Natalie and Rhiannon. Having a writer in the family is never easy, and without their unstinting support this book would never have been written.

I am greatly indebted to the staff of the research institutions from where the bulk of the book's material has been drawn. In particular I wish to thank the staff of the Alexander Turnbull Library in Wellington, the National Archives, also in Wellington, and the archive section of the Queen Elizabeth II Army Memorial Museum located at Waiouru.

I received invaluable help and advice from Chris Pugsley, who is only too happy to share his intimate knowledge of New Zealand's efforts in the Great War with others. Paul Lumsden produced the excellent maps. Joel Hayward, Paul Lumsden, Roger Mortlock and Piers Reid read drafts of the book and made many useful suggestions for its improvement.

The staff at the Queen Elizabeth II Army Memorial Museum, particularly Windsor Jones, were very helpful in providing most of the illustrations, including those for the cover.

I wish to thank Ian Watt and Sue Page of HarperCollins for their patience, support and encouragement during the course of this project.

I am grateful to the Commonwealth War Graves Commission for supplying the information on New Zealand graves in the Ypres Salient and for allowing me to publish the details in this book.

FOREWORD

Decades after the First World War, it remains nearly impossible to read about the experience of New Zealand soldiers in that conflict without feeling bewildered and angry: bewildered that the Imperial High Command seemed so determined to persist in the face of catastrophe; outraged that thousands upon thousands of New Zealand soldiers' lives were sacrificed, on so many occasions for a fleeting military advantage only, or for none at all.

Much of the war's conduct resulted in appalling casualty lists. Many small New Zealand towns lost a high percentage of all their young men. The aftermath of Gallipoli shocked the country. France was even bloodier. We came to understand that war was not, as we had once thought, an endeavour that had any glory in it. We came to understand, too, that even should armed conflict become necessary, it would inevitably be an evil experience, for combatants and non-combatants alike.

More than eight decades afterwards, New Zealanders of the early 21st century will have the great benefit of hindsight to judge the conduct of the First World War. Like the New Zealanders of the time, we can acknowledge that First World War military commanders were confronted with an enormous military problem — the immense defensive strength of dug-in or emplaced machine-gunners who were able, usually, to massacre infantrymen who were conventionally deployed. The Allied commanders learned, in time, that infantry assaults had to be supported by massed and coordinated artillery barrages, and that their tactical objectives should be realistic. But while they learned, they continued to expend thousands of the lives entrusted to them.

Massacre at Passchendaele is a short work: the 1917 offensive in Flanders was not as drawn out as some other campaigns in the war.

The length of the casualty list that follows the text, however, attests to the scale of the battles — page after page of names of men who would have been our countrymen and neighbours when alive in the years 1914 to 1918. Those sons, brothers, husbands, fathers vanished, never to make a normal contribution to the life of this country, their voices never to be heard.

I commend Glyn Harper's history to all those who wish to reclaim knowledge of an important event in New Zealanders; First World War experience. His book recounts an almost-forgotten tale, and reminds us why New Zealanders, ever since those black years, have been so wary of military entanglement.

The Right Honourable Sir Michael Hardie Boys GNZM, GCMG
Governor-General and Commander-in-Chief in and over New Zealand

Introduction

AN UNTOLD STORY

If you take the Zonnebeke road north of the Belgian town of Ieper (Ypres) and turn left at the major crossroads of the Passchendaele–Broodseinde road, after a kilometre you come across the Tyne Cot Cemetery. One of 174 British military cemeteries in the Ypres Salient for fallen soldiers from the First World War, Tyne Cot is a special place. It is the largest British military cemetery in Europe, containing 11,956 graves, 8,366 of them unnamed, and covering almost 36,000 square yards.[1] Located at this hauntingly beautiful resting place is a graceful wall: the Tyne Cot Memorial to the Missing. Fourteen feet high and some 500 feet long, this memorial wall bears the names of 35,000 men who fell in battle near here and who have no known grave. The list appears endless and is a powerful reminder of the tragic cost of war. While the missing from the Dominion armies are engraved on the Menin Gate at Ieper, the central apse of the wall is the New Zealand memorial, dedicated to New Zealand's soldiers who fell in two battles in October 1917 and whose bodies were never found. One thousand one hundred and seventy-nine names are recorded here.

Sir Philip Gibbs, a distinguished historian and a war correspondent in France from 1916 to 1918, wrote that: 'nothing that has been written is more than the pale image of the abomination of those battle-fields, and that no pen or brush has yet achieved the picture of that Armageddon in which so many of our men perished'.[2] The Armageddon to which Sir Philip Gibbs was referring was the Third Battle of Ypres, in particular the struggle for the heights of the Passchendaele Ridge in the battle's last phases. Sir Philip recognised the failure of words, no matter how powerful or how vivid, to record an event and experience that was in many ways unrecordable. Yet the historian of this particular battle must try to explain what happened and seek explanations for why things turned out as they did. The historian also aims to preserve the experiences of those caught up in this terrible battle, a battle which has came to epitomise the tragedy and suffering of all who were drawn into the Great War of 1914–1918. The experiences of those who fought at Passchendaele, and other battles like it, are central to the history of the nations that took part in the war, and they should not be forgotten. Unfortunately, most New Zealanders remain ignorant of this pivotal event in their country's history, which only adds to the tragedy.

This is the story of the New Zealand attacks at Passchendaele, one of which remains New Zealand's worst military blunder and the greatest disaster of any kind to strike this small and vulnerable nation. At Passchendaele in October 1917, the New Zealand Division took part in two great attacks. The first, on 4 October 1917, was a stunning success although costly in terms of casualties. The other, on 12 October, should never have gone ahead in the conditions then prevailing, and saw more New Zealanders killed or maimed in a few short hours than has occurred on any other day since the beginning of European settlement. Though Passchendaele would eventually be claimed as a victory for the Commonwealth forces involved, no victory was more hollow.

While Passchendaele, a tragedy without equal in New Zealand history, remains unknown to most New Zealanders, the name of that disaster 'has evoked more horror and loathing than any other battle-name' in the United Kingdom, according to the British historian John Terraine.[3] Mention Passchendaele in Britain or in Canada and the reaction, usually negative, is instant. For New Zealand, though, Passchendaele is truly an untold story.

It wasn't always so. On the day of the second New Zealand attack at Passchendaele, a New Zealand Sergeant, W.K. Wilson, recorded in his diary:

> Black Friday 12 [Oct.] A day that will long be remembered by New Zealanders. Our boys and the Aussies went over at 5.30 and got practically cut to pieces . . . This is the biggest 'slap up' the NZers have had. Far worse than the Somme I believe.[4]

And at a meeting of the Imperial War Cabinet in London in June 1918, an angry New Zealand Prime Minister, William Massey, berated his British counterpart, Lloyd George:

I was told last night by a reliable man — a man I knew years before he joined the Army — that the New Zealanders (he was one of them) were asked to do the impossible. He said they were sent to Passchendaele, to a swampy locality where it was almost impossible to walk and where they found themselves up against particularly strong wire entanglements which it was impossible for them to cut. They were, he said, simply shot down like rabbits. These are the sort of things that are going to lead to serious trouble.[5]

Yet since 1918, this battle has sadly been all but confined to the scrap heap of New Zealand history.

Passchendaele should, however, be much more than an unfamiliar name on a war memorial. In fact, one New Zealand historian has gone so far as to claim that, because of the large number of casualties with its subsequent impact on the New Zealand Division, Passchendaele 'must be considered the most important event in New Zealand military history'.[6] While not going to this extreme (similar claims have been made about Gallipoli, Crete and Cassino), it is indisputable that for New Zealand the experience of the battles at Passchendaele was an especially significant one. As has been written of Passchendaele in a recent history of the Great War: 'No British, Australian or Canadian chronicle of the war would be complete without an account of what took place there. For even more than the Somme, Passchendaele symbolises the futility of trench warfare.'[7] This is also especially true for New Zealand. Passchendaele deserves to be, and should become, as Sergeant Wilson believed it would back in October 1917, an experience 'that will long be remembered by New Zealanders'.

This book aims to tell the story of this New Zealand tragedy. It does so by using, as much as possible, the words of those who took part. It will examine in some detail the two New Zealand attacks made at Passchendaele in October 1917 and explain why their outcomes were so radically different. The book will then examine the impact of the disaster on New Zealand society, an impact that resonates to this day. The book will also try to offer some explanation of why the Passchendaele experience has been largely forgotten or ignored by New Zealanders. In writing this book, I hope Passchendaele will remain an untold story no longer.

Chapter 1

THE MILITARY BACKGROUND

No historical event exists in isolation. Before one can fully understand what happened at Passchendaele in October 1917, it is necessary to have an overview of how the war had unfolded up to that time.

In September 1914, the British and French armies finally succeeded in halting the advancing Germans at the Battle of the Marne. Both sides then became locked in and behind their trench systems, which stretched from the Belgian coast to the Swiss border — about 350 miles. There they would remain for most of the war. The length of those trenches, some 25,000 miles, cannot be imagined today, but for the soldiers of the war they provided a stark reality, prompting one influential writer to describe them as a 'troglodyte world'.[1]

After its defeat on the Marne, Germany adopted the strategy of remaining on the defensive on the western front while doing all in her power on the eastern front to knock Russia out of the war. This presented Britain and France with a tactical dilemma which they remained unable to solve until the last year of the war. The front-line trenches of the west could not be turned from either flank; diversions elsewhere, such as the Dardanelles expedition in 1915, served only to dissipate strength; and amphibious operations, being in their infancy, were not trusted to produce the desired result. This left only the prospect of full-scale frontal assaults on the enemy entrenchments, which would, it was hoped, eventually crack open the enemy front lines and allow a return to the more mobile and open type of warfare favoured by the Allies. In an attempt to transform the western front from siege to open warfare, the British and French mounted a number of large set-piece battles, all of which resulted in heavy casualties but only extremely limited gains on the ground. These efforts reached their climax in 1917, which for the Allies would prove the worst year of the war. The slaughter became so bad that 1917 was described by one influential writer as a 'carnival of death'.[2]

In July 1917, prior to the start of the great offensive in Flanders, the northern-most region, the 20 miles from the coast to the town of Boesinghe, was held by the British Fourth Army and a combined French–Belgian army. The next 90 miles, from Ypres to the River Ancre, were held by the four other British (including Dominion) armies, with the French holding the southern portion of the line to the Swiss frontier. The British section of the line comprised two main sectors: the Ypres Salient in Flanders and the Somme area in Picardy. In 1916, the British had made their main effort to break through the German front lines at the Somme. The results had been disastrous. The opening day of the attack had set an unenviable twentieth century record for the most men killed and wounded in a single day. In 1917, despite this being a year of almost continuous activity along the whole of the British line, the main effort would fall in the north centred around the Ypres Salient in Flanders.

When deciding to launch a major offensive in Flanders in 1917, the British high command aimed for a great strategic victory — the type of victory that so far had eluded both sides. Above all, British commanders hoped that victory here would lead to the end of the war. They had good reasons for launching a large offensive in Flanders. They had not done so before (the two previous battles of Ypres having been defensive for the British), and Field Marshal Sir Douglas Haig had long harboured the desire to launch a major attack from the region. As Trevor Wilson has commented, 'no aura of past failure hung over an attack here'.[3] Field Marshal Haig and his staff hoped, by breaking through the German defences in Flanders, to secure the channel ports and the whole Belgian coastline, break out of the Ypres Salient, which had imprisoned the defenders since 1914, and then strike at the Germans' extended right flank, possibly carrying the British armies into the Ruhr, Germany's industrial heartland. Any large offensive by the British armies in Flanders would also divert German forces from the French army, now demoralised and mutinous after the costly failure of the Nivelle offensive in April 1917. The great victory now to be won was to be primarily a British army affair; it was to be their moment of glory.

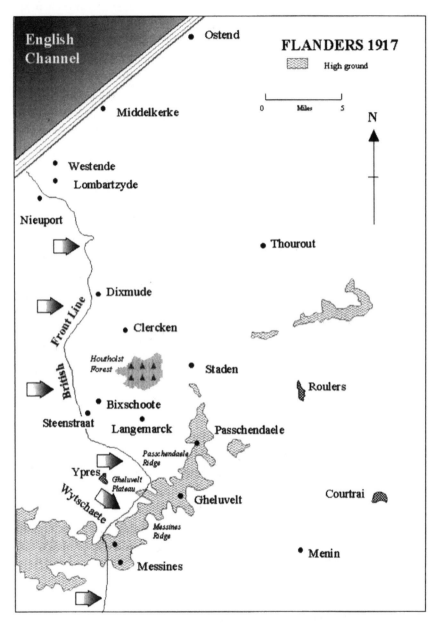

Flanders, the Ypres Salient and the Passchendaele Ridge, prior to the British offensives of 1917.

Such sweeping movements of troops looked easy on paper, and Haig felt confident of success. The 'fundamental object' of the attacks made after Messines, he explained in a memorandum on 30 June, was 'the defeat of the German Army', which would only be achieved after 'very hard fighting lasting perhaps for weeks'.[4] What became evident as the great battles unfolded was that the strategic victory for which the British had planned was soon forgotten. Once all hope of this type of victory had faded after 31 July 1917, the aim of the campaign became to inflict more casualties on the Germans than their own armies were suffering, and to secure the best position from which to renew the attritional struggle in the campaigning season of 1918. Though initially aiming to achieve a decisive breakthrough, Haig all too willingly settled for more dead and wounded Germans than dead and wounded Allied soldiers.

While Haig planned for a great strategic victory, there were pressing tactical reasons for striking from Ypres. The British line in the Ypres Salient was 'tactically about as bad as it could be',[5] with the British positions being overlooked from three directions — north, east and south. This meant 'no part of the Salient was safe from the enemy's guns, which searched our trenches with all the advantages of direct observation'.[6] The first stage of any great victory here had to be to eject the Germans from their present positions on the heights overlooking the town of Ypres. This would provide a tactical victory upon which an even greater victory could be launched.

To achieve this major triumph, two separate British armies were crammed into the Ypres Salient. They were the Second Army, commanded by General Sir Herbert Plumer, and the Fifth Army, under General Sir Hubert Gough. All told a total of thirty-five divisions would fight in this campaign, seventeen of them in the opening thrust. With so much committed to the offensive in terms of men and firepower, Haig and his commanders felt confident of success. Yet the German commanders, especially Field Marshal Ludendorff and the Bavarian Crown Prince Rupprecht, were prepared. They knew the British were planning to strike another large blow against them and felt certain it would be made somewhere in Flanders. Most divisions now being released from the eastern front were accordingly allocated to the Flanders region, and further reinforcements were moved to Flanders by thinning the front opposite the French army. Ludendorff and the Crown Prince, however, did not know — and did not learn until the second week of June 1917 — that the attack would be made from the Ypres Salient. The successful attack at Messines in early June, in which the New Zealand Division played a leading role, captured the vital Messines–Wytschaete portion of the ridge. After this it became impossible for the British to achieve surprise as to the location and direction of their next offensive — not that they bothered to try. On the basis of the build-up that could be readily observed by the Germans, and from their intelligence assessments, the Crown Prince and his Fourth Army headquarters agreed that the next British offensive must be made in the Ypres Salient. As well as strengthening his front with the additional divisions now available to him, from mid-June Rupprecht accelerated the construction of the concrete pillbox fortifications, thereby adding considerable depth to the Ypres frontage. As Winston Churchill commented in his history of this war:

> . . . the positions to be assaulted were immensely strong. The enemy was fully prepared. The frowning undulations of the Passchendaele–Klercken ridge had been fortified with every resource of German science and ingenuity.[7]

The British possessed several advantages in the Flanders offensive of 1917, but surprise, now considered so important it has been elevated to a principle of war, was not one of them.

The climate and terrain of the Flanders region had a major influence on the outcome of the campaign and must be examined in detail.

The Ypres Salient was 14 miles long and three miles at its widest point. As it formed a large bulge in the front line, every part of it lay exposed to the concentrated artillery fire of the Germans on the high ground to the north. Striking from three sides, the artillery made the Salient one of the most shelled spots on earth. In this deathtrap, the British, without taking any offensive action whatsoever, suffered casualties at the rate of 7,000 a week. By the end of the war the town of Ypres had been totally destroyed and became one of the enduring symbols in English literature of the destructiveness and inhumanity of the twentieth century. One New Zealand soldier reflected on marching up the line:

> A short march of three miles brought us to historic Ypres. What a

pitiful sight is a beautiful city in ruins! Everywhere the streets were lined with heaps of broken masonry and bricks. Not one house had escaped the smashing shell. On the left was a twisted mass of steel rails and the battered gaunt skeleton of a large building — all that was left of the Railway Yards and Station . . . Before us were the ruins of the Cloth Hall and the Cathedral. From the many pictures taken of this particular scene the sight appeared quite familiar to us. The battered tower still stood erect from amid the broken mass that once represented one of the architectural glories of the world.[8]

Something else immediately impressed itself on the senses of those moving into the Salient: the overpowering smell of death and decay. Dead men and horses were often not buried for months, so 'the stench of rotten flesh was over everything'.[9] Marching towards the front at Ypres, soldiers could smell it while still miles away.

With constant enemy shelling from three sides, so much physical destruction and the all-pervading stench of death, it is little wonder soldiers hated serving in the Ypres Salient, and that some were driven mad while doing so.

Two words provide an accurate description of much of Flanders: wet and flat. The Passchendaele soil is wet, dense clay, impervious to water and permitting no natural drainage. Rain water tends to lie on the surface of the ground, forming stagnant swamps and ponds if there is no artificial drainage. Furthermore, because Flanders is close to sea level, the region has an exceptionally high water table — on average only 14 inches from the surface even in summer. This can only be controlled by a complicated series of canals and ditches, which crisscrosses the region. While Belgium is largely flat, a low ridge curls round Ypres 'like a giant pruning hook'.[10] 'Ridge' is something of a misleading term for Australians and New Zealanders — it is really only a stretch of terrain slightly higher than the surrounding land.

Passchendaele was a tiny village on the crest of the highest part of the ridge, five miles east of Ypres. In 1917 it was a deserted ruin. The ridge there rises some 70 yards over several miles, an almost imperceptible elevation. It is the last high ground before open country, making it a vital piece of territory to any army operating in the region.

The terrain around the Ypres Salient therefore placed the British armies at a great tactical disadvantage, because all the high ground, - including the Passchendaele Ridge, lay in German hands. The Germans had good observation over nearly all of the battlefield, and, equally significant, the advancing British infantry would have to battle uphill if they were ever to eject the Germans from the heights. The German positions were also relatively dry, while the British front lines were waterlogged and extremely uncomfortable.

The Germans knew the great value of the ridge, and their defences were formidable. Because the high water table mitigated against the digging of deep trench systems as they had used in the Somme, the Germans constructed hundreds of pillboxes — low, squat concrete shelters many feet thick. Each pillbox was in fact a miniature fortress that could garrison between ten and fifty men. The advantage of these 'field fortresses', as the British press called them, was that they made small targets, on average no larger than 81 square feet, so were difficult for the artillery to observe. Their design, with overhead cover as much as 6 feet thick and with elastic cushions of steel rails and air, meant they were impervious to field artillery and could only be destroyed by a direct hit from a heavy-calibre gun of at least 8 inches. The pillboxes were so well camouflaged it was often difficult to detect them from ground level until almost right on top of them. The Germans had used thousands of them to fortify the Ypres positions into six separate zones of defence. As long as a number remained intact and were able to offer protection to their neighbours, thus preventing the enemy from outflanking them, their positions remained impervious to infantry assault.

The British were also very unlucky in that the weather of 1917 could not have been worse, with heavy rain and snow, a late, brief spring and no summer to speak of. As Colonel Charles Repington recorded in his diary: '1 April. Heavy fall of snow this morning. This winter seems endless.'[11] From July onward, rainfall was the heaviest in seventy-five years. In October, the month of the two New Zealand attacks, 4.5 inches of rain fell, compared with just over an inch in 1914 and 1915, and 2.75 inches in 1916. There were only five days in the month when it didn't rain, and it rained during both New Zealand attacks. By 1917, Flanders' drainage systems had been long destroyed by the millions of artillery shells that had fallen in the region, and the ground was a quagmire.

With all these factors — vital high ground held by the enemy and protected by such formidable defences, the going underfoot so glutinous and Belgium's wettest and coldest winter in seventy-five years looming — it is little wonder that, after the British offensive had begun, German warlord Paul von Hindenburg recalled:

> I had a certain feeling of satisfaction when this new battle began, in spite of the extraordinary difficulties it involved for our situation on the Western Front . . . It was with a feeling of absolute longing that we waited for the beginning of the wet season. As previous experience had taught us, great stretches of the Flemish flats would then become impassable, and even in firmer places the new shell holes would fill so quickly with ground water that men seeking shelter in them would find themselves faced with the alternative, 'Shall we drown or get out of this hole?' This battle, too, must finally stick in the mud, even though English stubbornness kept it up longer than otherwise.[12]

With all these disadvantages so obvious with the benefit of hindsight, did the British armies have anything going for them? Was there anything in their favour that could have made up for such tremendous disadvantages? Surprisingly, the answer is 'Yes'.

Contrary to popular notions, Allied commanders during the Great War did learn from their costly mistakes and adjusted their tactics accordingly.[13] It had become evident from 1915 that success in land warfare now depended on the correct use of artillery. That is, artillery had to be present in large quantities and its fire carefully directed to where it could do most damage to the enemy and provide the best protection for the infantry. New artillery techniques evolved as gunners, for the first time in the war, developed the principles of scientific gunnery. The creeping barrage had been largely perfected by the end of 1916 as the Allied gunners, with better-quality shells and more of them, honed their skills to a fine edge. A creeping barrage was a wall of exploding shells that moved ahead of advancing infantry, obscuring their presence and keeping the defenders' heads down. Another development was the standing barrage, a wall of artillery fire directed in front of existing infantry positions to provide them with protection. A third, equally important development in the scientific use of artillery was counterbattery fire, using the techniques of sound-ranging and flash-spotting. This involved detecting enemy artillery batteries by the sound of gunfire or the muzzle flash and then directing huge concentrations of one's own artillery fire onto that location. Through a process of trial and error, both techniques were proving very successful by 1917.

Protection for the infantry usually came from the supporting field artillery, which provided creeping barrages, smashed barbed wire and other obstacles and broke up German counterattacks. Field artillery's main weakness was a limited effective range of about 6,000 yards.

To provide maximum protection, it was vitally important that the final objective to be reached by the infantry was well within the range of their supporting guns. This simple requirement, as the battle of Arras testifies, had not always been observed — the direct cause of many British failures. Two further conditions needed to be fulfilled: there had to be time to carry out the detailed planning required for each operation, and good weather to enable the infantry to advance steadily under the direct observation of the artillery. By the end of July 1917, the British armies were running short on both counts.

Infantry tactics had also been modified as a result of the slaughter on the Somme in 1916. Infantry units now advanced across no-man's-land in smaller, nonlinear columns with emphasis on the technique of fire and manoeuvre. The units retained some of their strength to mop up pockets of resistance, or as a tactical reserve to plug weak points or reinforce success. Infantry units also trained with the artillery and now appreciated that their own chances of success and survival were vitally dependent on the skill and cooperation of the artillerymen. Infantrymen knew that without effective artillery protection they could not hope to move beyond the confines of their trenches without suffering massive casualties.

The success of improved British artillery and infantry tactics forced the Germans to experiment with an elastic system of defence, whereby troops were reduced in the forward areas but now lay in considerable depth, and with reserves close at hand for counterattacks. The first line of defence was in reality an outpost zone designed to cushion the shock of the initial assault and allow reserves to deal more easily with attacking troops in a deeper battle zone immediately beyond the front line. These tactics soon became evident to the British, who adjusted their tactics accordingly. As Haig explained to General Plumer on 10 May:

> I called his attention to the new German system of defence. The enemy now fight not in, but for his first position. He uses

considerable forces for counter-attacks. Our guns should therefore be registered beforehand to deal with these latter. Our objective is now to capture and consolidate up to the range of our guns, and at once to push on advanced guards to profit by the enemy's demoralisation after the bombardment.[14]

The Germans also began using obstacles, including wire entanglements and blockhouses of ferroconcrete (i.e. pillboxes). Both of these were used in abundance at Passchendaele in 1917, and had a major influence on the outcome of the New Zealand attacks there.

Two British offensives commenced in Flanders in 1917: Messines in early June, which captured the vital Messines–Wytschaete portion of the ridge, followed, after a long, fateful gap of six weeks, by the Third Battle of Ypres, lasting from July to November. The New Zealand Division played a leading role in the outstanding success of Messines, but its involvement in Third Ypres (sometimes known just as the Battle of Passchendaele) was limited to just two battles among the eight separate offensives launched. The eight battles of Third Ypres were:

> Pilckem Ridge (31 July–2 August)
> Langemarck (16–18 August)
> Menin Road (20–25 September)
> Polygon Wood (26 September–3 October)
> Broodseinde (4 October)
> Poelcappelle (9 October)
> First Passchendaele (12 October)
> Second Passchendaele (26 October–10 November)

While the New Zealand Division fought in only Broodseinde and First Passchendaele, a brief account of each of the preceding battles provides essential background to its involvement.

The campaign began with a mixed success. The attack of 31 July aimed to take 4,000 to 5,000 yards of territory in four stages to a line running from Polygon Wood through to Broodseinde and Langemarck. This was far too ambitious, as most of the Fifth Army attacks under the aggressive, impetuous, reckless cavalryman Hubert Gough proved. The preliminary bombardment began on 16 July, and for fifteen days the German positions suffered under more than 3,000 British guns of all calibres, 1,000 of them classified as 'heavy'. This was a ratio of one gun to every six yards of the front line,[15] and about 4.75 tons of high explosive ammunition to every yard of front.[16] Over four million shells together weighing more than 100,000 tons fell on the enemy positions, and in the reclaimed bog land of the Ypres Salient it created a formidable obstacle for the attacking troops. The Germans' front-line positions were destroyed, but the pillboxes just beyond remained intact because rain and heavy wind made it impossible to use aerial-spotting or sound-ranging to detect them. The attack, made by seventeen divisions totalling more than 100,000 troops over a 15-mile front, did not reach its final objective, but Pilckem Ridge fell and the advance reached the Steenbeek stream. All told, an advance of some 3,000 yards took place, but on the right (to the south), the advance reached only 1,000 yards. Casualties were heavy — some 31,000. The Battle of Pilckem Ridge managed to wrest 18 square miles of ground and two defensive lines from the Germans, but did not touch the main German defensive line. No ridges were taken, and none of the vital high ground of the the Gheluvelt Plateau to the south was touched. Haig pointed out this important deficiency to Gough on 2 August and directed him to deal with it in the next attack:

> I showed him on my relief map the importance of the Broodseinde–Passchendaele Ridge, and gave it as my opinion that his main effort must be devoted to capturing that. Not until it was in his possession could he hope to advance his centre. He quite agreed.[17]

Haig also urged Gough to have patience and not to put in an infantry attack until there had been two or three days of good weather with a subsequent improvement in the state of the ground. Unfortunately, in August just over five inches of rain fell, almost double the monthly average. There were only three days in the whole month when it did not rain, but the operations continued as the British sought to take more ground.

In the next attack, the Battle of Langemarck, launched on 16 August, some ground was taken in the north, but nothing from the centre nor to the south. The Fifth Army's average advance was less than halfway towards the final objectives of the previous attack. There were another 15,000 casualties. Small attacks were made on 19, 22, 24, and 27 August. These served little purpose other than to wear out Gough's Fifth Army. Failures resulted from the rain and mud, the effects of which Gough tended to ignore. By the end of August, casualties had amounted to 67,000, with 10,000 killed in action.

While the British gained little ground, the August battles had a serious effect on German morale. General Ludendorff recalled later how they

> imposed a heavy strain on the western troops. In spite of all the concrete protection they seemed more or less powerless under the enormous weight of the enemy's artillery. At some points they no longer displayed the firmness which I, in common with the local commanders, had hoped for.[18]

The Fifth Army's spirit broke in these attacks, though, and of the twenty-two divisions used, fourteen had to be rebuilt. The main effort of the British now switched from the low ground to the ridges in the northeast, and to the Second Army commanded by General Herbert Charles Onslow Plumer. For the remainder of the campaign, the role allotted to Gough's shattered Fifth Army amounted to providing flank protection for the main effort made by Plumer.

For the first three weeks of September there was little activity as Plumer undertook careful preparations. One of the most competent British field commanders, he had developed a doctrine suited to conditions on the western front and to Flanders in particular. Reluctant to take over the main effort of the campaign, he insisted he be given the freedom of action necessary to implement the measures he felt would bring success. His conditions, characterised by one writer as 'extreme deliberation',[19] were:

- that the infantry must not be made to advance too far — 1,500 yards was regarded as a prudent total if conducted in several stages
- that the artillery must support the infantry at all stages and to a depth of 2,000 yards beyond the final objective
- that any attack had to be made on a wide front
- that attacks must not be rushed, but were to be well planned and allow ample time for the infantry to familiarise themselves with the terrain over which they were expected to advance.

Professor Trevor Wilson has written of the Plumer formula:

> Here, then, was a true alternative to Haig's Flanders plan. Rawlinson, after Neuve Chapelle in long ago 1915, had called it 'bite and hold'. It consisted of a series of set-piece operations whose extent and frequency would depend on the range and mobility of the artillery. The objective of any infantry attack must lie within the hitting limit of the guns. Once the objective had been taken, that phase of the operation would be over. As soon as the artillery could assume new positions and register upon fresh targets, another blow would be struck.[20]

By limiting the length of any advance made, the infantry would be immune from German counterattacks, which could be easily broken by the wall of protection provided by massed artillery fire.[21] For each attack Plumer also insisted on a greater concentration of force — both artillery and infantry — in pursuit of more modest objectives than had been allocated by Gough. To ensure he could do this Plumer received artillery and men from the other British armies, and he commenced operations on 20 September with twice the fire power, against half the length of front, that had been available to Gough. He also used his artillery carefully. His Chief of Staff, General Sir Charles Harington, later recalled that at Messines, Plumer

> knew so well how much depended on the artillery plan. He viewed that from the Infantry point of view. Whilst the infantry were training in back areas or on our model . . . he was perfecting the artillery arrangements. We actually carried out artillery and machine-gun rehearsals on the enemy.[22]

One of Plumer's guiding principles was that 'His Infantry were not going to be launched at uncut wire.' At Messines, his Second Army had had to cut through 280 miles of barbed wire, and he had used all his artillery to do this, thus paving the way for the successful infantry assault that followed.[23]

At Messines and during the battles of Third Ypres Plumer insisted on one further measure. He placed an Anzac corps (and later, two of them) at the centre of his attacking force, thereby allocating some of the key objectives to 'the most offensively minded' troops in the British armies.[24]

The Battle of Menin Road, which started on 20 September, saw the first of the Plumer attacks. The long delay between this and the previous attack led some German commanders to hope that this particular Battle of Flanders had run its course.[25] Unfortunately it still had a long way to go. After the British artillery had fired 1.5 million shells in a five-day preliminary bombardment, 65,000 men from eighteen brigades advanced from their forward positions. They moved behind five belts of protective fire, three of high explosive, one of shrapnel and one of machine-gun bullets, all fired to a depth of 1,000 yards. The objectives were easily taken. This battle is notable for several reasons. For the first time in history two Australians divisions fought side by side, the 1st and 2nd Australian Divisions now fighting as part of I ANZAC Corps. According to John Terraine, the battle was 'a model of forethought and precision',[26] a rarity for a western-front attack at this time. The artillery barrage worked extremely well and was the best of the war to date. 'The power of the attack,' Ludendorff later wrote, 'lay in the artillery, and the fact that ours did not do enough damage to the hostile infantry.'[27] Despite the Menin Road offensive being a success it still cost 21,000 casualties to secure 5.5 square miles and advance the British positions an average of 1,250 yards. Pouring rain and the boggy ground across which the infantry had to advance compounded the difficulties.

Polygon Wood was Plumer's next battle, starting on 26 September. This attack aimed to take the wood and Zonnebecke using a shallow advance of around 1,000 to 1,250 yards on a narrow front of 8,500 yards. Seven divisions participated, and, once more, two Australian divisions (the 5th and 4th) fought side by side. It was another success, with nearly all objectives taken, but yet again it was no easy effort and saw much hard fighting as the Germans launched nine counterattacks in an effort to recapture lost ground. The end result was 15,375 casualties and the capture of 3.5 square miles. Polygon Wood passed into British hands and the line advanced to the foot of the main ridge. Ahead lay Broodseinde and Passchendaele.

The two September victories had cost 36,000 casualties to advance some 2,750 yards. The British front line was still 4,500 yards away from Passchendaele, and with each successive battle, artillery support had grown progressively weaker. Yet the German Army was suffering heavily. General Ludendorff wrote after the last attack that

the 26th proved a day of heavy fighting, accompanied by every circumstance that could cause us loss. We might be able to stand the loss of ground, but the reduction of our fighting strength was again all the heavier. Once more we were involved in a terrific struggle in the West, and had to prepare for a continuation of the attack on many parts of the front.[28]

Haig had seen his plans for a great strategic victory evaporate, but he felt delighted by what Plumer had achieved in his two attacks. After three years of almost total disasters, Haig and his headquarters were electrified by two successive victories and believed they had achieved something significant. Haig convinced himself and those around him that the high ground of Passchendaele held the key to victory, that the German army was near collapse and that he was close to beginning the end of the war. Seizing the high ground, especially that of the Gheluvelt Plateau, would greatly accelerate the British victory. On the eve of the next big attack, Haig's views were expressed by his chief intelligence officer:

> Continued defeats, combined with the long duration of the war, has tended to lower the enemy's morale. The condition of certain hostile divisions was known to be bad. The time may come shortly when the enemy's troops will not stand up to repeated attacks, or when he may not have sufficient fresh troops immediately available to throw into battle. The enemy failed to take advantage of his opportunities on 31 October, 1914, and did not push forward when his repeated attacks had exhausted the British forces on the Ypres front. We must be careful not to make the same error. It was essential that we should be prepared and ready to exploit success on and after the 10th October, and that all the necessary means for this purpose should be at hand.[29]

Twice now Plumer's Second Army had broken clean through the German defence systems. Could they do it a third time? Clearly Haig, Plumer and others believed they could and felt the next attack should follow hard on the heels of the second. It had been noted by the commanders how effective the use of two Australian divisions side by side had been, so it was planned to repeat the formula in an attack on 4 October, but to double the dose. For the final push on to the Passchendaele Ridge, planned for execution in two more phases, there would be an injection of fresh Dominion troops. I Anzac Corps was sidestepped north to allow II Anzac Corps, consisting in part of the untried 3rd Australian Division and the experienced and well-regarded New Zealand Division, to move alongside.

At this stage in the war, the New Zealand Division had not experienced a military failure and, as a result, had a formidable reputation. The Corps Commander of I ANZAC wrote to the New Zealand Minister of Defence prior to this attack:

> I know well it will do as well as it always has done and that is saying a great deal, for I am not flattering when I say that no division in France has a higher reputation than yours.[30]

Before examining the two New Zealand attacks, a brief description of the command structure under which the New Zealanders would be fighting is in order. At the head of the British armies in France was the newly promoted Field Marshal Sir Douglas Haig. Haig's soldierly qualities included determination, industry and resolve, but he lacked imagination and humour and, according to one influential writer, his defects have convinced all intelligent people of today 'of the unredeemable defectiveness of all . . . military leaders'.[31] Yet Haig was not an uneducated soldier. Unlike his peers he had actually devoted considerable time to the study of warfare, and especially the study of military history. But a little knowledge indeed proved a dangerous thing. As General 'Boney' Fuller wrote of Haig's military education:

> Unlike so many cavalrymen of his day, he had studied war, and, strange to say, this was to his undoing, because he was so unimaginative that he could not see that the tactics of the past were as dead as mutton. We are told that he held that the 'role of the cavalry on the battlefield will always go on increasing', and that he believed bullets had 'little stopping power against the horse'. This was never true, as an intelligent glance at past battles would have made clear to him.[32]

From 1916 Haig had become convinced that the war could only be won on the western front and by the forces of the British Empire, with the French playing a subsidiary role. He believed the Flanders campaign of 1917 offered his best opportunity for victory. One thing he retained throughout those long months was an eternal optimism that the Germans were almost defeated and one further 'push' would do the trick. Fed intelligence reports by his senior intelligence officer, Brigadier General John Charteris, that bordered on sheer fantasy, Haig believed the German forces in the second half of 1917 were barely hanging on and were ready for the coup de grâce. The Germans certainly were suffering under the repeated attacks. Ludendorff recalled after the war: 'The fighting on the Western Front became more severe and costly than any the German Army had yet experienced.'[33] While few Allied commanders shared Haig's optimism, the attack of 4 October did provide reasonable grounds for encouragement.

Under Haig's command were fifty-five British and Dominion divisions organised into five armies. Of these, two fought at Third Ypres: the Fifth Army under General Sir Hubert Gough and the Second Army under Sir General Herbert Plumer. Plumer's unmilitary appearance and age — he was sixty in 1917 and his hair had turned completely white after two years in the Ypres Salient — disguised an astute military brain, one that recognised the importance of surprise and of the logistics needed to sustain a large military venture.

Within the Second Army for the attacks at Passchendaele were two Anzac corps, I Anzac commanded by General W.R. Birdwood and II Anzac commanded by General Sir Alexander Godley. Godley had done much to prepare the New Zealand army for war and had established a solid reputation as an administrator and trainer. He was also ambitious, aloof and undemonstrative. New Zealand soldiers hated him. As the popular and astute Birdwood wrote before the New Zealand attacks at Passchendaele, Godley was 'a good soldier, and I am sure means most extraordinarily well, but somehow or other, he does not seem able to command the affection of officers or men'.[34] Godley's unlikable character would provide the New Zealand soldiers of the time, and New Zealand historians ever after, with a convenient scapegoat for the disaster ahead.

The New Zealand Division, under Major General Andrew Russell, formed part of Godley's II Anzac Corps. Though born in New Zealand, Russell was a Sandhurst graduate with five years' service in the Indian army. Since 1892, he had been a sheep farmer in the Hawke's Bay region but had maintained his military knowledge and experience by serving in the Volunteers and Territorial Force. A perfectionist and workaholic, he established a solid reputation as a trainer, administrator and commander who set high standards and ensured they were reached. He was also ambitious and determined to produce the best division in France.[35] To achieve this he drove himself and his commanders extremely hard.

The New Zealand Division at this time was a most unusual military formation. From May 1917 until February 1918, it was a 'superheavy' division with sixteen battalions organised into four brigades, instead of the usual twelve battalions spread across three brigades. This structure had been imposed upon the New Zealand General Officer Commanding instead of New Zealand raising a second division. It proved an unpopular measure. Rather than the extra brigade acting as a kind of superreserve, it was usually sent away from the division and used as an additional pool of labour. Having an additional brigade also increased the likelihood that the division would be called upon more often than its lighter counterparts. The heavy losses experienced during the forthcoming operations greatly contributed to the short duration of the 'superheavy' experiment. In the long term such a formation proved impossible for New Zealand to sustain.

Preparations for Plumer's next attack were rushed. The British high command knew the current spell of good weather was not going to last and believed the Germans to be staggering under the weight of the British attacks and close to breaking point. For the Germans, October 1917 would be 'one of the hardest months of the war'.[36] The New Zealand Division, out of the front line since the attack at Messines in June, was about to go 'over the top' again. It, too, was about to experience its toughest month of the war.

Chapter 2

SUCCESS: 4 OCTOBER

On 24 September 1917, the New Zealand Division was ordered to move to the Ypres battle area. This meant a six-day trek for most of the 23,000 troops, marching more than 20 miles a day, at the regulation three miles per hour. The weather had been fine for the previous three weeks, the longest spell of good weather in 1917, and, as a result, the roads were hard and dusty. The long march severely tested the troops. To ease the strain, the men 'marched easy' and sang songs along the way, but:

> By late afternoon the songs were few and far between. Even conversation lagged. The packs upon our backs in some unaccountable way were fully three times as heavy as when we carelessly hoisted them to our shoulders many, many hours before.[1]

As the New Zealanders passed through Ypres, the ruins of the city made a lasting impression:

> We passed through Ypres, my first time in this town which is perhaps one of the most well-known on the Western Front. It is a great place now, shell shattered and in ruins . . . As I passed through for the first time I marvelled and wondered at the immensity of the war, the ruins of Ypres and the wonderful organisation of the army.[2]

The extent of the destruction of this once proud and beautiful town together with its 'gaunt ruins and deserted streets', according to one New Zealand history, 'suggested some city of the dead'.[3]

If Ypres made a lasting impression on the New Zealanders, the front-line positions had an equally powerful impact:

> The ground is covered with shell holes as close together as pebbles on

the beach; the dead from the last two pushes were being buried at half a dozen places en route, but were still lying about the battle front in large numbers, a dreadfully gruesome sight, and the smell struck one forcibly when at least two-and-a-half miles away.[4]

A New Zealand private recorded after the war:

No words can give any adequate impression of a Flanders battle-field, even the pictured page fails lamentably to adequately impress . . . Picture an expanse of black mud as far as the eye can reach. Shell craters everywhere! There is not a square yard of the Ypres salient upon which a shell has not fallen. The craters have merged one into the other and perhaps a stormy sea, suddenly converted into semi-liquid mud, would hint at the configuration of the land. Every house, every shed has been smashed to splinters, but dotted over the landscape were the squat concrete 'pill-boxes' erected by the enemy. Not a single tree remains, only a few jagged, splintered stumps remaining. Not a leaf, not a blade of grass but everywhere the debris of war, human and inanimate.[5]

Such was the impression made by this war zone, another New Zealand soldier wrote something almost identical:

. . . nothing but utter desolation, not a blade of grass or tree, here and there a heap of bricks marking where a village or farmhouse had once stood, numerous 'tanks' stuck in the mud, and for the rest, just one shell hole touching another.[6]

It was, as another New Zealander recounted, 'a place where no-one in his right senses would want to venture',[7] while the Commanding Officer of 3 Wellington Battalion believed that 'the Mark of Cain seemed upon the land . . . Every square yard of it seemed foul with slaughter.'[8]

The New Zealand and 3rd Australian Division, the two attacking divisions of II ANZAC Corps, were given just three days to prepare for their next action. One soldier in 1 Auckland Battalion scrawled a hasty note to his sister in New Zealand and caught the mood of the time. He hinted of the important events ahead:

I am in a terrible hurry so please excuse scribble. Well since long before this ever reaches you we will have been in another 'Dustup' so I most likely wont be able to write to you for a few days.[9]

II Anzac took over its sector of the front on 28 September, only to learn that the attack had been moved forward two days in order to take advantage of good weather. Both divisions lacked familiarity with the ground over which they would have to attack, yet they felt elated that at last the two Anzac corps were to fight side by side.

Nothing was left to chance despite the haste of the preparations. The corps war diary tells of a huge build-up for the coming battle, with 'a continuous stream of lorries and transport taking material to the forward area'.[10] Brigadier Hart of 4 Brigade recorded in his diary that 'convoys of lorries reached as far as the eye could see'. On 30 September he wrote:

> Conference all the morning outlining dispositions and issuing instns for the forthcoming attack. A very busy time all day preparing maps, orders, arranging further moves, obtaining requirements for the offensive, bombs, ammn, flares, rockets, entrenching tools, etc.[11]

By 2 October, all the guns of the New Zealand artillery were forward in their new positions and calibrated ready to fire with plenty of ammunition on hand.[12] The Machine Gun Corps was also well prepared with their firing programme completed and the necessary orders issued on the afternoon of 2 October. To support the infantry in the attack, all five companies of the New Zealand Machine Gun Corps would be used. They would provide a very effective protective barrage, utilising over sixty machine guns and firing some 600,000 rounds on the day of the attack.[13]

The infantry battalions had two days to prepare and used the time wisely. The 2nd Auckland Battalion recorded on 3 October: 'officers and NCOs reconnoitred all ground to the Assembly area and carefully studied the ground of the advance'.[14] All New Zealand battalions did the same. On 2 October, General Russell visited his two brigadiers and all the commanding officers who were to take part in the forthcoming attack. He left the meeting well pleased. He recorded in his diary, 'I fancy we have got most of the work done and everyone seems confident'.[15]

Numerous spurs run from the main Passchendaele Ridge. The two now facing the New Zealand Division were Gravenstafel, the smaller of the two, and Bellevue. These two low hills were to be the scene of the New Zealanders' fighting at Passchendaele. Small streams had drained them but the intense shell fire had turned the region into one large quagmire in a countryside now bearing the scars of war. Numerous pillboxes peppered both locations, especially amongst the destroyed farms. Broodseinde, the section of the ridge east of Ypres, was the main enemy stronghold and the site of an enemy regimental headquarters and an observation post (OP) which overlooked the whole salient. This important feature faced I Anzac Corps and became the main objective of the offensive.

The attack aimed to seize the first low ridge in front of Passchendaele as a preliminary to taking the village on the next ridge in a subsequent push. It would be opened on 4 October by twelve divisions along an eight mile front. For the only time in history, four Anzac divisions, making the main thrust in the centre, would be attacking side by side. They formed 'a single solid phalanx in the centre of the battle-line . . . the greatest overseas force which had ever simultaneously attacked the enemy'.[16] I Anzac Corps would attack Broodseinde on a 2,000-yard front, while II Anzac would take the Gravenstafel Spur on a front of 3,000 yards. The planned advance varied from 1,200 to 2,000 yards — 'strictly limited' objectives.[17] The three Australian divisions were to take Broodseinde Ridge and Zonnebecke, while the New Zealanders were to concentrate on taking the Abraham Heights (the eastern slopes of Gravenstafel) and the spur itself. It was a formidable task because the divisions would have to advance up open slopes chequered with strongpoints. If the final objectives were taken, the British army would be back on its old line of 1914, which had been lost in the German offensive of 1915.

To preserve the element of surprise, no preliminary artillery bombardment would be used in the attack, but at zero (Z) hour a devastating artillery barrage would take place, firing to a depth of 1,000 yards. Artillery support for the Second Army, using the field guns of five divisions and some corps and army 'heavies', amounted to an impressive 796 heavy and medium guns, and 1,548 field guns and howitzers. While there was no preliminary barrage, practice barrages broke the silence from 1 October and were fired twice a day until Z hour. These swept over the ground of the planned attack and beyond.

The New Zealanders' share of this artillery was generous. They would be supported by one hundred and eighty 18-pounders, sixty 4.5 inch howitzers and sixty-eight machine guns. There were to be four distinct artillery/machine-gun barrages to assist the assaulting infantry. The first would begin 150 yards in front of the start tape, and then lift 50 yards every two minutes for the initial 200 yards. The rate would then change to a lift of 50 yards every three minutes until the Red Line, the first objective, had been reached. A hundred and fifty yards past this the barrage would pause for an hour before moving on at a rate of 50 yards every four minutes until the second and final objective, the Blue Line, had been reached. The barrage would finally halt 150 yards beyond the final objective, during the vital period of consolidation, protecting the infantry while they dug new trenches. The machine-gun group in support of the final advance planned to fire a barrage out to 400 yards from the final objective and then remain ready to offer instant support to the infantry on the Blue Line.[18] As one New Zealand historian noted, this attack was to be 'a limited advance with unlimited explosives to blast out a way. If the weather held it must succeed.'[19]

Few of the unreliable, slow Mark IV tanks were to be used in the attack, but there were none in the II Anzac Corps sector. These steel monsters were not suited to the terrain around Ypres and they were committed to the various attacks in a piecemeal fashion without any consideration of the state of the ground over which they would have to pass. Slow-moving, high-profiled and unreliable, they were easily destroyed by the German artillery, and Ypres became known as the 'tank graveyard'. Sick of being squandered for heavy casualties and no gains, the tank officers protested to GHQ after the 4 October attack about the way their machines were being used. They were not employed again at Ypres, but the tank commanders were given freedom to plan an operation on ground of their own choosing. They found suitable ground some 40 miles to the southeast at Cambrai. Attacking on the misty morning of 20 November on dry, downward-sloping ground, 381 tanks achieved a stunning, though short-lived, victory.

The New Zealand Division was allocated a wide 2,000-yard front and would be attacking to a depth of just over 1,000 yards. Facing it was the 4th Bavarian Division. The New Zealanders planned their advance in two stages: first, to the Red Line, which ran approximately along the crest of the ridge just short of Gravenstafel village; then on to the Blue Line, at the foot of the Bellevue Spur in the Stroombeek valley, about 500 yards east of Gravenstafel.

Four battalions — 1 Auckland and Wellington from 1 Brigade, and 3 Otago and Auckland from 4 Brigade — would cross the Hannebeek stream and take the enemy trenches, shell holes and pillboxes as far as the Red Line. They would then be leapfrogged by four more battalions — 2 Wellington and Auckland from 1 Brigade, and 3 Wellington and Canterbury from 4 Brigade — which would carry the attack to the Blue Line.

Both brigades were in position on the evening of 2 October and used the next day to carry out last-minute preparations, such as reconnoitring the battleground, establishing approach marches and tapping the start lines. The men were well briefed and understood the task ahead of them despite the short preparation time, which had permitted only two planning conferences. The commander of 1 Brigade was to write after the battle: 'I am satisfied that every man knew his job and the result of recent training was clearly proved.'[20] This would be 4 Brigade's first (and only) action of the war, and it felt determined to prove itself the equal of the other three New Zealand brigades.

On the evening of 3 October, the weather broke, bringing rain and gale-force winds. The long march, followed by the necessity of digging in, had exhausted many of the soldiers, and the dismal weather made for a cold night. With the uncomfortable conditions, and each man's private thoughts focused on what the next day would bring, few of the New Zealand infantry slept well.

On the day of the attack the temperature was 60°F, the sky was overcast and a quarter of an inch of rain fell. Despite the deterioration in the weather the ground underfoot remained firm throughout the day.

At 5.20 a.m., while the whole attacking force was crammed in the front line, a heavy German barrage fell on the front of II Anzac Corps. Most of the rounds fell to the rear of the New Zealand Division, although machine-gun and sniper fire did do some damage, causing about eighty casualties prior to Z hour in 1 Auckland Battalion alone.[21] Many of the sheltering troops believed the shelling indicated the Germans had detected their attack, but the German commander General Sixt von Armin, with three fresh divisions from Ludendorff's general reserve, had also planned a strike for the morning of 4 October, and this was his opening barrage. When massing for their attack, however, his troops were caught in the open by the British artillery barrage which erupted at 6.00 a.m. They were slaughtered by the tremendous weight of fire, and general confusion followed, from which they never recovered.

The artillery barrage had opened on time and the New Zealand infantry advanced behind it. 'You couldn't hear a thing,' reflected one soldier more than seventy years later, 'the air was just quivering.'[22] A New Zealand writer eloquently expressed the feelings of those taking part in an infantry assault. It was 'the deepest and most soul-searching ordeal that men can undergo'.[23] According to one of the attacking brigades, the artillery barrage 'opened to the second and was very intense'. It was 'excellent and all ranks were full of praise and admiration for it. It was easily followed and very few shorts were experienced'.[24] A New Zealand stretcher-bearer experiencing his first action of the war recalled that the artillery barrage was 'hell . . . let loose . . . The din was deafening and awe-inspiring, just one terrific roar.'[25] A soldier who had found the night of 3 October 'rather terrifying' reflected in his diary:

> Going over the bags in the morning. I am in the hands of God. So are we all. Preserve us Lord.[26]

He died on 6 October from wounds sustained during the attack.

The New Zealand infantry followed the barrage, 'like horses behind the hounds', according to Brigadier Hart.[27] It proved to be an easy advance for the 200 yards to the first enemy line, which had suffered badly during the opening barrage. Resistance was scant and easily overcome.

4 Brigade on the right, covering an 800-yard front, aimed to take the Abraham Heights. Starting with 3 Auckland and 3 Otago, it took its first objectives — Duchy Farm and Riverside — with very little opposition. The two battalions were then held up by the large pillbox known as Otto Farm. This was eventually outflanked and then cleared using the powerful Mills bombs. Mills bombs were the perfect weapons against pillboxes. According to Ormond Burton, 'they burst in the confined space with a ghastly effect'.[28] Fifteen prisoners and four machine guns were captured.

A New Zealand soldier, Private Stewart Callaghan, lined up on the tapes at 3.00 a.m. and followed the artillery barrage keeping 50 yards behind the line of shells bursting in front of him. He recorded:

There were huns getting out of shell holes every where you looked and unless they put up their hands and came in to be taken prisoner they were shot down straight away. I shot one bloke I know of and fired a lot more shots but I don't know whether I got any more or not . . . There were a fair number of our chaps caught it but it can only be expected in an advance such as that was . . . I have wondered since how we got through at all as there were shells and bullets flying everywhere.[29]

Private Callaghan wrote that he came through this ordeal 'without a scratch' and described 4 October 'as a day I will not forget for a lifetime'. Unfortunately he did not have a normal lifetime left to him. He was badly gassed the following year and never recovered, the mustard gas having seared his lungs beyond repair. He died in Trentham Military Hospital in 1920.

One young Otago soldier, Gordon Neill from Outram, found that morning's attack anything but the 'great adventure' he had expected war to be. He recalled it seventy years later:

Now, at six a.m. that morning we were all lined up on this tape — just in a long row. The barrage came down I would think fifty yards in front of us and it played on there for so many minutes and then it lifted another fifty yards and while it was lifting we moved forward and so barrage after barrage we moved up the hill protected as far as possible by the artillery fire that was in front of us. The idea, of course, is that any enemy between us and our objective was being subjected to heavy destructive fire from the artillery. Right, it was a steady incline. Anybody who was wounded and dropped could very easily perish in the mud. There were times where you had to drag out, almost to your knees, out of soft mud — ghastly conditions. And it pelted rain all the time. There were some spectacular sights, you know you see them painted by the artists. You know you'd see a man throw his hands up and down — finish! That was happening all round us because as we went up the rise we were subjected to heavy machine gun fire from the Germans up the rise . . . As we went up the hill, we encountered heavy machine gun fire from a pill box, a German pill box, and one of my mates, Tommy, received a wound in the thigh and he went down . . . it was in just about the same place that we lost our skipper. He was killed. We had very heavy casualties up at the top. In fact, we made our objective anyway and rooted the Germans out . . . We took our objectives there and we spent the night in the trenches.[30]

3 Auckland and 3 Otago had pushed on to the Red Line, where

they were covered by a protective artillery barrage. They were followed by 3 Wellington and 3 Canterbury, which advanced over the Abraham Heights, suffering heavy casualties from the direct fire of the German machine guns on the high ground to the north and northeast. An officer in one of the following battalions penned in his diary:

> At 5:50 the Bn commenced to move forward. At 6 am our barrage of thousands of guns opened fire and we advanced into the Germans under the cover of their fire. The Germans shelled us fairly heavily. We advanced in company in columns of single file. At 6:20 am Colonel Weston was wounded and a message came to me to take command of the Bn which I did . . . I led Bn Hdqrs and established Hdqrs in a machine gun emplacement. Hundreds of German prisoners coming in . . . Rained at times. Poor Mitchell my batman was killed near me. A great victory.[31]

Both battalions continued their advance down the eastern slopes of the heights to the Blue Line, 3 Canterbury having to subdue two pillboxes, which slowed their 2 Company. By 9.10 a.m. Berlin Wood and Berlin Farm had fallen and the battalions were on their final objective. There they immediately began the process of consolidating their hard-won gains.

1 Brigade, on the left, covering a 1,200-yard front, planned to advance to Korek. 1 Auckland and 1 Wellington led the way. Both battalions experienced considerable difficulty crossing the bog that had once been the Hannebeek stream but were fortunate the heavy mud softened the impact of the German artillery or they would have suffered severe losses. 1 Auckland drifted to the north in the early stages of the attack, receiving heavy fire from the pillboxes and farm houses, but managing to subdue them one by one with flank attacks and Mills bombs. The battalion ended up fighting in the 48th Division's sector and cleared the entire Red Line in that area. Meanwhile 1 Wellington had also pushed on to the Red Line in its sector and cleared the whole brigade area. As its regimental history states:

> By . . . acts of individual gallantry and by the grim determination of all ranks, allied with skilful leadership of officers and non-commissioned officers, 1st Wellington pushed on to the Red Line, capturing the whole brigade frontage on schedule time.[32]

It was an outstanding feat of arms. But it didn't stop there. With a party from 3 Otago, 1 Wellington took the ruins of Korek village 120 yards beyond the Red Line. Machine-gun fire from two dugouts there had caused casualties in both battalions and therefore had to be subdued.

Sidney Stanfield, a 16-year-old serving in 1 Wellington, recalled that the attack was very hard work and that he had a peculiar sensation of being alone on the battlefield:

> You're loaded down with 220 rounds of ammunition in your pouches . . . two bandoliers of fifties, one slung over each way, one this way . . . Forty-eight hours' rations, a full water bottle, a shovel or a pick shoved down your equipment at the back, and a rifle and a bayonet and one thing and another — I think they calculated round eighty pounds, so . . . this business of charge boys, charge the blighters boys, give them cold steel and all that was a lot of bunkum. You just blundered along, blundered along. And . . . if you came under heavy fire from a machine gun you'd immediately take shelter in a shell hole or something like that, or any bit of broken ground you see, to size up the situation. Groups of you in twos and threes. You weren't packed close together. It was basic, not to bunch . . . Immediately you bunched you drew fire you see. So, there'd only be perhaps two of you at most, or three of you, in one shell hole at a time . . . with the shell holes nearly all full of water . . . [For] My part, in . . . Passchendaele I seemed to be alone mostly. Alone, I felt I was alone if you understand, when I think of it now. Although I know there must have been men on either side of me.[33]

Little wonder one commanding officer later remarked 'Don Quixote was not more heavily laden than a modern "digger" '.[34]

The Red Line was consolidated before the leapfrog battalions arrived. These— 2 Auckland and 2 Wellington — fought through the German positions beyond Korek to the final objective. While resistance was often strong, especially for 2 Wellington at Kron Prinz Farm, they were soon in possession of the whole of the Blue Line. Once there, the professionalism of the New Zealand soldiers became evident. With great urgency, they immediately began the process of consolidation and soon had all troops on the final objective well under cover and prepared for the inevitable counterattacks.

The following summary of events is from 2 Auckland Battalion's war diary:

Strength Battalion 1 Oct: 26 Offrs, 780 ORs
3–5 Oct LtCol S.S. Allen wounded and 12 other officers, inc 2IC
Bn CO for most 4 Oct Lt E.A. Porritt A/Adj
4 Oct: advanced through enemy HE barrage. Casualties not heavy,
but direction in many cases badly kept.
8:05: RED Line reached.
8:10: Barrage lifted and Bn advanced behind it.
9:26: BLUE LINE reached and held.
2:00 pm first counterattack reported and destroyed by arty fire
4:00 pm enemy again counterattacked in three waves in front of
PETER PAN. Artillery barrage was excellently placed completely
smashing up counter-attack.
Another counterattack at 8:00 pm similarly dealt with.
Total casualties 3–5 Oct
KIA 41
Wounded   179
Missing   40
Strength on 5 Oct: 12 Offrs, 561 ORs
New Major took over Bn at 7 pm 4 Oct
Took 290 POWs, 9 machine guns
Relieved 5 Oct[35]

The New Zealand Division had secured all of its objectives by
11.00 a.m. and was safe behind the wall of artillery and machine-
gun fire that protected it in its new positions. The German
counterattacks, which came at at 8.15 a.m., 10.00 a.m., noon and
2.00 p.m., were 'disjointed and were not pressed home . . . and were
satisfactorily dealt with by our artillery'.[36] A New Zealand gunner
left an account of the fate of the German attackers:

> We had quite a nice shoot but he [the enemy artillery] spotted us and
> got onto us with a very fast gun, made rather a mess, but when he
> counterattacked in force about 10 we were there and I believe they
> saw the troops get out of the train and form up for it and cut them
> down in hundreds.[37]

Three more counterattacks in the evening were similarly dealt
with.[38] The sixty-eight machine guns of the New Zealand Corps were
all in position to offer instant support to the infantry. They answered
three calls on 4 October and another three in the early hours of the
following morning. The machine gunners responded instantly,
spraying the entire New Zealand Division front with thousands of
rounds. Such support 'won high praise from the infantry'.[39]

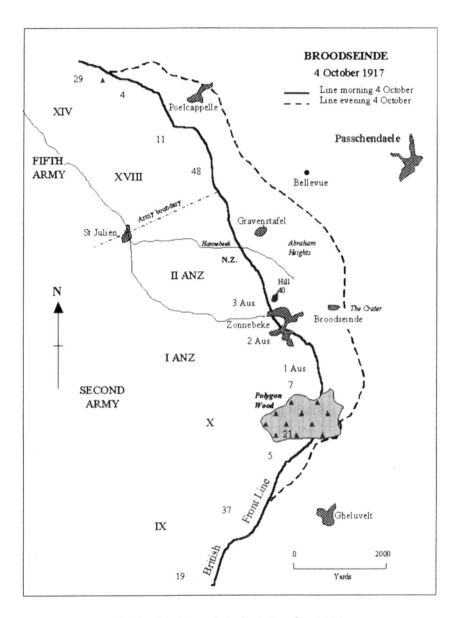

The Battle of Broodseinde, 4 October 1917.

The New Zealand attack had been highly successful and advanced the line by 1,900 yards. It had taken 1,159 POWs from four different divisions, out of a total of 5,000 POWs taken that day. The aggressive New Zealanders had also killed many Germans, 800 in 1 Brigade's sector alone. The commander of 1 Brigade concluded his report of the operation by stating: 'I cannot express myself too highly of the work of all ranks. Their dash and elan were magnificent.'[40] The brigade major of 4 Brigade could not 'speak too highly of the splendid conduct of officers, NCOs and men during these operations. Under the most appalling . . . conditions they displayed the utmost perseverance, bravery, endurance.'[41]

New Zealand casualties numbered 192 dead and 700 wounded in 1 Brigade, and 130 killed and 600 wounded in 4 Brigade. The New Zealand Artillery had lost eight killed and twenty-three wounded. Around 200 New Zealand soldiers were listed as missing. While the total of 1,853 casualties was regarded by the official historian as 'not excessive',[42] it could hardly be regarded as light. The New Zealanders had experienced a casualty rate of around 25 per cent, or one in four of all participating soldiers. In 1 Auckland Battalion, because of its unfortunate start, the casualty rate had been over 40 per cent. Yet this was a battle in which everything had gone according to plan and the New Zealand infantry had received maximum artillery and machine-gun protection. In their next attack they would not be so fortunate.

Despite the relative ease of the victory — a 'walkover' as one soldier expressed it[43] — the attacking troops were exhausted by their efforts. While looking for his cousin, Gunner Bert Stokes visited 3 Otago immediately after the attack:

> The poor old boys looked dead beat. Here they were lying asleep in an open paddock, in the rain, wet through. By Jove; they must have had a hard time of it and looked as if they did not care what happened!

Unfortunately, Gunner Stokes learned his young cousin had been killed half an hour after the battalion had gone over the parapet.[44]

Meanwhile, at a regimental aid post (RAP) a New Zealand padre recalled:

> We were going hard nearly all day long. I helped to place in splints I can't tell how many broken thighs, and found at last I could be really useful if given the opportunity.[45]

Removing the wounded from the battlefield proved difficult. Working four men to a stretcher, it took about four hours to cover the three miles to safety. Lieutenant Colonel C.H. Weston, Commanding Officer of 3 Wellington Battalion, was wounded by an artillery shell in the early stages of his advance and had to be carried from the battlefield on a stretcher. He described this experience as 'the hottest corner I had ever been in' and felt it would be 'nothing short of a miracle if we escaped'.[46] Weston did escape, but not unscathed. He suffered another wound when a shell fragment punched a hole through the back of his steel helmet.[47]

After three days of backbreaking work by teams of stretcher-bearers, the battlefield was cleared of the wounded of both sides. As Linus Ryan, one of the stretcher-bearers at Passchendaele, recorded: 'It was the proud boast of the NZ Division that they never left a sector whilst one of their wounded remained.'[48] Once again, this tradition was maintained, although at the end of their ordeal the stretcher-bearers were 'too tired to talk . . . we got back — crawled into our bivvy, sat down and just ached. We were too tired to sleep — very near down and out'.[49]

Gravenstafel Spur, of which the Abraham Heights taken by the New Zealanders formed part, was a good tactical gain. It provided excellent observation of the Passchendaele Ridge and was the logical starting point for any attack on Passchendaele. On the high ground ahead the New Zealanders could see the pillboxes of the Flanders I Line on Bellevue Spur, an obvious objective for the next attack. But not one of those New Zealanders who gazed across to the spur on the morning of 4 October could have guessed that in just over a week's time it would be the site of indescribable suffering and total defeat for their fellow soldiers in the New Zealand Division.

The Australians of I Anzac had taken the Broodseinde portion of the ridge, and for the first time since May 1915, the British held some of the high ground and could look down on the Flemish lowlands beyond. Australian losses had not been light either — 6,500, with 3 Australian Division suffering 1,810 of these.

Broodseinde, the name by which this battle is known, and Gravenstafel Spur were vital ground; the Germans had been driven from some of the most important positions on the western front. It was a victory of significance, as the Germans had no obvious solution to the step-by-step advances of Plumer's Second Army, especially when the attackers stayed well within range of their supporting artillery. The Germans had been powerless to prevent the attack from succeeding, and the ten counterattacks they had launched that day had failed to regain any ground and had been easily dispersed by the supporting artillery. That their new tactics were failing them was evident to the German High Command:

> Once again the losses had been extraordinarily severe . . . The new combat methods had not proved themselves successful on 4 October. The more heavily manned front line which had suffered heavy losses from artillery fire had been overrun by enemy infantry who had attacked in superior numbers with tank support . . . The Army High Command came to the conclusion that there was no means by which the positions could be held against the overpowering enemy superiority in artillery and infantry. Loss of ground in these heavy enemy attacks was unavoidable.[50]

The attack of 4 October was the third hammer blow against the Germans in a fortnight. It was one of the greatest victories of the war to date. Certainly those who had taken part believed they had won a great victory and hoped the Flanders campaign might now reach a successful conclusion. The Germans had been badly shaken. A German regiment on the receiving end of the New Zealand attack recorded in its history after the war: 'The 4th of October arrived. The blackest day in the history of the regiment.'[51] The Australian official historian commented: 'An overwhelming blow had been struck and both sides knew it.'[52] So heavy had the German losses been that Crown Prince Rupprecht considered a general withdrawal from the Flanders front beyond the range of the vicious British artillery.[53]

The reasons for the success were obvious to those who had participated. By attacking without a long preliminary artillery barrage, a tactical surprise had been obtained. Artillery support throughout had been almost perfect, paving the way for the infantry. Despite the change in the weather the ground underfoot had remained firm, so although the infantry's task had by no means been easy, it had not been made harder by having to battle though mud and slush as well. Despite the lack of preparation time, individual units had carried out a thorough reconnaissance of the ground across which they would have to assault and had detected no major obstacles in their way.

Because the Germans had suffered heavily in the attack, many people in the Allied camp believed they were on the verge of defeat. A sense of anticipation of great events mounted in the headquarters of the higher formations. At Corps Headquarters, General Godley's personal messenger recorded the sense of excitement:

> Great reports re the advance have been coming in all day. From all accounts they have a great crowd of prisoners . . . The GOC is very pleased with his Anzacs. They did far more than he expected them to do. If only it keeps fine for a few more days Fritz will get the scare of his life but I'm afraid it will rain before long . . . Good reports are still coming in and everyone is excited about the haul of prisoners we have got.[54]

Reflecting this euphoria, on 7 October, General Godley wrote to Allen in New Zealand:

> They [the New Zealand Division] took Gravenstafel and Abraham's Heights, and had a wider front and very nearly as far to go as anybody, and, as usual, did it excellently. They took over 1,000 prisoners, and I am glad to say that the casualties are much lighter than they had ever been before, and, in fact, are not much more than the number of prisoners taken . . . it will not be long before the other two brigades are attacking again and you will hear of them . . . there is no doubt that the Boche is becoming very demoralised, and if the weather will only hold up for a bit longer and we can deliver a few more blows before the weather sets in, it will go a longway towards the end. The best sign of all was the demoralisation not only of the troops but of the enemy's commanders and staffs . . . The whole of the battlefield of our successive advances is covered with dead Huns, and there is no doubt that a very large number have been killed since the beginning of this third battle of Ypres.[55]

General Monash, the Australian commander of 3 Australian Division, also believed that the enemy was 'staggering' and that, provided sufficient artillery was in place for the next attack, 'Unless the weather balks me I shall capture P— village on 12th.' Monash felt 'very much elated and not a little excited' by this prospect.[56]

The condition of many of the German prisoners greatly reinforced the view that the enemy was suffering severely and scraping the bottom of the barrel. One New Zealander wrote in his diary:

At 6:45 am the first of the prisoners started to come in in droves . . .
Some of the prisoners, or the majority of them, were very poor types
indeed; we managed to find out that some of them were only 17 and
18. One of the little chaps was crying . . . [57]

Gunner Bert Stokes also recorded his poor impressions of the
prisoners as they walked past:

They were a motley crew, some old looking, young boys and all
exhausted and worn. A very poor specimen of Germans they were,
and all were lacking colour, they were awfully pale and looked as if
they had spent some hard times under our bombardment.[58]

Another New Zealander noted:

The prisoners are a miserable looking mob and one German I was
talking to told me that London is a heap of ruins, England was
starving and it was impossible to get troops across the Channel — the
poor fools.[59]

Leonard Hart regarded the German POWs taken on 4 October as:

. . . the poorest looking lot I have ever seen . . . Many of them were
mere boys of sixteen and seventeen and plenty of them were not an
inch over five feet high. This certainly looks as though Germany is
falling back to her unfit material to keep up the strength of her
armies.[60]

Little wonder, then, that British commanders from Haig down
believed the Germans were nearly exhausted as a fighting force and
that one more success would finish them off.

Yet the weather had broken, and the heavy rain soon turned the
battlefield into a sea of mud. This would save the Germans from
certain disaster, and they knew it. A relieved Crown Prince Rupprecht
wrote: 'Most gratifying, rain: our most effective ally'.[61]

General Russell felt well pleased with his division and noted in
his diary:

. . . we gained all objectives advancing our line some 1900 yards on
NZ front and this division captured 1100 prisoners. Our casualties I
estimate at 1500/2000, they make it less. All battns (1st and 4th Bde)
fought well especially latter.[62]

In spite of the success of the New Zealand Division, though, and unlike his Australian counterpart, General Russell had a sense of foreboding about his men's future operations:

We've been having one of our periodic battles today and so far have done well. Casualties not so heavy as at Messines, nor nearly so heavy as the Somme which was the biggest battle, and the hardest fighting that we shall ever see I hope. The more I see of it the less I like it. These big casualty lists, with all they mean, do not lose their effect thro' familiarity. It seems so futile tho' one knows it isn't. Unfortunately it is raining, and the sun hasn't got the power to dry the ground so late in the year. We've got a very muddy time in front of us, and that means a lot. The mud is a worse enemy than the Germans who did not today put up much of a show of resistance, tho' I shall not be surprised if he tries to get us tomorrow.[63]

Exhilarated by the success of 4 October, Haig was keen to follow with another big attack, despite the heavy rainfall and the arrival of fresh German troops. He had wanted to push on to Passchendaele village on 4 October, but as this would have taken the infantry beyond the range of the British artillery, the idea had been opposed by both Plumer and Birdwood. Yet Haig could hardly wait to come to grips with the enemy again and brought the date of the next big attack forward. The offensive would continue, with a fresh attack planned for 9 October.

49 Division relieved the New Zealanders on 6 October, and the exhausted troops had a long march to an area west of Ypres. Brigadier Hart wrote of the relief:

The night was dark, wet, muddy and miserable troops were weary and worn and had a four mile march to the Goldfish chateau area. We got out as dawn was breaking, the shattered and torn town of Ypres looked extraordinarily sombre and weird at that hour to the eyes of all of us who were winding our weary way back after three sleepless nights and a strenuous battle thrown in.[64]

While this action proved 4 Brigade's only battle of the war, within a week the New Zealand Division would be marching back to the front-line trenches for the attack on Passchendaele village, now only a mile-and-a-half away but still beyond the range of most British guns.

Those New Zealand troops who had taken part in the attack of 4 October were aware of how well they had performed:

> I have not yet seen the newspaper reports of this little 'push' and I don't suppose it will be much more than mentioned but all the same it was one of the most complete successes our side have ever had and even General Godley doled out a little praise to the New Zealanders . . . a thing which must have caused him a severe strain.[65]

Newspaper reports in New Zealand raised the attack to something more than a substantial victory, reporting of 'Thrilling Dispatches From Flanders' where the 'Anzacs Fought Like Tigers'.[66] They described it as 'The Turning Point of the War', the New Zealanders' 'greatest and most glorious day',[67] 'Germany's Biggest Defeat' and 'The Most Slashing Defeat Yet Inflicted'.[68]

The New Zealand Division had secured all its objectives and, as far as the troops were concerned, 4 October had been a textbook operation in which everything had gone according to plan. One young soldier wrote after the attack: 'It's marvellous the way these 'Stunts' as we call them are got up, everything run like clockwork.'[69] To date the New Zealand Division had not experienced a military failure, and all its members felt immensely proud of this achievement. One soldier, Peter Howden, wrote to his wife after 4 October:

> . . . it is a thing to be proud of being a New Zealander I can tell you when you realise and see and know how our chaps behave over here. People do not perhaps realise that the NZs have the record of being the only troops on our side who have always taken their objectives, who have always done it to time and who have never yet lost a place they have taken. Just think what that means.[70]

A New Zealand newspaper editorialised on this theme on 8 October. Describing the Australian and New Zealand attack on the fourth as 'rivalling Wolfe's ascent to the plain of Quebec', the paper quoted Haig:

> Sir Douglas Haig has said that he looks to the New Zealanders 'to carry out with complete success every task set,' and once more that high confidence has been justified. The division's record is one of which New Zealand is justly proud.[71]

Unfortunately, the New Zealand Division's record was about to end. Its next great attack of the war would prove far from a textbook or 'clockwork' operation. Peter Howden, writer of the proud letter above, would be just one of many New Zealand casualties in the country's worst-ever military disaster.

Chapter 3

PRELUDE TO DISASTER: 9 OCTOBER

From 4 October, rain in Flanders turned the ground into thick, glutinous mud. While the rain turned to drizzle on the fifth, constant showers fell on the sixth and seventh and torrential rain soaked the ground on the afternoon of the eighth. A young New Zealand officer wrote:

> It sure means business when once it does commence to rain in this country. The last two days have been bitterly cold, but now it has set in very wet, such rain as you never see in New Zealand.[1]

The rain obliterated all landmarks and washed away roading and tracks. Three months of constant shelling had destroyed the natural drainage of the region and the thousands of shell holes now filled with muddy water. The entire valley facing the two Anzac corps, and across which they would soon have to fight, became, in the words of one divisional engineer, 'a porridge of mud'.[2] Describing the mud as 'terrible', one Canterbury soldier complained that 'I always thought Oxford was bad enough for mud but it's not a patch on this.'[3]

The heavy rain was also falling on the Germans, who likewise struggled with the mud in their wet trench systems, yet it was easier to occupy high ground from which water would drain. It was also easier, if decidedly uncomfortable, to sit tight in the prevailing conditions than attempt to advance through them. The British army commander decided this would be the fate of his men.

The state of the road leading to the front line which the New Zealanders had to use was extremely poor and did not reflect the mountain of work being done on it by the engineers and assault pioneers. The war diary of the New Zealand Engineers recorded on 6 October that 'bad weather continues and roads have become too soft for transport. Sappers and Pioneers are working continuously day and night repairing roads.'[4] The New Zealand (Maori) Pioneer Battalion had been struggling since 4 October to make adequate roading for the forthcoming attacks. These experts at road-making, bridge-building, trench-digging and the myriad other manual tasks required of an army at war worked harder than most infantry battalions at these backbreaking tasks and often produced double the output of their more glamorous counterparts. The pioneers made good progress until 6 October, when the wet weather and the constant stream of mule-drawn supply trains turned earth roading 'into a quagmire'. From 7 to 10 October there was:

> . . . a steady fight with mud. All available men have been carrying fascines [bundles of sticks] . . . BUT guns and horses are bogged everywhere. We have pulled many guns out and into position but the road is in a fearful condition . . . Many of our guns were bogged on the road and never got into action.[5]

Despite their best efforts the road remained 'a shaky bog'. In the Pioneer Battalion's view, the two attacks of 9 and 12 October failed primarily because of 'the failure of roads, light railways and tram lines'. A tram line to Gravenstafel Hill, for example, 'would have been invaluable if only for supply of ammunition and evacuation of wounded'. The overriding lesson of the New Zealand Division's October operations, according to the pioneers, was the 'vital necessity' of establishing roads, rail and tram lines after an advance 'with all possible speed'.[6]

One of the officers in charge of the road-building teams in II Anzac Corps was New Zealand engineer Stanley Rogers. It was a hard, dangerous and thankless task. Rogers wrote to his brother before 12 October:

> There has never been a stunt like this before; for instance, yesterday we had 42 horses to drag off the road and bury. I phoned for more men, but at the moment manpower is a premium.[7]

Rogers did receive an additional twenty men and was able to have the road cleared and the horses buried in one strenuous night of activity. From 10 October, the priority became shifting ammunition forward for the artillery. To do this, Rogers and his team worked forty hours straight without meal breaks or rest.

Road-clearing also proved dangerous work, and a number of Rogers' men were killed and wounded by enemy shell fire. Rogers himself had many close calls. One of these occurred while talking to an old friend, Mark Farington, a veteran of the Somme and Messines. A German shell landed between them and catapulted them into the mud. Rogers felt at the time that 'I would suffocate — had I swallowed any mud I would have.' He dragged himself clear of the mud with great difficulty, then located Farington. Rogers pulled his friend from the mud and 'when I went to clear his mouth, his lower jaw was gone and the head split open'. Farington had been killed instantly by the stray shell. Naturally, Rogers felt ill after this very close shave and, being covered in mud from head to foot, he took off the rest of the night. The next day, though, he was back at work and soldiering on.[8]

In this cold, wet, muddy environment the New Zealand Division began to suffer. It was impossible to keep dry and the mud penetrated everything. There was one small comfort. A soldier's diary notes that on 6 October 'the rum ration was recommenced'. This was 'very acceptable too as cold weather set in and we were up to out knees in mud most of the time'.[9] Work still had to be done, no matter what the conditions, and the digging, road-building and shifting of material, especially ammunition, continued. With only one blanket, one pair of boots and two pairs of socks issued per man, the men's health and morale soon plummeted. The end of the war seemed as far away as ever:

> I can't say I feel like writing and saying I am feeling fit and things are going well because that would be lies, but I am a good deal better off than a lot of the fellows as I have the top boots and waterproof overcoat . . . The Army is a queer place at the present moment. I feel pretty fed up. I am really getting rather sick of it. I honestly believe we are winning but I never do believe now that we will force him to unconditional surrender.[10]

The two commanders, Gough and Plumer, were worried about the bad weather and its effect on the troops. On the evening of 7 October they told Haig that while they could continue the campaign, they would both prefer to suspend it for the winter. Despite their concerns, Haig and others felt so buoyed by the results of 4 October they decided to press their advantage with more attacks in an effort to secure the Passchendaele Ridge as the campaign's last gain. The longer the enemy was left unmolested, Haig believed, the stronger his defences would be and the more rested his troops. After three crushing blows against him, now was the time to strike. The Australian official historian commented:

> Let the student looking at the prospect as it appeared at noon on October 4th ask himself, 'In view of the results of three step-by-step blows, what will be the result of three more in the next fortnight?'[11]

Haig felt convinced, and not without good reason, that the Germans were on their last legs, so Allied pressure must continue. He cited the Germans' failure to push home their attacks at Ypres in 1914 and was determined to avoid making a similar mistake. His enthusiasm proved infectious and easily swayed Plumer. Plumer's Chief of Staff, General 'Tim' Harington, recalled:

> It is, therefore, inconceivable to me that his [Plumer's] agreement with the views of the Commander-in-Chief was anything but one of 'utter loyalty' and desire to carry out his Chief's orders to capture Passchendaele. He knew well what that ridge would mean to his beloved troops and I am sure that once within his grasp, as it was after his successful capture of the Broodseinde Ridge on 4th October, he never gave a thought to stopping and turning back.[12]

General Godley of II Anzac Corps was also an enthusiastic supporter and all for continuing the attack. Haig wrote in his diary on 8 October:

> I called on General Plumer and had tea. It was raining and looked like a wet night. He stated that 2nd Anzac Corps (which is chiefly concerned in tomorrow's attack) had specially asked that there should be no postponement. I ordered them to carry on.[13]

The request that there be no postponement can only have come from General Godley. Ironically, the reckless, impetuous Gough remained unconvinced about continuing the campaign. His experiences in August had filled him with a sense of foreboding and pessimism that made him cautious about forcing troops to fight in heavy rain.

Another factor influenced Haig's decision to continue. The British front could not remain where it was, at the foot of the slope of the most prominent ridge in the region. The choice was to advance or withdraw. A withdrawal would be tantamount to admitting failure and, after so many casualties suffered for the little ground taken, would cause an outcry by the British public, with political consequences. Haig knew the British prime minister, Lloyd George, considered him incompetent and wanted an excuse to remove him. Such an admission of failure would provide Lloyd George with just such an excuse. Haig therefore refused to consider the option of withdrawal, instead insisting that the British try to capture the Passchendaele sector of the ridge, where the troops would be able to overlook the Steenbeke valley and winter on higher, dryer ground. At least this would look like some kind of victory. Haig's decision to continue after 4 October when the weather had broken remains 'the most questioned decision of his career'.[14]

The next move was to capture the village of Passchendaele. It was to be done in two steps. The first, in an action that was to be known as the Battle of Poelcappelle, was to occur on 9 October, just five days after Broodseinde, and was to be the shorter of the two advances. It would pave the way for a much larger advance three days later. The main objective of the 9 October attack was to secure two spurs leading up to the Passchendaele Ridge.

Immediately noticeable about the planning for both attacks is the lack of preparation time. They would be very rushed affairs. The first attack by the Second Army, back in September, had taken three weeks to prepare. The third attack, that of 4 October, had been given only eight days, but the attacking divisions still had the maximum artillery and machine-gun protection. For the 9 October push, the attackers had just five days of preparation, while 12 October had only two days, and the vital artillery could not be made ready with such short lead times given the dreadful conditions prevailing in the salient.

The decision to go ahead with the attack on 9 October ignored all the conditions that had led to the previous successes, especially the role of the artillery. Also ignored were the weather and terrain. As the Australian official historian would aptly comment: 'the brilliance of the Second Army's success appeared to be tempting its leaders to forsake their tried methods'.[15] It had taken three years and horrific casualties to perfect these methods. A 'sorry decline'[16] was occurring in the quality of Second Army's preparations and it was about to learn the terrible cost of abandoning its tried and tested formula.

Most soldiers believed that, with the heavy rain, the chance of a decisive, knockout blow had vanished. One Australian subaltern, who would be killed in the attack on 12 October, wrote on the eighth:

> I believe that if the weather had only held over another two or three weeks we would have Fritz well on the run in Flanders, and would have had numerous opportunities of following him up and further knocking him about with our cavalry. Now I fear that it must be a wash-out for the year — tough luck, but we take things as they are and keep plugging away.[17]

On 8 October, General Harington held a press conference. The Second Army, he stated, could not be stopped in its step-by-step approach and the attack the next day would bring further success. The sandy crest of the ridge was 'as dry as a bone' and the cavalry were on standby to pass through the big gap the Second Army would punch in the German positions. Newspapermen listened with scepticism. One later recorded his impression of the conference:

> I believe the official attitude is that Passchendaele Ridge is so important that tomorrow's attack is worth making, whether it succeeds or fails . . . I suspect that they are making a great, bloody experiment — a huge gamble . . . I feel, and most of the correspondents feel . . . terribly anxious . . . The major-generals are banking on their knowledge of German demoralization . . . I thought the principle was to 'hit, hit, hit, whenever the weather is suitable'. If so, it is thrown over at the first temptation.[18]

Both British armies would attack on 9 October, the Second Army with six divisions, the Fifth Army with five. In II Anzac Corps, two British divisions would be used: the experienced 49th (West Riding), a veteran formation that had fought in the Somme the previous year, and the untried 66th (2nd East Lancashires). Both divisions planned to use two brigades. I Anzac's 2 Australian Division would also be used. The brigades of II Anzac were to advance along two parallel spurs towards Passchendaele village. Between the spurs lay the saturated and impassable Ravebeek valley, dividing the formations, which would therefore be unable to offer each other support. The attack aimed to swing the Allied line to the left by taking the Bellevue Spur and the high ground opposite. This was an advance of 600–900 yards, which would take the British line to the foot of the slope just below Passchendaele village. The attack of 12 October would take the village itself.

The attacking divisions of II Anzac had a march of four miles through a quagmire of mud and slush just to reach their start line. In fact, this march was so arduous some troops never completed it, and there were large gaps along the jumping-off tapes when the infantry finally moved forward. The effort to get on the start lines in time exhausted both divisions. There was also inadequate artillery support, as few guns had been moved within range. The 66th Division, for example, had only twenty-five field guns in support of its attack. The opening barrage was so weak and patchy it proved impossible for the infantry to establish where the shells were meant to fall. It thus provided no guide, and even less protection, for the advancing infantry.

49 Division attacked from the New Zealand frontage secured on 4 October. Bellevue Spur, facing it, projected north of a sunken road which led to the highest part of the ridge. Uncut wire flanked the sides of the slopes, the steel and concrete walls of pillboxes crowned the spur, and the attacking battalions had to cross the flooded Ravebeek stream, now 50 yards wide and waist deep. The Germans were on the last bit of vantage ground and fought desperately to hold it. The two brigades of 49 Division came under withering fire from machine guns the moment they crossed the start line. The British official history records, ominously: 'No previous attack organised by the Second Army in the War had such an unfavourable start.'[19] Both brigades were then delayed by the dense unbroken wire and pillboxes on Bellevue Spur and suffered heavy losses. They failed to reach their objectives. 148 Brigade, on the right, took no new ground at all, while 146 Brigade, on the left, managed an advance of just 300 yards and held this ground until the next day. The division suffered more than 2,500 casualties in this abortive attack.

On the right wing of II Anzac, 66 Division, in its first major action of the war, had a somewhat easier task. Fighting on firmer ground and striking no wire obstacles, its infantry took its final objective, and a patrol from 3/5 Lancashire Fusiliers entered Passchendaele village, finding it a deserted ruin. The division had to abandon these hard-won gains, though, to conform to the front of 49 Division and avoid the heavy enfilade fire from machine guns and light field pieces now being poured into both its brigades from the strongpoints on Bellevue Spur. It withdrew to a line about 500 yards in front of its starting line, having suffered more than three hundred casualties.

2 Australian Division, of I Anzac, also failed to make any progress and suffered 1,253 casualties. Only on the left flank of the Fifth Army were the final objectives taken and held. In general, progress on 9 October was slight while casualties were excessive.

Many of the wounded from the attack lay in the open and would not be retrieved until days later, especially those of 49 Division. Some lay on the battlefield for three days and their injuries 'turned septic; in some cases the wounds are filled with maggots'.[20] Many died of exposure or drowned in the shellholes in which they had sought shelter. A New Zealand stretcher-bearer recorded on moving back to the front line:

> In the ordinary course of events we should have been able to spell ourselves until the commencement of the stunt, but we found that the Division who had just left this sector, had left their wounded lying about in shell holes and all our bearers had to set to and clean the place up. We carried out poor little Tommies who told us they had been lying out in shell holes for four days, and their wounds, absolutely black, bore out their words.[21]

There were about two hundred stretcher cases requiring evacuation from the battlefield, no easy task under the prevailing conditions. A New Zealand soldier commented on the task that had been left to him and his fellow compatriots:

> To make matters worse the 49th Division, whom we relieved, went out leaving 200 stretcher cases for us to shift — most of whom had been out 4 or 5 days. Stretcher bearing was exceedingly hard owing to mud and shell holes and the boys were done before the stunt started.[22]

The attack on 9 October was clearly a dismal failure — a 'total repulse', to use the phrase of the Australian official historian.[23] General Russell lamented in his diary:

Attack this morning a failure — carried out by 29th and 66th Dn on our Corps' front — troops held up early and arrived at Assembly point exhausted.[24]

In three days' time his own troops would be in exactly the same situation.

Losses in both II Anzac divisions amounted to more than 5,000, and total Allied casualties for the day to more than 13,000, of which just on 4,000 had been killed. Yet enough ground had been taken — even if it was only a paltry 500 yards and none of it vital — to justify, in the minds of the senior commanders, another attempt as soon as possible. Haig, demonstrating no grasp of reality, wrote the briefest entry in his diary:

> Tuesday, 9 October. A general attack was launched at 5.30 am today from a point S.E. of Broodseinde on the right to St. Janshoek (1 mile N.E. of Bixschoote). The results were very successful.[25]

Plumer, presumably after consulting with General Godley, informed Haig's headquarters:

> I am of opinion that the operations of the 49th and 66th Divisions, carried out today under great difficulties of assembly, will afford the II Anzac Corps a sufficiently good jumping off line for operations on October 12th, on which date I hope that the II Anzac Corps will capture Passchendaele.[26]

Not only Haig wanted the attack at Passchendaele renewed — so did General Plumer, despite his earlier misgivings, and Godley. None of these senior commanders, and few divisional commanders, had gone forward to speak to the junior officers responsible for conducting the attack. Even Monash and Russell, both of whom received negative reports, did not check conditions facing their men for themselves, nor did they take any other action. Despite the obviously atrocious conditions, General Godley felt keen for II Anzac to be used and again asked that there be no postponement. His soldiers would attack through the Flanders battlefields, now a sea of thick, glutinous mud resembling in its consistency something akin to lumpy porridge. Relying on second-hand information would cause an appalling tragedy for those at the sharp end of the battle plans. The British official historian admitted after the war that the task given to

New Zealanders on 12 October was 'beyond the power of any infantry with so little support'.[27]

On the eve of attack several senior officers had grave misgivings. Without any change in the weather, and well aware of the difficulties ahead for his troops, General Gough considered asking for the attack to be cancelled. After consulting with Plumer he concluded, however, that it was now too late to do so. The New Zealand Division would have welcomed a postponement, but felt powerless to initiate one. The system of command lacked flexibility and granted little power to subordinates to express their doubts or refuse an order.

Those Anzac divisions responsible for the outstanding success of 4 October were now to be used in another attack on the twelfth. To the objectives of this push would now be added those that had eluded the attacking divisions on the ninth. General Birdwood protested that the conditions on his front, and the exhaustion of I Anzac Corps, meant his troops would be able to do little more than offer flank protection for II Anzac. Yet General Godley said nothing. His silence condemned II Anzac Corps to making the main effort. The New Zealand Division, along with 3 Australian Division, would again enter the cauldron of battle. The senior commanders, Haig, Plumer and Godley, anticipated another stunning success. They were about to be terribly disappointed.

Chapter 4

DISASTER: 12 OCTOBER

On the night of 10/11 October the attacking brigades of the New Zealand and 3 Australian Divisions marched from Pilckem to the front line. The march of five miles through driving rain proved difficult, and to stray from the duckboards meant becoming stuck in knee-deep mud with the risk of drowning. Progress was slow — one mile every four hours. A New Zealand machine-gunner recalled the painful journey:

> We had to go about 6 miles on duck walks and then after leaving the boards it took us 4 hours to go a quarter of a mile. It was raining, we lost the track and the boys were getting bogged. I myself was bogged down to the waist twice. We eventually reached the end of our journey about 4:30 am this morning and as we were in an exposed and dangerous position we had to set to and dig ourselves in.[1]

A corporal of the Rifle Brigade also remembered the march without affection:

> Issued out with bombs, shovels, etc. ready for the attack on Friday morning. Moved off to within 1000 yards of the front line at 6:30 pm. Awful road congested with traffic of all description. Nothing but a veritable sea of mud to walk. Dug a hole to live in that night and next day.[2]

Another rifleman recalled:

> Got on to the duckboards and a few shells dropped near killing three. We took a long time going up, there were constant halts. Of course Bricky took HQ off the duckboards about a mile from the end of our journey and we had to struggle through mud to Calgary Grange. Arrived there about 11 pm and dug ourselves holes to live in. It came on to rain and Fritz started shelling so we had a rotten night.[3]

Little wonder that a machine-gun officer, a 'valued and trusted leader' of the Machine Gun Corps[4] who died of injuries sustained next day, wrote in his last letter home that moving up to the line was 'more like a nightmare than anything I can think of'.[5] Another soldier accurately remarked: 'no one will ever forget that dark passage amongst the shell-holes and swamps'.[6]

By 3.00 a.m., most troops were on their start lines ready for the attack, but were thoroughly exhausted. Others had gone astray in the night. One veteran recalled how the troops on his battalion's left flank failed to appear at dawn. He blamed the terrain:

It was broken, not high ridgy country, but broken rolling country with those canals and streams bust up, and it was very easy for people to do a circle almost if they kept going at night, falling into shell holes . . . in the dark it was very hard for the troops to get up if they didn't know the way.[7]

Haig, meanwhile, claimed in his diary on 10 October:

The 3rd Australian Division and the New Zealand Division go into the line again tonight. Gough told me they are determined to take Passchendaele in the next attack and will put the Australian flag on it! The advance will be then over 2,000 yards. But the enemy is now much weakened in morale and lacks the desire to fight.[8]

Haig's determination not to miss what seemed a prime opportunity meant the 12 October attack was hurried. The divisions involved not only had much less planning time — just two days — but were given deeper objectives than any of the preceding attacks. The New Zealand Division only took over its sector at 1000 hours on 11 October but was to attack the next morning. This allowed little time to determine the tape-line for the attack, to draft and issue orders, for commanders at all levels to brief their troops, for artillery barrage tables to be calculated and disseminated to infantry battalions, or to carry out the other vital tasks necessary to prepare an attack of this scale. A British history written shortly after the war caught the mood:

The sands were fast running out, and if another attempt was to be made to develop the success of October 4 it was clear that it would have to be made quickly. It was decided to attack again on the 12th, a brief two days' interval since our last assault.[9]

A New Zealand junior officer recalled:

As far as the 3rd Battalion was concerned, the whole affair from the beginning appeared to be rushed. This was seen in the little time allowed officers to import to the other ranks the meagre information received about the essential features of the attack, and in the belated issue of bombs, flares, etc.[10]

A senior New Zealand officer recorded similar misgivings in his diary:

We all hope for the best tomorrow, but I do not feel as confident as usual. Things are being rushed too much. The weather is rotten, the roads very bad, and the objectives have not been properly bombarded. However, we will hope for the best.[11]

The hasty preparations affected the troops, including an often ignored unit, the New Zealand machine-gunners. Describing preparations for the attack as 'hasty and imperfect', the official history of this unit clearly indicates plans and decisions were constantly changed until the last minute before the attack. This forced the machine-gunners to prepare three different sets of fire plans and orders, a time-consuming and frustrating task. The final set of orders was not complete until 2.00 p.m. on 11 October, which meant 'barely thirteen hours were left to the Commanders to get ready for the operation'.[12] Only thirty-eight machine guns participated in the opening barrage, compared with the sixty used on 4 October.[13]

The New Zealanders also knew artillery support would be far weaker than it had been on 4 October. The New Zealand artillery commander, Napier Johnston, was worried and warned Russell that little support would be available to the infantry. Russell noted in his diary on 11 October:

Napier Johnston came to see me after lunch. The guns are all forward but he evidently feels uneasy about the attack — says preparation inadequate.[14]

The guns were not all forward. The problem was that, as a result of the gains of 4 October, most of the field artillery was now out of effective range (6,000 yards) and would have to be moved well forward to be of any use. Because of the haste with which the attack was being thrown together and the dreadful conditions of the front, the enormous efforts being made to move the guns were mostly unsuccessful. The attack would take place with less than half the artillery support provided on 4 October and normally provided in an attack of this nature. Effective counter battery fire had ceased from 4 October because of limited visibility and bad weather. Johnston plainly stated to Russell that effective artillery support for this next attack was not possible, but Russell ignored the information and did not pass it on to Second Army HQ or GHQ.

Not only were few field guns in position by 12 October, it took seventeen hours to move shells from the rear to the gun lines by pack animal. Each time an animal became stuck, its load of eight shells had to be removed and the animal dragged clear. The shells were then repacked and the animal loaded again for its next few steps. Then the whole exhausting process had to be repeated. A New Zealand sergeant saw a donkey loaded with two 18-pounder shell cases fall into a shell hole where it 'sank like quicksand'. Even probing the hole with six-foot rods failed to find the donkey. It had sunk without trace.[15] A New Zealand gunner later wrote:

> I knew the ground around our guns as I had been there daily with ammunition and I knew how impossible it was to move the guns in time for the second attempt. Horses were useless in such mud so the guns had to be inched forward by manpower — pulled out of the muddy water in one shell hole to slide into another.[16]

Brigadier Hart noted in his diary that many of the guns 'had been unable to get forward to their proper positions and were stuck in the mud at all angles along the road between their original and their new lines'.[17]

For an attack of this magnitude each artillery battery usually had thousands of rounds at its disposal. Yet on 12 October most were lucky to have a few hundred. This was especially true of the heavy artillery. Captain Rogers recalled meeting an artillery forward-observation officer who was very concerned about the uncut wire and the lack of heavy ammunition:

> . . . he was of the opinion that the stunt should be held up for two days longer. I was of the same opinion and I did get notice that the stunt would be on the 14th, but HQ is HQ, and the stunt went over

on the 12th. I can only say it was a failure, the heavies never got up half the ammunition they should have.[18]

With such problems being experienced with the field artillery, there could be no question of moving the heavy artillery until the ground hardened.

Another problem was the lack of stable platforms for the forward guns owing to the state of the ground. Proper gun platforms consisted of a double deck of hardwood supported by a solid foundation of fascines and road metal. It took two days to make such a platform and a plank road connecting it to the main roadway for supplying ammunition. Even then, many platforms remained unstable,[19] and their guns were useless after firing a few rounds as the recoil pushed them even deeper into the mud. Moreover, the limited supplies of ammunition had to be carefully cleaned before they could be fired — every single artillery shell. Ironically, given the state of the weather, clean water for this purpose was also in short supply.

The attack aimed to take Passchendaele village, a task given to 3rd Australian Division with the New Zealanders protecting their exposed flank. The Fifth Army's 9th Division was on the New Zealanders' left flank. The direction of the attack was northeasterly, and the attacking divisions were allocated unrealistic objectives, requiring an advance of more than 3,000 yards, a distance not considered possible even in dry weather. This was 1,000 yards more than any of Plumer's previous three advances, and this attack would be made in abysmal weather with only two days of preparation! The Australian official historian was critical of Godley about the depth of the attack:

Had Godley really known the conditions of October 9th . . . how could he have hoped for success with deeper objectives than any since July 31st, shorter preparation, and with the infantry asked to advance at a pace unattempted in the dry weather of September?[20]

Godley planned the advance in three phases. The first objective, the Red Line, was 1,200 yards from the start line. The second, the Blue Line, was more than a mile from the start line and 1,000 yards beyond the first objective. The final objectives, the Green Dotted Line and the Green Line, were about 800 yards in advance of the Blue Line and 400 yards beyond Passchendaele village. The 3rd Australian

Division would use its 10 and 9 Brigades to take the village, while the New Zealanders used their 3 (Rifle) and 2 Brigades to take Bellevue and Goudberg Spurs on the Australians' left flank. Goudberg Spur, which the New Zealanders would not even see on the morning of 12 October, was designated as their main objective. To reach it they would have to advance over the Gravenstafel Ridge, down into the small Ravebeek Valley, cross the Strombeke stream and then advance up the slopes of the two spurs, wading through thick mud and into the driving rain and gale-force winds. Bellevue Spur was about 1,000 yards from the New Zealand positions and projected from the Passchendaele Ridge into the Ravebeek Valley. The German positions there were well protected by the many concrete pillboxes on the crest of the spur, by concealed machine-gun posts and by two formidable and continuous belts of wire entanglements, more than 30 feet thick. A New Zealand gunner recalled:

> The whole country side was dotted with these Boxes, walls 6 ft thick of reinforced concrete, not many of them were hit. Each one had been a fort on its own with barbed wire right around it and loops for machine guns on each side.[21]

These obstacles were well known to all senior commanders, including General Russell, on the eve of the attack. The day of 11 October was described as 'ominously quiet' by one New Zealand history, which also noted that 'The great belts of wire ahead were apparent to the most casual observer.'[22] Gazing across no-man's-land in the dawn's growing light on 12 October, one New Zealand soldier noted in his diary that 'it was possible to discern the chief details of the slope above us, the broken trees, the torn ground, and on the summit "pill-boxes", black and threatening'.[23] Patrols sent out on the night of 10/11 October by 2 Otago, including one led by the legendary Sergeant Dick Travis, revealed the extent of the entanglements, but little action was taken. Travis reported:

> No-man's-land is in very bad order — one mass of huge shell holes three parts full of water, a large amount of old wire entanglements scattered about makes it very awkward for patrolling. It is very heavy to patrol on account of the ground being so ploughed up by shell-holes. It is very hard to keep your feet as it is so slippery . . . The enemy posn just below sky line commands a great field of Machine Gun fire and the observation is excellent.[24]

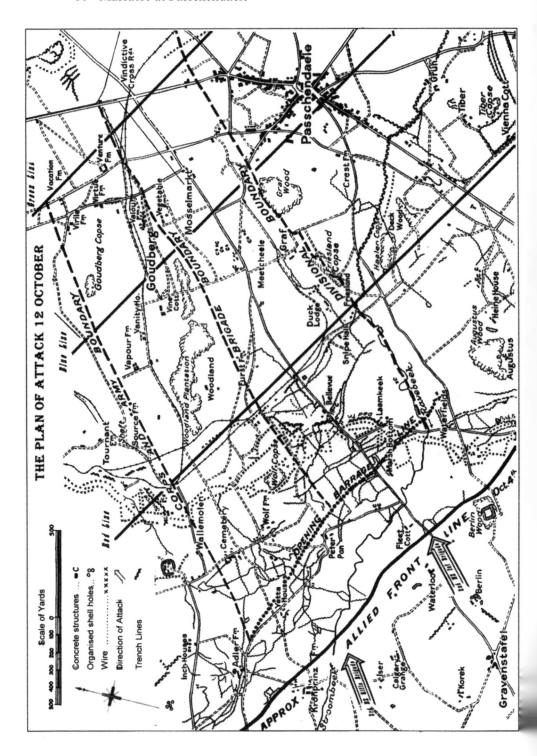

THE PLAN OF ATTACK 12 OCTOBER

Other patrols revealed the extent of the entanglements: 30 yards thick and well protected by many pillboxes and hidden machine-gun posts along the Flanders I Line. Sergeant Travis detected eight pillboxes in 2 Otago Battalion's sector alone, the nearest only 150 yards from their forward posts.[25] This came as bad news to the attacking brigades, and attempts to cut the wire using heavy artillery were half-hearted at best and produced poor results. Prior to the successful attack on Messines in June, General Haig had told Plumer: 'No attack should even commence until the barbed wire has been cut.'[26] Ignoring this sensible precaution would now doom the New Zealanders to failure.

Little wonder morale in the attacking brigades was low. The state of the New Zealand Rifle Brigade illustrates the severity of the situation. Its men were exhausted by a month's backbreaking work, often under fire, burying more than 60,000 yards of cable and constructing more than 30,000 yards of banking three to six feet high.[27] They had not completed any training whatsoever in preparation for this attack. The brigade's official history reveals:

It would be idle to pretend that the prospect of an engagement within a few days could be regarded with absolute equanimity. Battalion commanders knew only too well how much their men were in need of both rest and training . . . but since September 4th they had been almost continuously employed at the trying and wearing work of cable burying and road-making, well up in the Ypres Salient. These duties had entailed long marches over difficult shell-hole country; and most of the work had been done at night, and sometimes in gas masks under shell-fire. Exactly 200 casualties had been sustained. The weather, at first fair, became bitterly cold, and as the men had neither blankets nor warm underclothing, they got little sleep. Throughout the period they had literally slaved at their tasks, and now they were almost worn out and certainly unready for immediate combative action.[28]

One wonders whether Russell knew of the condition of this brigade and, if he did, why he foolishly insisted on committing it to the forthcoming battle.

The Battle of Passchendaele: the plan of attack, 12 October 1917.

Both New Zealand brigades suffered seriously from the exhausting march to the front, the miserable weather conditions, the sight of the great masses of unbroken wire now facing them and the knowledge that the previous attack had failed, with heavy losses. One New Zealand history noted:

> There was overwhelming and gruesome evidence of the disastrous results of the British attack launched on the 9th. To say nothing of the dead, scores of men, wounded and near to death, still lay out over the country, unattended and without protection from the weather.[29]

Those New Zealanders making the attack on 12 October glumly realised that the difficulties ahead were formidable and their prospects of survival poor.

General Gough also knew their prospects of success were minimal. On the evening of 11 October he telephoned Plumer and asked him to postpone the attack until the weather improved. Plumer refused to consider this request and insisted the attack commence on time the next morning.

The New Zealanders again planned to use two brigades: 2 New Zealand Infantry Brigade, commanded by Brigadier W.G. Braithwaite, and 3 New Zealand Rifle Brigade, temporarily commanded by Lieutenant Colonel A.E. Stewart. Each brigade was to attack on a narrow front of 750 yards, but the attack was to be made to considerable depth with a battalion being allocated to each separate objective.

2 Brigade planned to use 2 Otago Battalion to take the Red Line, to be followed by 1 Otago allocated the Blue Line, while 1 Canterbury received the task of securing the Dotted Green and Green Lines. 2 Canterbury served as the brigade reserve, with each company allotted a specific task. Each battalion, other than the lead one, was to leapfrog the others once they were established at their objectives. 3 Brigade, on the far left of II Anzac Corps, also using the leapfrog system, allocated the first objective to 2 Battalion, to be followed up by 3 Battalion, with the final objective allocated to 1 Battalion. The assembly for the attack commenced under cover of darkness on the evening of 11 October, so most units were in position by dawn of the twelfth.

The attack opened at 5.25 a.m., 'Barely daylight. A cold, miserable morning.'[30] The opening barrage was so weak and erratic many of the infantry barely noticed it. It was universally condemned by the battalions that took part as 'very feeble'.[31] Worse still, many shells dropped short, landing among the New Zealand infantry and causing death and chaos. One soldier recorded:

> Through some blunder our artillery barrage opened up about two hundred yards short of the specified range and thus opened right in the midst of us. It was a truly awful time — our own men getting cut to pieces in dozens by our own guns. Immediate disorganisation followed.[32]

A sniper with one of the Otago battalions recalled the 'terrible affair' at Passchendaele when the guns of the artillery had sunk into the mire: 'We were firing into our own men, that's how bad it was.'[33] Soldiers in 10 Company of 1 Otago Battalion, for example, were killed by their own artillery shells when still 100 yards behind the starting tape.[34]

This weak artillery protection resulted from the lack of guns forward, the impossible task of establishing stable platforms for the few that were, and the scanty ammunition supply. After firing each round the guns had to be realigned, which affected the density of the barrage. At eight minutes per 100 yards, the rate of advance of the barrage was much too fast for the hapless infantry, and those shells that did land in front of them became buried in mud, showering the pillboxes with fountains of mud but doing little real damage. As one account stated, 'Naturally neither the inaccuracy of the fire nor the scanty sprinkling of shells tended to increase the confidence of the infantry.'[35] General Russell later wrote of the barrage on the New Zealand sector: '. . . owing to the state of the ground after wet weather, only a proportion of the guns had been able to get into position, so that the fire was weak and patchy, and at places it was almost impossible to see the barrage'.[36] The New Zealand official historian commented: '. . . it was at once apparent that the infantry must rely on their own efforts'.[37] Despite the obvious lack of protection, the infantry advanced from their shelters to be met by a storm of hot metal.

The enemy artillery burst into life as the infantry moved forward. So did the much more dangerous German machine-gun barrage, which sprayed the front of the hillside and the Ravebeek Valley. Each German machine gun spat out between 300 and 450 rounds a minute, and there were hundreds in action that morning. They swept the assaulting infantry from both flanks and from their immediate front. According to an eyewitness, they 'rattled through belt after belt while the New Zealanders fell by the scores'.[38] A veteran of the battle recalled:

> Machine gun fire. That makes your ears ring if you're close to it. When it cracks in your ears it's very close. Both ears were ringing there on Passchendaele.[39]

The official history of the New Zealand Rifle Brigade praises the German defence:

> The enemy's reliance on his machine-gun barrage, however, was not misplaced, for here was a perfect example of the use of machine-guns in the defence, an intense and deadly grazing cross-fire sweeping the front of both the New Zealand Brigades.[40]

2 Brigade jumped off at Waterloo Farm, on a bend in the Gravenstafel Road. 2 Otago struggled across Marsh Bottom, waist deep in mud, unable to move beyond a slow shuffle. The attack initially seemed to make progress, and the first farms fell, although New Zealand artillery shells dropping short caused considerable casualties. The Otagos then reached the top of the first ridge and saw, with dismay and shock, the uncut wire at the Gravenstafel Road some 25 to 50 yards wide. This wire was well protected by machine-gun fire from undamaged pillboxes beyond. The only gap was on the Gravenstafel Road itself, but this was a death trap, protected by heavy machine-gun fire from both sides. It was 'a veritable lane of death'.[41] The wire proved an impenetrable obstacle and many men from this gallant battalion died trying to get beyond it. As one of those who took part recalled with obvious pain:

> What was our dismay upon reaching almost to the top of the ridge to find a long line of practically undamaged German concrete machine gun emplacements with barbed wire entanglements in front of them fully fifty yards deep . . . Even then what was left of us made an attempt to get through the wire and a few actually penetrated as far as his emplacements only to be shot down as fast as they appeared. Dozens got hung up in the wire and shot down before their surviving comrades' eyes.[42]

At the end of the day this soldier's 180-strong company had no surviving officers, one sergeant, one corporal and thirty men. It had been cut to pieces. Other companies in the battalion suffered similar losses. A private soldier who 'hopped the bags' with 2 Otago Battalion at 5.29 a.m. summarised the day's events:

> . . . attack a failure on acnt [account of] wire encountered. Casualties extremely heavy. Hun machine guns and snipers play havoc. Absolute hell . . . Brigade practically wiped out.[43]

By 6.00 a.m. it became clear that 2 Otago could get no further, but 1 Otago joined their sister battalion at the wire and tried to push through. Men tried to crawl under the entanglements, and some actually got beyond the first two belts of wire to within yards of the German pillboxes. Two junior officers died while valiantly attempting to hurl their Mills bombs through the loop holes of the boxes. Very heavy casualties occurred in these courageous attempts to get beyond the wire. The left company of 1 Otago was cut from 140 to twenty-eight men, with every officer either killed or wounded.

To the deadly volume of machine-gun fire was added the crackle of well-concealed German snipers hiding in shell holes and behind tree stumps, who also exacted a heavy toll. A soldier of 4 Company of 1 Otago who survived the attack recalled that 'you couldn't see any enemy . . . never even saw a German there. But they were there and the German snipers were just having a field day.' When his close friend next to him was killed by a sniper, the soldier threw himself into a hollow in the ground and stayed there. This undoubtedly saved his life:

> The snipers just simply had a day out. They were on the alert all the time and any man that moved, I must have seen a dozen men killed that way just dodging to what they thought was a better position.[44]

When the men of 4 Company were able to withdraw under cover of darkness only thirty-four remained of the morning's 140.

The company on the right of 1 Otago suffered heavy casualties from two pillbox fortresses. The Otagos took the pillboxes and over eighty prisoners in hand-to-hand fighting, mainly through the sheer heroism of 2nd Lieutenant A.R. Cockerell, but his platoon was wiped out in the process.

1 Canterbury Battalion joined the two Otago battalions at the wire, but the New Zealanders could still not break through. The Canterburies lost their headquarters, probably to a New Zealand artillery shell dropping short, a few minutes after crossing the start tape. Wiped out in this one tragic blow were the CO, Lieutenant Colonel George King, the RSM and the entire staff of the battalion's headquarters. One soldier stated that while they could have taken Messines 'with a wet sack', Passchendaele was an entirely different matter: 'In less than no time we were practically extinct — they had wiped us out . . . All our crowd got killed [in] my section.'[45] Another soldier recorded, somewhat laconically, in his diary:

> Arrived 1st position 7 am wet through and covered with mud, latter knee deep. Moved on after spell, across flat swept by Fritz's machine guns which caused a fair amount of casualties. Dug in for life . . . Things very lively and heavy stuff all around. Raining: retired to our 1st position . . . at 5 pm and dug in for the night . . . Wet night and mud nearly knee deep. In open trench but dozed a little.[46]

For Harry Highet, a junior officer of 1 Canterbury Battalion, one of only seven to survive the attack out of the twenty-three officers of the battalion who had started, the events of the day had a rather surreal quality. Describing himself as 'acting entirely by the sub-conscious', Highet at first thought he was he was advancing through a large field of pumpkins, then 'realised they were the packs of dead soldiers I could see'.[47] Percy Williams, a soldier in 1 Canterbury Battalion, recalled seeing dead and dying all around him at the start line but felt he had left this 'fringe of death' behind him when he managed to get some yards beyond the starting positions.[48] He grimly realised his mistake when he reached the formidable pillboxes and belts of wire on the crest of the slope. He records: 'One saw the Otago Battalion melt away; then as the Canterbury's moved in, they too were mown down ruthlessly.'[49] A private in 13 Company witnessed his whole section 'mowed down to a man, to a man. What a hell of a sight that was.'[50]

Back at Brigade Headquarters, Signaller Leonard Leary witnessed an attempt to renew the advance, but 'as soon as the men got to their feet machine guns opened up and it was just like a scythe going along the line'.[51] Every unit of 2 Brigade had now flung itself at the enemy and suffered in this harvest of death. Party after party of New

Zealand infantry 'undauntedly threw themselves against the impenetrable wire, raked by the heaviest machine-gun fire',[52] some even reaching as close as 15 yards from the pillboxes. But not one soldier managed to get right through the wire. Private David Grant recalled how, during the advance, 'the boys were dropping on all sides' so that he reached the wire with only one other member of his infantry company, who soon fell victim to a sniper's explosive bullet. After the attack, only thirty-two of Private Grant's company remained, and only six from his platoon.[53] The infantry of this brigade had been cut down in droves and their attack had clearly failed. The survivors of the three battalions dug in where they could.

The Rifle Brigade, on the far left of II Anzac, led off with 2 Battalion, which had experienced great difficulty reaching its start line and arrived in a state of exhaustion. They had been on the move since 1.00 a.m. One soldier later lamented: 'It was raining and things were in a Hell of a mess. I fell down innumerable times and it was all I could do to get up.'[54] The lead troops set off at 5.25 a.m., taking each obstacle one at a time. Rifleman Jervis advanced from the start line at 6.00 and noticed 'a fair number had been smacked as I went up . . . Machine gun and rifle fire was very hot.'[55]

After taking the Wallemolen cemetery on the left, Wolf Farm in the centre fell, but the battalion could get no further. Ahead of them lay a line of pillboxes, impervious behind a sea of barbed wire and deep mud, with even more concrete fortresses on the slightly higher ground beyond those to their immediate front. Each pillbox had a strong garrison, and machine-gun rounds poured from the fire positions. These, and enfilade fire from the crest of Bellevue on the right, halted all forward momentum and forced the battalion to dig in at Wolf Farm just after 8.00 a.m.

3 Battalion tried to leapfrog this position and made almost 150 yards through the swamp, where it attracted heavy fire, which forced it also to dig in. There were heavy casualties when 1 Battalion reached them. One officer from 1 Battalion managed to penetrate some 200 yards into the German lines before 'he was shot to pieces'.[56] All battalions would remain in these positions for two 'cold, wet and miserable nights'.[57]

An excellent account of the disaster was written by Corporal Harold Green of C Company, 3 Battalion, New Zealand Rifle Brigade:

At 6 am a tremendous bombardment opened and we went over in a sea of mud. The fire from the German pill boxes was hellish and our barrage failed. The emplacements for the guns were not solid enough and the guns tilted causing trouble in our ranks from the shells of our own 18 pounders. The barbed wire entanglements, the mud and the pill boxes prevented any success. C Company lost heavily and the 3rd Battalion lost about half its number in casualties. Our Colonel, Winter-Evans, was killed. 150 of C Company went over and casualties numbered 82, including all the sergeants except Goodfellow. The attack was an impossible attempt. The ground was swampy and very muddy and the heavy cross fire from the pill boxes did not give us a chance. The Black Watch on our left were in exactly the same position. The stunt should never have been ordered under such conditions. It was absolute murder.[58]

More than eighty years later, Mr Bright Williams of Havelock North recalled the death of Colonel Winter-Evans. As battalion runner, Rifleman Williams had just been sent by the colonel to locate the adjutant and inform him where the battalion HQ was:

Well I went so far and a machine gun got me. So he [Winter-Evans] said 'All right, I'll see what I can do. And away he went. And they got him. It cut the artery on the inside of his leg and he was fading away when two of our C Company Signallers came on him and he said, 'You boys stop with me. I might want you'. He was going then. So they went about their own business as soon as he was gone.[59]

A party of six men and an NCO from 3 Battalion later spent three hours after the attack trying to locate Winter-Evans' body. They never found it.[60]

Some of the casualties in 3 Battalion resulted from snipers who lay concealed and waited for the infantry to advance before shooting them from behind. Lieutenant George Brunton, the only officer left in the battalion, was hit in the side by a sniper's bullet and initially believed his spine had been shattered:

That's a lovely way to end your life. I'd been shot in the spine from a bullet that had come from the back of me.[61]

Receiving confirmation from his batman that the wound was serious but not life-threatening, Lieutenant Brunton met Lieutenant Colonel Puttick on the battlefield and was ordered to report to an RAP.

Corporal Duthie, also of 3 Battalion, recalled in his diary an experience that must have been commonplace:

> We moved forward 6 am through that awful sea of mud until held up by machine gun fire. Hit in left shoulder about 8:30 am. Could not get out until 2 pm. Arrived at dressing station where we had tea and soup. A God send.[62]

While Corporal Duthie suffered an agonising wait of almost six hours until he could receive basic medical attention, he could be counted as fortunate among the New Zealand wounded. Some had to wait days before reaching an RAP.

Corporal A.D. Bridge wrote a detailed account of his horrific experiences in a letter to his wife in New Zealand. He described how 3 Battalion had been on fatigues for more than a month prior to 12 October 'and this job alone was enough to make the hardest of men tired and knocked up'. The barrage that opened at 5.25 a.m. was 'like all hell let loose' but was obviously inadequate: '. . . we could see gaps in the line of advancing fire even then and guessed that a gun or two was missing'. Corporal Bridge led his section forward behind the other two battalions of the Rifle Brigade. At the foot of the Passchendaele Ridge their problems began:

> All went well until we commenced the incline up the ridge. Then it was that we all became literally bogged. One leg would sink to the knee and many seconds were lost each step pulling it out . . . Our barrage was well ahead of us as we started up the hill. Too far unfortunately and it was seen that it had gone past the Hun 'pill boxes' and left them unharmed. Now was Fritz's chance. He opened on us with every available machine gun and sniper. Comrades fell by the dozen so I decided to plant my section in a shell hole and go forward myself to investigate.

Corporal Bridge found New Zealand troops at the brigade's first objective, but machine-gun fire and poor artillery protection prevented them from advancing further. Realising open movement was suicidal, Corporal Bridge kept his section in the shell hole until it could withdraw to the rear after nightfall. From there he and his section volunteered to help shift the hundreds of wounded men from the battlefield, 'the hardest task in the Army'. Corporal Bridge later stated bluntly to his wife:

> Never before has there been so many casualties to NZers . . . The whole affair was horrible from start to finish and a great sacrifice of life.

Bridge also noted in this revealing letter that he was 'very thankful to God that I am here today able to write to you as a sound and able man'.[63] He had been through the fires of Passchendaele and escaped unharmed, but just over one month later he was not so lucky. The popular and gallant corporal fell to a sniper's bullet while on a minor raid on 25 November 1917.

At 8.00 a.m. Lieutenant Colonel Puttick arrived at Wolf Farm and immediately grasped the extent of the tragedy. He ordered the three battalions to dig in where they were and decided not to commit the reserve battalion (1 Battalion). He quickly realised progress would be impossible, as any movement brought immediate fire. The battalions dug in along the hill and along Marsh Bottom with fewer than 500 men. The machine-gun fire on the Rifle Brigade's front was so great that, at one stage, all went quiet as the guns stopped for twenty minutes, their supplies of ammunition exhausted.[64]

While the New Zealanders could not pass beyond the wire and the German pillboxes, 3rd Australian Division advanced about 1,000 yards but became bogged in the mud of the Ravebeek Valley below Passchendaele, just short of their first objective. There they suffered withering flanking fire from Bellevue Spur. Twenty Australians from 38 Battalion actually reached the ruins of the church at Passchendaele, but were forced to withdraw. General Monash blamed the failure on the state of the ground, the lack of adequate artillery support, the lack of time for preparation and the inclement weather. He believed the plan could have worked only if the weather had been fine and 48 hours of preparation time available to the attacking divisions. He condemned the decision to proceed on 12 October as 'hare-brained'.[65] His 3rd Australian Division casualties numbered 3,200, or 62 per cent of those involved, similar to the New Zealand losses. The 4th Australian Division also had 1,000 casualties.

New Zealand losses for the morning's action were catastrophic, reaching to nearly 3000 within a few hours. The attack carried the

The Battle of Passchendaele: position of New Zealand troops on the morning of 12 October 1917.

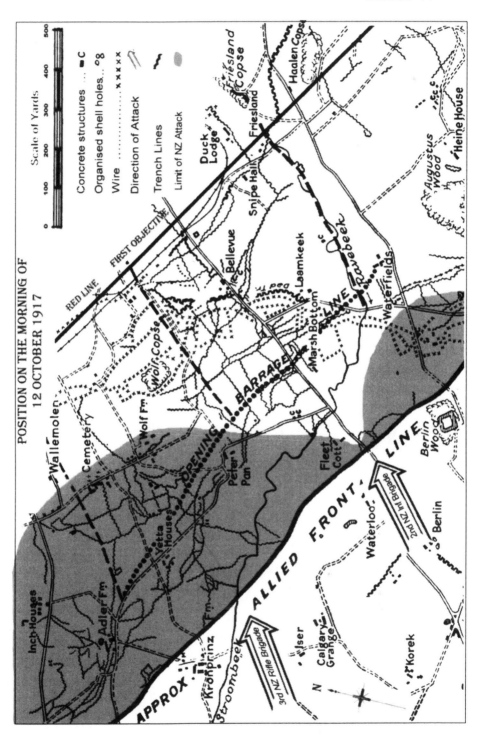

POSITION ON THE MORNING OF
12 OCTOBER 1917

Scale of Yards

0   100   200   300   400   500

Concrete structures .... ■ C
Organised shell holes... °8
Wire .... x x x x x
Direction of Attack
Trench Lines
Limit of NZ Attack

British positions forward from their original line 500 yards on the left and 200 yards on the right. Many New Zealanders had died to make these paltry gains. More than 800 bodies lay in swathes about the wire, buried in the marsh and along the road. The ratio of killed to wounded was unusually high if those listed as missing are added to the numbers killed. Most of those listed as missing had in fact been killed, but their bodies were never located. [66] The death toll reached 846, nearly a third of the total casualty figure, and probably reflects the care taken by the Germans to prepare their killing zone as well as the influence of the well-trained, extremely efficient snipers. One New Zealand soldier testified: 'The marksmanship of the Hun Snipers was deadly.' [67] Over the next week a further 138 New Zealand soldiers died of their wounds. [68] This is 'a loss unequalled by any other disaster in the nation's history'.[69] It makes 12 October 1917 the single bloodiest day in New Zealand's military history.

Despite these losses, the extent of which he had yet to learn, General Russell, believing 3rd Australian Division had secured its objectives and now had a dangerously exposed left flank, ordered the attack to start again at 3.00 p.m. There now occurred a clash of commanders on the battlefield which many troops believed was responsible for the removal of Brigadier Braithwaite from command of 2 Brigade. When Braithwaite received the message to renew the attack at 3.00 p.m., 'all COs in consultation with the Brigade Major . . . were unanimous that such an operation was impossible under the existing conditions'. Two of his COs communicated to him by note and telephone, making it clear their men were exhausted, the ground was impossible to cross, casualties were very heavy, especially amongst the officers, and the men were trapped at the wire.[70] A battalion war diary recorded: '. . . such an attempt would be absolutely disastrous . . . To advance against it [the uncut wire] would have meant practically annihilation of the Brigade.'[71] One of the New Zealand official histories is also emphatic that those on the spot agreed that 'any attempt to renew the attack would be suicidal'.[72]

Braithwaite told Russell this via a signal at 1.45 p.m.:

Have consulted my Commanding Officers on the spot and am of opinion that owing to very severe casualties and especially among officers and also to the close proximity of our men to the German wire it is impossible for this Brigade to continue the attack without incurring abnormal additional losses. Reorganisation is absolutely out of the question in daylight owing to snipers and machine gun fire and my men are so closely dug in under the enemy wire that the heavy bombardment of the Pill Boxes is also impossible.[73]

Braithwaite was therefore somewhat shocked when, 'In spite of this message, the G.O.C. Division ordered the advance to take place at 3:00 pm.'[74] This later changed at 2.10 p.m. to an attack using only 3 New Zealand Rifle Brigade on the left. The battalion commanders of this brigade, however, 'with their first-hand knowledge of the situation, were unanimous in their opinion as to the fruitlessness of any immediate attempt to get forward',[75] and were relieved when the order to renew the attack was cancelled at the very last minute once the true state of progress on the 3rd Australian and 9th Division front was revealed.

Russell glumly noted the day's results in his diary:

Attacked this morning at daybreak —we, and indeed all other divisions, were held up from start by M.G. Evidently the artillery preparation was insufficient, the barrage poor, and it goes to show the weakness of haste — our casualties are heavy, Geo King amongst others — I am very sad.[76]

Evidence buried in the New Zealand archives, and the testimony of participants, reveal the Germans almost certainly knew the New Zealanders were to attack on the morning of 12 October and, as a result, the two New Zealand brigades walked into a well-prepared trap. Pinned down in no-man's-land by a German sniper who seemed to take a special interest in him, Lieutenant Harry Highet reflected that the Germans 'had had eight days to set this very obvious trap, his machine guns had the range of every prominent piece of dirt that might shelter an enemy'.[77] Yet there was more than good preparation evident in the Germans' response to the attack. They had been forewarned. A captured German document of 2 Battalion, 29 Infantry Regiment, reveals in its morning report for 12 October that, 'At midnight a deserter (Scotsman) was brought in by 7 Coy 29 IR. He said that they had been since previous evening in line and would attack at 6 am.'[78] The division on the Rifle Brigade's left flank was the 9th Scottish Division, and the practice of receiving valuable information from deserters was not uncommon on either side.[79] Other evidence supports the view that the Germans were expecting the attack of 12 October and were well prepared to meet it. Brigadier Braithwaite noted in his report that on the night of the eleventh, 'The enemy . . . was very jumpy, and evidently expecting an attack, used a lot of flares.'[80] The intelligence report of II Anzac Corps also suspected the Germans had prior knowledge of the attack:

> It seems evident from a number of prisoners' statements that a large number of Machine Guns were actually in position prior to our attack, but with orders not to fire until the actual assault.

The report also noted that opposite the corps were two Jaeger regiments, elite, fit troops with high morale and twice the number of machine guns of other German units; that is, seventy-two heavy and seventy-two light machine guns per regiment.[81]

A British newspaper history of the war also commented on the very large concentration of machine guns well prepared for the New Zealand attack and attributed it to a new German method of defence:

> The shells thundered with less precision and density than usual along the main road running into Passchendaele village and swept the flanking ridges where the German commander had massed his men and machine-guns in extraordinary number, according to a new method of defence . . . As before explained, he [the enemy] had taken machine-gunners from reserves and supports, and placed them on the hills, hoping that sufficient would survive the British bombardment to check the attack. As the British bombardment was unexpectedly feeble, the German gunners survived in practically undiminished strength. They poured out such a fire between the Lekkerboterbeek and the Ravebeek as made the situation of the attacking troops impossible.[82]

This report is confirmed by a dispatch from the distinguished war correspondent Philip Gibbs, which also reported in New Zealand:

> All the machine-guns from the supporting lines were sent to this front. The enemy had never massed so many machine-guns on his front. Many were posted in trees. There were never so many riflemen scattered among the shell craters. The machine-gun fire and rifle fire

never ceased for an instant during the attack. Our men, floundering in the bogs, were unable to keep up with the barrage. The German snipers and gunners shot with a cool aim while our men struggled forward.[83]

No German commander would have denuded his reserves and support troops of their main firepower unless he had felt absolutely sure that something big was about to happen and that this firepower would be desperately needed. The evidence is therefore overwhelming that the German commanders knew an attack was due on the morning of 12 October and they had prepared themselves accordingly. One of the New Zealanders in the attack later stated: 'We should never have been sent there. They were so ready for it that we never got any distance . . . Oh, it was slaughter. They had everything all ready'.[84]

The deaths of the two senior officers, Lieutenant Colonel George King of 1 Canterbury Battalion, and Lieutenant Colonel Winter-Evans of 3 Rifle Battalion, were 'both very great losses' to the division, according to General Godley.[85] This is especially true of Lieutenant Colonel King, an outstanding commanding officer who had only joined 1 Canterbury at the end of August 1917. King had been the first CO of the New Zealand (Maori) Pioneer Battalion, and only through his outstanding leadership had that disparate organisation become an effective military unit and the great asset it now was to the New Zealand Division.[86] King's death is recorded with some shock and deep regret in the war diary of the Pioneer Battalion, which when the battle was over, recovered his body and buried it in front of the ramparts of the ruins of Ypres. A witness to the tangi recorded:

> I do not think I will ever forget that service, a cloudless sky and an aeroplane scrap overhead, the shallow grave, the body sewn in a blanket and covered with the New Zealand flag, the surpliced Padre, the short impressive burial service and finishing up with the beautiful Maori lament for a fallen chief, 'Piko nei te Matenga' ['When our heads are bowed with woe'] sung by the Maoris present, and with its beautiful harmonies and perfect tune, it seemed to me the most feeling tribute they could offer.[87]

General Russell also attended King's tangi and later described him in his diary as 'a fine good man, one of the best who lies buried in

Ypres'.[88] The New Zealand Division had indeed lost many fine, good men in this battle.

Evacuating the thousands of casualties from the battlefield proved a nightmare for the wounded and the stretcher-bearers alike, a slow, difficult task. It took eight men to manage each stretcher on an agonising three-and-a-half-mile journey to the nearest dressing station. As one soldier recorded: 'The wounded have had a rotten spin so far, many have died from exposure and a lot were shelled when down at the dressing station and killed.'[89]

The wounded George Brunton, ordered back to the RAP by Puttick, felt shocked on reaching it:

> There . . . must have been a hundred men lying there on stretchers and as the shells would come over I could see them shiver. Boy, they could hear the shells coming over and landing.

One particular case haunted Brunton for the rest of his life. A man whose leg had been shot off turned green from gas gangrene:

> And I saw him die. [Mr Brunton broke down here]. Oh boy, you know it's a terrible war, a terrible war. To see all those men lying there.[90]

Linus Ryan recalled being sent out as part of a four-man team to bring in a man with a serious leg wound:

> Not a dozen steps had we taken before the whole squad were bogged to our thighs in clinging slime. We rested the stretcher on the mud, whilst the two leaders extricated themselves then shoved the stretcher forward a few yards and waited whilst the bearers in the rear crawled out of the slime. It took us over an hour to bring that man a distance of 300 yards . . . Every step you would sink to the knees at least , and when without warning you struck a bad patch, you would feel yourself sink, sink and wonder if you were ever going to stop. Then the struggle would begin and pushing and sliding the stretcher along the surface we would fight to regain the comparative solidity of knee deep mud. It was gruelling heart-breaking work.[91]

Little wonder one New Zealand official history stated that 'the plight of the wounded was particularly pitiful'.[92] The plight of the stretcher-bearers was hardly much better.

The stretcher-bearers of the Army Medical Corps worked the rest of the day and throughout the night to clear the wounded from the battlefield. Yet there were not enough of them. On 13 October, during an informal armistice, more than 3,000 extra troops, 1,600 from 4 Brigade and 1,000 from 49 Division, went forward to remove the wounded of both sides.

One of the bearers from 4 Brigade was the Otago soldier Gordon Neill, who had experienced a rough time in the previous attack. With a party of eight men, Neill stumbled upon a wounded English soldier with both legs broken by shell fire. He had lain out in the rain and cold for three long days. It took Neill and the others twelve hours to move him to the nearest advanced dressing station, whereupon Neill, himself wounded in the arm, collapsed in the mud and slept for three hours.[93] Neill later learned that his eldest brother, an ambulance driver in the New Zealand Medical Corps, had received a very severe head wound and been left with a mate in a shell hole waiting for the stretcher-bearers to collect them:

> They never found the body of the man who was left behind and my brother was reported missing, missing for ages and ages and ages, and eventually missing believed killed, so eventually the final of it was when he was buried in Tyne Cot cemetery on the Passchendaele ridge.[94]

At the Casualty Clearing Station (CCS) at Waterloo Farm there were nearly five hundred stretcher cases lying around the German pillboxes, sinking into the mud and exposed to the driving rain and hail, 'just dying there where they were dumped off'.[95] Some of these lay in the open for three days. On 14 October Brigadier Braithwaite could not stand to see these men suffer any more. He made a personal appeal to Russell to have the last seventy-five of them moved, which duly happened at noon that day.[96] The same conditions prevailed around the CCS at Kron Prinz Farm.

Gunner Alfred Stratton volunteered for work as a stretcher-bearer and was able to observe the ground over which the infantry had been expected to advance:

> There was a flat muddy bog in front of our trenches and the ground sloped uphill to some pill boxes which completely dominated the position; as our shell fire had not reached these concrete shelters or the barbed wire entanglements, what chance had our infantry to get

out of that mud and climb that bare hill against machine gun fire? It was just pure murder.[97]

Sidney Stanfield, the young boy who had taken part in the earlier New Zealand attack, also worked as a stretcher-bearer after the attack of 12 October. He remembered they 'just carried till you couldn't carry any more. You just went until you couldn't walk really. You just went until you couldn't walk.'[98] By the afternoon of 16 October all surviving wounded had finally been evacuated. It had taken four days of backbreaking work. The stretcher-bearers were physical wrecks:

> Our feet were so swollen and painful that we had to cut our boots off, and not one of us could raise our voice above the merest whisper. Our uniform was concealed beneath a solid casing of mud to our arm pits. Bloodshot eyes shone from haggard faces, so that we could hardly recognise ourselves in a mirrored reflection. Every bone and muscle ached with pain.[99]

Despite the magnificent efforts of the stretcher-bearers, evacuation from the battlefield did not necessarily guarantee survival; it was only the first step. A nurse working at No. 3 Australian CCS, near Poperinghe, noted despairingly: 'I thought I had seen terific [sic] wounds and badly gassed Patients untill [sic] I looked in the resuscitation ward at the CCS. The poor boys came in and died like Flies'.[100]

Both 2 and 3 Brigades were relieved on the night of 14 October and the pitifully few survivors faced another weary journey to the rear. One soldier described the relief as 'a hellish experience coming out thro mud, arrive in middle of night . . . Absolutely done when arrived out. Mud from head to foot.'[101]

The responses of Generals Russell and Godley to this tragedy reveal much about their characters. Inspecting the battlefield for the first time on 16 October, Russell felt shocked to see the heavy strands of wire clearly visible on the forward slope and the strength of the German positions on Bellevue Spur. He was somewhat consoled when General Plumer visited him on 16 October and 'expressed his entire satisfaction with the way our men had fought and attributes no blame for our failure'.[102] Russell condemned the attack on Bellevue Spur and blamed himself and his staff. His diary entry for 24 October recounts a conference at his headquarters, at which he explained the lessons of the two attacks at Passchendaele:

> The chief one [lesson], applying especially to Div. Staff and Self, is that under no circumstances in war is one justified in assuming anything which can possibly be verified — and that where there are certain known conditions necessary to success it is a great risk, however justifiable, to attack before they are fulfilled.[103]

As Russell wrote to Allen, the attack of 12 October, 'though not an entire failure, was very nearly so'. As to its cause Russell frankly accepted a large measure of blame:

> I am confident that our men would have got forward excepting for the insuperable difficulties of the wire. You cannot fight machine guns, plus wire, with human bodies. Without the wire to check them the men would have tackled machine guns in spite of their losses. As it was, they tried to tackle both. This was humanly impossible . . . We, as a Divisional Staff, assumed that the wire had been cut. Assumption in war is radically wrong if by any means in your power you can eliminate the uncertain. This, of course, is pure theory, but we made a mistake.[104]

As a result of an earlier portion of this letter explaining the weakness of the artillery barrage, Allen replied to Russell that: 'We regret this as much as you do, and personally I feel sure that no possible blame can be attached to the New Zealand Artillery.' He went on:

> Rumours have been circulating through parts of New Zealand that the situation was not properly appreciated and that it was known to some senior officers, at any rate, that it would be impossible for the Artillery to clear up the wire and to preserve the barrage as they had done in previous attacks. I quite understand your position, namely, that your Divisional staff assumed the wire had been cut, and I lay no blame on you, nor indeed do I blame anybody, but there is a feeling of unrest and I have it myself. There is no use denying it.[105]

Russell replied: 'I hope you do not think that I throw any blame on the New Zealand Artillery for our failure on Bellevue Spur. That would be the last impression I would wish to convey.' Russell also reported to Allen with much relief that the New Zealand Division had now left Ypres which he regarded as 'a disgusting spot'.[106]

While accepting some responsibility for the disaster, as indeed he should, Russell also felt there were mitigating circumstances. At a conference of commanding officers held after the Passchendaele operations, Russell stated that the Division had not received timely and accurate information about the enemy's entanglements or the strength of his defences then facing the division. He added that, even if this information had been available, it would have made no difference:

> . . . even if the position had been known earlier, and it had been possible to make representations to G.H.Q. on the subject, he [Russell] doubted if the likelihood of the non-success of one Division would have effected any alteration in the programme already determined upon in respect of the fronts of two Armies.[107]

Russell was less than frank at this conference. The strength of the German positions and the depth of the German wire were known as a result of the abortive attack of 9 October. As many accounts testify, the wire was clearly visible to anybody who cared to visit the front line positions. Russell did not do this until after the attack. When doubting whether the attack would be held up because of the qualms of one division, Russell was also on shaky ground. The New Zealand Division had been allocated a key role in the attack, and 3 Australian Division could not possibly succeed in their thrust at Passchendaele village unless the New Zealanders were guarding their left flank. Before 12 October 1917, the New Zealanders had not experienced a military failure in France and, as a result, General Russell and his division had a formidable reputation. The recent triumphs at Messines and on 4 October at Gravenstafel had firmly cemented this. Any concerns or doubts expressed by Russell then were sure to be taken seriously by GHQ, no matter how unwelcome.

The point is that Russell never raised these doubts, nor did he bother to learn the true conditions under which he was expecting his men to fight. He was adhering to the British imperial system, like all other commanders at the time except Birdwood and Monash, and on 12 October this outdated approach failed the New Zealanders miserably. They were consequently forced to make an attack that lacked any possibility of success.

Godley's response, however, was different. Immediately after the attack he felt deeply affected by the disaster. Sergeant Wilson's diary entry of 14 October shows Godley was 'working day and night in his office lately and looks terrible worried over recent events'.[108] Even so, in his official correspondence dealing with the attacks of his corps at Passchendaele, Godley sought to minimise the casualties suffered while exaggerating the importance of the successes gained. Nowhere in this correspondence does he accept any responsibility for the failures of 9 and 12 October, nor does he acknowledge them as the disasters they truly were. Writing to the New Zealand Minister of Defence on 16 October, for example, he stated that in the 'big fight' of 12 October the New Zealand Division had had to attack 'a very difficult piece of country'. While they had gained about 500 yards of enemy territory, they 'did not quite succeed in getting it all'. He went on:

> . . . so, though not such a big success as Messines or the battle here of the 4th, it was a very good day's work, and the Division again did it excellently. The casualties were about the same as the last time, and the two added up together, though not unduly heavy, necessitate the provision of a good many reinforcements . . . no troops, except British, could have attacked as our men did over such incredible difficulties in getting to their assembly positions, and starting as tired as they consequently did.[109]

The astute Allen, though, as revealed in his letters to Russell, was not deceived by Godley's dishonesty, and, in fact, remained appalled by the extent of the losses suffered on 12 October.

Writing to Lieutenant Colonel Clive Wigram, assistant private secretary to the King at Buckingham Palace, the ambitious Godley stated: 'I hope it may interest His Majesty to hear something of the performance of my Corps during our share of the advance on Passchendaele.' Detailing the three attacks, Godley claimed them as successes which amounted to a total advance for II Anzac of some 3,000 yards. He continued:

> I hope and think [this success] will enable the Canadians, who are now taking over from us, to get into Passchendaele without undue difficulty. We are, of course, very disappointed at not getting into Passchendaele ourselves . . . The courage and tenacity of the men is beyond anything that one can describe. No other troops in the world could have attacked under such conditions as they did on the last two occasions, and, though all four Divisions are very exhausted, their spirit is very high, and in a very short time they will be quite fit to come in again where required.

In this letter Godley either lied or did not know about the true state of the divisions of his corps, especially that of the New Zealanders. With his extensive touring of the battlefield after 12 October, he must have seen the condition of the troops, so the former accusation is probably the correct one. Godley also stated in the same letter that the casualties were 'not unduly heavy'.[110] With the casualty rate for the New Zealand Division and 3 Australian Division around 60 per cent, and as high as 85 per cent in some New Zealand units, this was an astounding statement to make.

Godley's letter did the trick, though. On 16 October, he received news that must have been music to his ears. Wigram wrote that the King and Queen 'are delighted to hear how well your Corps has done during the recent operations'.[111]

The attack of 12 October should never have gone ahead. It failed for many reasons: poor reconnaissance, the lack of time to prepare, the exhaustion of the troops involved, the weakness of the artillery support, the muddy terrain, and a forewarned enemy who prepared very strong defences utilizing a maximum of firepower. That the attack should not have gone ahead under the conditions then prevailing was also the German view. Failing to detect the tragic irony in his statement, Godley had written to James Allen that a German officer, now a prisoner of war, saw the state of the road behind the front line and the lack of artillery and 'exclaimed in astonishment that no troops in the world would have attempted an offensive with such facilities of approach'.[112] The German officer was right. No troops in the world should have been made to attack in such unfavourable circumstances.

In the New Zealand sector the direct cause of the failure can be attributed to the unbroken wire entanglements through which the infantry, despite numerous attempts, could not break. These should have been destroyed by heavy artillery fire, but there were too few shells available for the heavy batteries to do a proper job and, of the few shells available, 'the heavies . . . had concentrated on the pill boxes and not the wire'.[113] General Russell remained adamant on the matter:

> The direct cause of failure was strong and continuous wire entanglements . . . the formidable nature of the wire entanglements in BELLVUE was not known until the evening of the 11th by the Bde holding the line when a patrol report was received which fully

disclosed it. This information 24 hours earlier would have been invaluable.[114]

A junior officer closer to the action believed there was another overriding cause for the failure:

There can be no doubt that the sole reason for the failure of the attack lay in the inefficient support given by the artillery in relation to the enemy machine gun positions. The German machine gunners had practically a free hand as they were unmolested by the artillery fire.[115]

Brigadier Hart, while not a participant, was a keen observer of the tragedy. The reasons for the New Zealand failure he recorded in his diary are remarkably detailed and astute:

This attack by the 2nd and 5th Armies on a 12 mile front was the most ambitious of the many made since 31 July last, and must be written down as a failure. Again it was the weather and not the enemy that rendered victory impossible. The country is now so absolutely shattered, ploughed up and pockmarked by shell fire, that movement is impossible beyond the roads trams and duckboard tracks we construct as we advance, unless the weather is dry.

There were 3 attacks within 9 days, the 4th, 9th and 12th. In the meantime much rain had fallen. Tanks, caterpillars, lorries, wagons, guns, mules and ammunition are stuck and were slowly being engulfed in the morass in all directions. Consequently the artillery preparation was incomplete. Uncut wire was met and was insurmountable under such conditions. Mud and wire prevented our men keeping up to the barrage. Hun machine gunners, protected in concrete pill boxes during the bombardment, came out with their machine guns after our barrage passed on and shot down our men while still struggling to get through and over the mud and wire.[116]

The failure of 12 October can never be blamed on lack of courage, tenacity or sheer heroism on the part of the troops who took part. The commander of the Rifle Brigade made this clear:

In conclusion, I cannot speak too highly of the splendid courage and devotion to duty of all ranks under my command, as they went into action in an exhausted condition and did everything that was humanly possible to attain success.[117]

A New Zealand stretcher-bearer remained in absolute awe of the infantry who had 'jumped the bags' on the morning of 12 October. This First Battle of Passchendaele

> . . . tells a story of almost unbelievable courage. Our citizen soldiers faced impossible odds. They knew what they were up against. They saw death staring them in the face — they saw no possible chance of success and with unfaltering courage, Officers and Men walked to their deaths, because it was their job.[118]

As the Australian official historian perceptively commented, given what faced the New Zealanders in the attack of 12 October, 'No infantry in the world could have succeeded.'[119] This was the New Zealand Division's one large-scale failure in Belgium, and the defeat was deeply felt.

The attack had almost mirrored that of 9 October, and was 'surely one of the lowest points in the British exercise of command'.[120] It was an unmitigated disaster without any redeeming qualities. As a British newspaper history described it:

> The result was in effect as serious as the reverse at Aubers Ridge in May 1915 . . . In both cases the urgency of the need for striking at the enemy seems to have prevented adequate preparation . . . there was again a failure in artillery power which prevented some of the most gallant forces in the world from achieving what they had fiercely determined they would do.[121]

What the newspaper history did not detail, however, was how many of these gallant soldiers, many of them Australians and New Zealanders, had died trying to fight this impossible battle.

The extent of the tragedy was never accurately reported in New Zealand newspapers, which concentrated on the small nation's 'Honoured Place'[122] in the attack and blamed the lack of success on the weather: '. . . had the rain held off [they] would have gallantly reached and held their objectives'.[123] The attack was portrayed as a limited success rather than the absolute disaster it really was. The accounts reported in New Zealand also made light of the dreadful conditions the men were having to endure. A good example of this was a dispatch from an Australian correspondent, Keith Murdoch:

The correspondent of the United Press [Murdoch] says that the rain reduced the battlefield to a perfect quagmire, but the British and Anzacs navigated the mud seas and mud mountains like miracle men. He talked to Sir Douglas Haig yesterday. The British leader was full of admiration for the men, and said that the entire history of Flanders shows that mud is always the soldiers' worst enemy. This is true to a greater extent now than ever, because the natural drainage is stopped. Nevertheless the British troops from all over the Empire, and also the French, were undaunted by either mud or Germans. The Field-Marshal concluded that they were all simply splendid.[124]

Walking to the battlefield three days later with General Godley, Sergeant Wilson was shocked by what he and the general saw:

I won't forget my experience today if I live for a thousand years . . . As we got further along we began to come to the part where all the recent fighting took place and where no salvaging had yet been done. Immense quantities of fighting material littered the ground. Graves were thick and bodies with only a few shovels full of earth protruded in every direction you looked and the further we advanced over the famous Abraham Heights the worse things got. Such a sight is impossible to describe. The Somme was pretty bad I'll admit but this is worse. I have never seen such destruction. It is hard to imagine that 4 years ago, peaceful people tilled this same soil and that it was one of the most prosperous districts in Europe. Now, as I saw it today, well its simply an awful nightmare, a hideous reeking swamp seething with living (and dead) beings. A place that stamps itself on one's mind and memory like a red hot iron.[125]

The New Zealand attack of 12 October 1917 was an intensely emotional and bitter experience for those who survived. Despite this experience now being all but lost to the New Zealand collective memory, the battle did leave an indelible mark on New Zealand, as if made by a red-hot iron. The following pages explore the destructive legacy of Passchendaele.

Chapter 5

THE LEGACY OF PASSCHENDAELE

After 12 October 1917, the Australians and New Zealanders were a spent force. Yet General Haig still refused to give up the offensive at Passchendaele. Six days later he brought in the Canadian Corps as the shock troops to finish the job. Haig had finally learned a valuable lesson from the disaster:

> The Army Commanders explained the situation; all agreed that mud and the bad weather prevented our troops getting on yesterday . . . We all agreed that our attack should only be launched when there is a fair prospect of fine weather. When the ground is dry no opposition which the enemy has put up has been able to stop our men.[1]

The Canadians planned to take in three stages what II Anzac Corps had been directed to achieve in just one. Given two weeks of preparation, the Canadians attacked on 26 October and took Bellevue Spur, before, on 30 October, securing Passchendaele village. On 6 November they went on to take Goudberg Spur (which had been the New Zealander's final objective), and on 10 November they secured the last of the high ground. All attacks proved successful, but cost the Canadians 13,000 casualties, including 4,000 killed, to take just over 3,000 yards of ground.

The greatest land battle of 1917, a year of almost constant fighting for the British armies, was Third Ypres. There were eleven major attacks, five of them spearheaded by Anzac troops with the final four spearheaded by the Canadian Corps. In good conditions the Germans had no answer to the step-by-step approach employed by Plumer and were defeated each time. Yet by persisting when the weather was bad, and without adequate artillery support, these attacks petered out into costly failures. The six attempts in the mud and slime after 4 October 'made the name of this battle one to shudder at'.[2]

The fighting around Ypres in the third battle to bear the town's name advanced the British line by almost six miles towards the objectives that had been set for the first two weeks of the campaign. The cost to achieve this ground was 275,000 casualties, of which 70,000 were killed. The British army lost the equivalent of ten to twelve divisions from its total of sixty. Many of those divisions still intact after November 1917 were in no fit state to continue fighting. Persisting with the battle after the success of 4 October produced effects opposite to those intended. The British armies were worn down after the fourth, and, as a result, German morale rose while that of the attackers — British, Australian and New Zealand — plummeted to the depths of despair.

German casualties were also heavy, caused mainly by an insistence on repeatedly counterattacking any time ground was lost. Many forget the Germans were fighting in the same appalling conditions as the British. Ludendorff wrote:

> Enormous masses of ammunition, such as the human mind had never imagined before the war, were hurled upon the bodies of men who passed a miserable existence scattered about in mud-filled shell-holes. The horror of the shell-hole area of Verdun was surpassed. It was no longer life at all. It was mere suffering. And through this world of mud the attackers dragged themselves, slowly, but steadily, and in dense masses. Caught in the advanced zone by our hail fire they often collapsed, and the lonely man in the shell-hole breathed again. Then the mass came on again. Rifle and machine-gun jammed with the mud. Man fought against man, and only too often the mass was successful.[3]

These muddy, freezing, damp conditions took a heavy toll on the German defenders at Passchendaele. Such was the extent of their wastage, it became evident that a change of tactics was required when the weather improved. Ludendorff later stated:

> The Army had come victoriously through 1917; but it had become apparent that the holding of the Western Front purely by a defensive could no longer be counted on, in view of the enormous quantity of material of all kinds which the Entente had now at their disposal . . . The condition of all allies and of our Army all called for an offensive

that would bring about an early decision. This was only possible on the Western Front.[4]

At the earliest opportunity in 1918, the Germans launched an offensive which broke the deadlock of trench warfare on the western front and almost won them the war. The experience of 1917, especially around Passchendaele, 'had given us valuable hints for an offensive battle in the West, if we wished to undertake one in 1918'.[5]

The disasters at Passchendaele caused the British army, the New Zealand Division included, to lose its confidence and optimism. Its good spirits were replaced by a 'deadly depression'.[6] For the survivors of Passchendaele the war seemed never-ending and ceased to have a purpose. As one New Zealand soldier wrote after the battle: 'I can't see Unconditional Surrender in the Peace Terms or the end even in sight.'[7] Soldiers had long ceased betting the war would be over by Christmas. Now they believed it would last a lifetime and sardonically joked that 'The first seven years will be the hardest.'[8] A future major general in the next great conflict, but a captain in the Machine Gun Corps when he witnessed the fateful attack of 12 October, wrote to his fiancée in New Zealand that his 'secret self' wished to get a minor wound that would finish his war 'and take him back to all the things he longs for'. Lindsay Inglis confessed: 'I hate the war, I'm sick of it, I have had enough; but I can't leave til I'm forced to.'[9] In his next letter he regained his composure and apologised to his fiancée for being so sentimental, but his letter of 26 October reveals his true feelings and is indicative of how the Passchendaele experience affected those who fought there. George McLaren, the soldier who had hastily scribbled his sister a note on the eve of the 4 October 'dust-up', wrote in his first letter to her after Passchendaele:

> It will soon be three years since I left NZ, there was a time when I thought I would have been home by now but I don't know what to make of it just now. The old Hun is still going strong in places and at present is wading into Italy at a great pace. I often wonder when he is going to give this front one of his wild visits . . . at any rate I am darned lucky to be alive ain't I . . . a man might have been pushing up the cowslips lots of times only for a terrible run of good luck.

His next letter contained more doubts about the direction of the war:

it is hard to say at times who is winning, but never mind Tina there is no question about who is going to win in the end, the only question is how long it is going to take the Allies to win.[10]

At the end of 1917, a year of disasters and huge sacrifice on the western front, this was the question to which no answer was immediately apparent. Morale in the whole British army suffered as a result. Victory was far, far away; death near and probable.

Yet the British army soldiered on, and, remarkably, no large mutinies occurred within its ranks. As the British official history freely admitted:

> The chief cause of the great discontentment during this period of the Flanders fighting was, in fact, the continuous demands on regimental officers and men to carry out tasks which appeared physically impossible to perform, and which no other army would have faced … That the attacks were so gallantly made in such conditions stands to the immortal credit of the battalions concerned.[11]

The historian is quite right. Such gallantry, while carelessly wasted at Passchendaele, should not be forgotten.

One of the divisions most affected by the horrors of Passchendaele was the New Zealand Division. The New Zealanders had suffered a huge defeat and they knew it. Ormond Burton accurately described the 12 October attack:

> The Huns kept their nerve, and the result was the inevitable massacre. For the first time New Zealand Brigades had completely failed, and their defeat had cost them as tragic a price as the barren victory on the blood-stained slopes of Sari Bair.[12]

As Stewart has commented, 'it is difficult to describe the troop's mortification and chagrin' at this failure.[13] One soldier noted:

> This is the first occasion when NZ troops have failed. The whole affair failed on account of the awful weather conditions and also through lack of sufficient preparation and coordination with the artillery.[14]

The casualties had been very heavy, but that alone had not caused the damage to morale. After the experience of two world wars, General Freyberg aptly commented:

> We had taken part in two forlorn hopes [Greece and Crete] . . . It was most important that we did not have another failure. It is a fact in war that troops can have heavy casualties, so long as the heavy casualties are not linked with failure.[15]

No longer able to boast of their proud reputation of always securing their objectives, the men of the division felt bitter at the losses associated with this futile attack. They were also much relieved when word came they were to leave the accursed Passchendaele swamp. Bert Stokes wrote:

> We suffered fairly heavily and I can tell you nobody was sorry when orders came to move out of the line. We had been looking forward to this day ever since we pulled in and all our eyes sparkled and we smiled a treat when we turned our backs on that part of the line which had treated us so badly.[16]

A gunner recorded that, while they didn't withdraw until 4 November and had to leave their guns behind for the Canadians to use, it was 'a happy day for us all, we were not sorry to leave the Ypres sector'.[17]

Morale in the New Zealand Division after its attack of 12 October reached an all-time low. All brigades were exhausted, and sickness within the various units was rife. The division had been pushed to the limits of endurance. General Russell's aide-de-camp recorded after Passchendaele that the New Zealanders were 'a Division somewhat shattered, dismally looking ahead to winter in frozen and damp trenches'.[18] One veteran believed that as a result of Passchendaele the New Zealand Division had slipped to being a C-class division, which was only to be expected. He stated years later: 'We'd been hammered too hard and of course your morale got low.'[19] The official history of the Machine Gun Corps readily admits that, after spending five days in the front line of Passchendaele under appalling conditions, combined with the 'nerve-wracking experience' of 12 October, its troops left the line 'completely exhausted . . . broken and worn out'.[20] In early November Russell witnessed the Rifle Brigade marching along a road and recorded that they were 'a sorry sight — this Bde wants looking after'.[21] Before Passchendaele, such a comment about a New Zealand infantry or rifle brigade was unthinkable. Passchendaele, the division's first and greatest failure of the war, when combined with the heavy winter of 1917, almost destroyed it. The division reached the nadir of its fortunes, similar to that suffered by 2 New Zealand Division at Monte Cassino in March 1944. Ormond Burton later wrote: 'There is a limit to what men can endure and during the winter of 1917–18 this limit was very nearly reached.'[22]

The extent of the disaster is reflected in the admission rates of the main New Zealand hospital in the United Kingdom, the No.1 New Zealand General Hospital at Brockenhurst, Hampshire, 14 miles from Southampton. This hospital had been established to receive sick and wounded New Zealand soldiers in June 1916, and most New Zealanders in need of hospitalisation found themselves there. The hospital continued to receive New Zealand soldiers until it closed in 1919. With a peak capacity of 920 patients, its monthly admission rates for 1916 and 1917 were:

1916 Admission Rates

July	522
August	422
September	1,306 (Somme)
October	662
November	389
December	545
Total	3,846

1917 Admission Rates

January	661
February	368
March	348
April	215
May	275
June	1,303 (Messines)
July	529
August	815
September	458
October	1,451 (Passchendaele)
November	719
December	720
Total	7,862

The admission rate for October 1917 was the highest in the hospital's history, and Brockenhurst ran out of bed space, having to set up an additional fifty beds in the local YMCA. Private Gwynne Potts was sent to Brockenhurst in early October suffering the effects of breathing mustard gas. He wrote home at the end of the month:

> The Hospitals are full up after this last stunt, suppose you have seen the casualty lists by now, the biggest smack New Zealand has had in some time. I don't think I have a mate left now, I was very lucky to miss it.[23]

The highest rate for 1918 was in September, with 1,308 admissions. Total admissions during the hospital's life amounted to 9,701.[24] What is also notable about the last three months of 1917 is that not only was the hospital's admission rate at its highest, but in the first two months of 1918, the admission rate was also well above the 1917 average of 655. The impact of Passchendaele was still being felt, these figures giving an indication of the health of the New Zealand Division. One historian has estimated that when the wastage rates from sickness are added to the battle casualties, the figure for New Zealand's losses reaches as high as 7,500 men for the month of October 1917, a figure confirmed by a New Zealand government publication of 1919.[25]

Major General J.F.C. Fuller, one of the most influential military thinkers of the 20th century, believed Third Ypres was 'a tactically impossible battle' and that to persist after August 1917 'was an inexcusable piece of pig-headedness on the part of Haig'.[26] Certainly many people have blamed Haig for the Passchendaele débâcle, one New Zealand writer going so far as to claim: 'As the officer in overall command, Field Marshall Sir Douglas Haig was responsible for the death of every New Zealander (not to mention the British casualties).'[27]

It is, therefore, a tragic irony — one almost impossible to explain — that on 15 October the British War Cabinet decided to send a message of congratulations to Haig, which he duly received on the sixteenth. The message declared the cabinet's desire 'to congratulate you and the troops under your command upon the achievements of the British Armies in Flanders in the great battle that has been raging since 31 July'. Even Haig was puzzled by the message and its appalling timing:

This is the first message of congratulation on any operation by the War Cabinet which has reached me since the war began! I wonder why the Prime Minister should suddenly have sent this message.[28]

As if to confirm the words were real, Haig copied the entire message into his personal diary.

While Haig must take a fair degree of the responsibility for the disaster of 12 October, there were plenty of other 'guilty men'. Many New Zealand soldiers believed Godley, not Haig, was personally to blame: 'A bad thing it was. You can thank old General Godley for that lot . . . One of Godley's mistakes. Everybody hated Godley. He was severe.'[29] Certainly the aloof, universally unpopular Godley made a convenient scapegoat. Most New Zealand soldiers after Gallipoli had come to regard him as both incompetent and foreign, a true-blue British officer in command of a division that by 1917 was largely anti-British. One soldier believed Godley had personally ordered the renewal of the attack on 12 October and that 'it was absolutely, utterly impossible. There wouldn't have been one of us left if we'd tried to do that.' Braithwaite, he believed, had refused to obey this order, and Godley had then had him sent home: 'That was Godley. I have no time for Godley at all. The troops didn't have much of an opinion of him.'[30]

While Godley, certainly not blameless, was the object of much criticism, General Russell, not blameless either, seems to have escaped the hatred and disdain of the troops who had suffered through his lack of action at Passchendaele. There were, however, some extenuating circumstances. Russell's diary reveals that from 5 October he was suffering from a severe cold which he could not shake off and which grew increasingly serious.[31] Years later his aide-de-camp recorded that:

The severe winter — the strain and the sorrow of the Battle of Passchendaele — the continuous work of building up the Division — the preparation for the Polderhoek Chateau assignment must have told on General Russell's health. He went to medical specialists . . . The General's chest was suspect and bronchitis was diagnosed.[32]

Despite this, General Russell must share much of the guilt for the events of 12 October. He had not gone forward prior to the attack to examine the ground over which he was about to send his soldiers, and, while he knew obstacles faced them, had naively assumed these would be destroyed by the heavy artillery. It was a dangerous assumption to make, and it proved a fatal one for many of his soldiers. If Russell had any doubts about the viability of the attack, he certainly did not voice them openly to his superiors. On the day of the attack he was not forward with the action, did not appreciate the huge difficulties facing his New Zealand troops — the terrible mud, the depth of the enemy wire, the withering machine-gun fire cutting them down en masse — and did not fully grasp the extent of his losses until well after the battle. He, not Godley, ordered the renewal of the attack at 3.00 p.m., before calling it off at the last minute when he learned the Australian division had also failed to secure their objectives and did not need flank protection from the New Zealanders.

Certainly many of the senior British commanders remained haunted by the experience of Passchendaele. General Harington, Plumer's Chief of Staff, later recalled:

> Those stages up to Passchendaele have always been a nightmare to me as they were to my Chief. They were all right up to and including Broodseinde, 4th October. After that Fate was very cruel to us. It is easy to say now that everyone knew it was going to rain like that except those at G.H.Q. and that the whole operation was an 'unjustifiable gamble.' I do not know how any operation of war can be anything else but a gamble unless the enemy tells you what he has got the other side of the hill and in what state his troops are.[33]

So painful a memory did this battle become that twenty-seven years later, in the third attempt to take the town of Cassino in southern Italy, Lieutenant General Sir Bernard Freyberg had only to utter the name 'Passchendaele' to bring all current operations to a close.[34]

Godley, Russell and Haig were only the most obvious of those to share the blame, but there were others. Above all, it was the British imperial system of command — a system that did not insist higher commanders lead from the front, and in which any doubts about the viability of an attack had to be locked away and internalised rather than openly voiced — that was at fault. This system failed the New Zealanders making the attack on the morning of 12 October 1917. Men like Godley, Haig and Russell were steeped in its culture, were products of it and could not escape from it. On the fields of

Passchendaele, just below the Bellevue Spur, a great many New Zealanders paid the ultimate price for its inadequacies.

In early November 1917 Russell wrote to James Allen of the Passchendaele disaster:

> We cannot always expect to succeed, but I feel very sorry about it all when I think of the numbers of men who were lost. My chief fear is that the men may lose confidence in the arrangements made for them as they had always been taught that, provided the Staff arrangements are good, they are able to do anything that is asked of them.[35]

Russell's fear was justified. An angry entry in Gunner Ward's diary caught the general mood of the New Zealand troops:

> Our boys went over at 6 AM . . . A bad, bad business — someone has blundered and our boys pay the price.[36]

Leonard Hart also believed a whole series of blunders were made and would never be brought to light:

> Some terrible blunder has been made. Someone is responsible for that barbed wire not having been broken up by our artillery and Someone is responsible for the opening of our barrage in the midst of us . . . Someone else is responsible for those machine gun emplacements being left practically intact, but the papers will all report another glorious success, and no one except those who actually took part in it will know any different.[37]

Indicating the huge gap between the commanders and the commanded, Gunner Stratton in his 'Recollections' was savage about the person who ordered this second attack:

> It was stated sometime later that some General or high person gave the order for us to attack the second time. Obviously he knew NOTHING at all about the conditions there nor did he heed the warnings of those that did know. Strange that we never heard when they shot him.[38]

Leonard Hart, whose infantry company lost 148 of its 180 members on 12 October, wrote to his parents:

> . . . we have nothing to be ashamed of as our commander afterwards

told us that no troops in the world could possibly have taken the position, but this is small comfort when one remembers the hundreds of lives that have been lost and nothing gained.[39]

Such an admission, if true, must have led many survivors to ask why their commanders allowed the attack to take place at all. It did not help matters either when the popular Brigadier 'Bill' Braithwaite left the New Zealand Division in December 1917 and did not return. Braithwaite was in a state of nervous exhaustion after Passchendaele, but had to command the division in its next action — the failed attack at Polderhoek Chateau. After Polderhoek, Braithwaite's health broke down and he was evacuated to England and hospitalised there. Yet rumours soon circulated that he had been sacked because of his refusal to sacrifice more of his men on the afternoon of 12 October:

Finally he [Braithwaite] refused to order his men to be murdered and of course that was the end of his military career. He was returned to England and we never saw him again.

This soldier added that 'the older we get the more bitter we feel about the needless suffering and the loss of so many of our friends'.[40] Another soldier, who lost a brother at Passchendaele, reflected in his old age: 'In many respects it makes me so angry when I think of the terrible loss of life and the things we had to put up with in war.'[41] Survivors of the battle took this bitterness back to New Zealand, where it took root and grew.

Anger generated by the Passchendaele attacks never died and, in Britain, some fifty years later, an 'explosive and abrasive' debate was conducted in the daily newspapers, with one contributor summing up the attitude of most veterans: 'The useless sacrifice is remembered by all those still living who took part in the actual fighting.'[42] This bitterness felt at the time grew dramatically when the ground won with so much blood and suffering in 1917 proved impossible to hold the following year. What had taken four months and 275,000 casualties to win was lost in just three days.

The experience was so painful for one soldier that even to this day he does not acknowledge that the battle of Passchendaele on 12 October was a disaster or could have been avoided:

It was the fortunes of war. Once it starts, it's got to go ahead doesn't it . . . I never heard it discussed that it had gone wrong. I think that is the armchair critics myself. I don't consider, never did consider it went wrong. It was a well-planned battle![43]

At least one participant believed Passchendaele was a positive experience, as painful as it had been:

In one way . . . when we came out of Passchendaele, we knew from the general higher authorities, we can't risk that again. So you knew you weren't going to be put in the same conditions . . . The troops at Passchendaele could talk about the hard times if they got out of it. But they didn't want it again!![44]

While the next New Zealand attack was also a failure, albeit on nowhere near the scale of 12 October 1917, there were no more Passchendaeles for the New Zealand Division.

In his letter of 7 November Russell had warned Allen: 'In these days of Parliamentary criticism, questions may be asked as to the operations I refer to.'[45] This did not happen. Allen spoke of the Passchendaele casualties in the House of Representatives on 1 November 1917. The number of New Zealand casualties suffered from 4 to 30 October appeared as 957 dead, 3,052 wounded and a further 1,300 unaccounted for. Allen stated that he 'regret[ed] very much this heavy casualty list', but no comments or questions emerged about the figures given. Allen's short comment is the only mention of the battle in the House records.[46] Despite Russell's concerns, Passchendaele did not provoke a political reaction in New Zealand. It did, however, provoke a reaction of another kind, one that has left an enduring legacy.

Passchendaele remains New Zealand's worst military disaster and as such is a pivotal moment in the country's history. Military history is not just about generals and battles in faraway places; it is also, in every sense, family history. The distinguished military-social historians of World War I, Jay Winter and Blaine Baggett, have commented: 'War is always the destroyer of families, and the Great War was to date the greatest destroyer of them all.'[47] This catastrophe at Passchendaele affected more New Zealand families and shattered more lives on a single day than any other event in the nation's history. Two stories, neither unusual, encapsulate the extent of the tragedy.

Private Wilfred C. Smith, a carpenter from Wellington, was a young New Zealander separated from his beloved wife and four young children. On the journey from New Zealand to England and France he wrote many long, tender letters to his family. Writing to 'My Dearest Ethel' on 23 September 1917, Private Smith mentioned the 'special training' the New Zealanders had been receiving and described how they would soon be in action:

> . . . we are expecting marching orders any hour and it is for something big too dearest and my only hope dear is to be spared to return to you all. The prospects of an early peace are much brighter now as we have been giving 'Fritz' a good thrashing right along the line.

Smith's letter also reveals a strong awareness of his children pining for an absent father and how deeply this must have affected them:

> Poor old Noni. I expect that she is tired of her Daddy being away from home for such a long time, and I can assure you dearest that I am tired of it too and would give anything if I knew for certain when I was going back to my own home.

Smith concluded by putting into words what many other soldiers must have felt at the time but lacked the ability to express:

> I am not afraid dearest and am certain that I will come through all right — But if I don't dear you will always have the satisfaction of knowing that your Husband has done his duty and that his last thoughts were of his wife and children.[48]

One is left to speculate whether this last letter was of much comfort to Ethel Smith. Private Smith never got to fire a shot at the enemy. He suffered a grievous wound from shell fire while moving up to the line on the evening of 3 October 1917 and died five days later at the 44th Casualty Clearing Station. Ethel and her children spent the rest of their lives aching for a lost husband and father who had done his duty to New Zealand, but for which this family had paid an almost unbearable price.

The Knight family, farmers and sawmillers from Dannervirke, was large, with ten children. The three elder sons, being of military age, went away to the Great War to do their bit. Not one of them

Private Linus T.J. Ryan. A keen observer of events at Passchendaele and one of the long suffering stretche-bearers of the New Zealand Army Medical Corps. (Anne Smyth).

Field guns firing from shell holes at Kanzas Farm. Note the ammunition mules ready to unload their burden. (1993.1032 H300, Kippenberger Military Archive and Research Library, Army Museum, Waiouru).

Jacking up a field gun at Passchendaele in an attempt to move it forward. (1999.929, Kippenberger Military Archive and Research Library, Army Museum, Waiouru).

Artillery position at Passchendaele. (1999.930, Kippenberger Military Archive and Research Library, Army Museum, Waiouru).

The desolate scene across one small part of the Passchendaele battlefield. The quagmire added to the death toll due to exposure or drowning as the terrain made it virtually impossible for stretcher-bearers to reach the wounded, especially at night. (Publishers collection).

'A hard task to be the mother of soldiers.' Nellie and Herbert Knight (second and third from the left) who lost three sons in the war. This photograph was taken in Dannevirke in 1916. (Nancy Croad).

A natural leader of considerable ability and charm. 2nd Lieutenant George Knight, killed at Passchendaele 12 October 1917. (Nancy Croad).

'Piko nei te Matenga.' (When our heads are bowed with woe). The tangi of Lieutenant Colonel George King, killed at Passchendaele 12 October 1917. (1993.1032 H346, Kippenberger Military Archive and Research Library, Army Museum, Waiouru).

New Zealand soldiers on their way to the NZ No.1 General Hospital, Brockenhurst, Hampshire, England. (Anne Smyth).

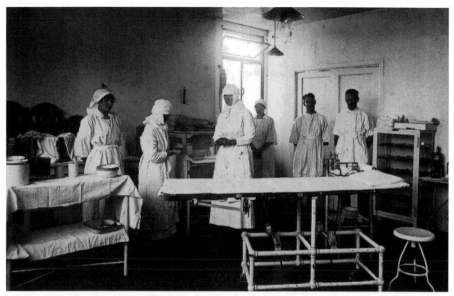

The operating theatre at Brockenhurst Hospital. During October 1917, many operations were performed each day here and the hospital staff were exhausted in the process. (Anne Smyth).

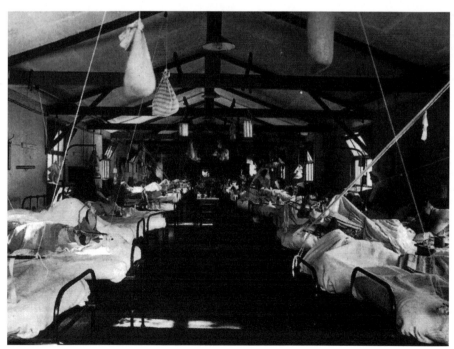

The No.1 Ward at Brockenhurst. This ward was reserved for serious leg cases. During October 1917 the hospital ran out of bed spaces, having to set up an additional fifty beds at the local YMCA. (Anne Smyth).

Winter in Passchendaele, Christmas 1917. The two soldiers are standing on the ice sheet over a shell crater. (1993.1951, Kippenberger Military Archive and Research Library, Army Museum, Waiouru).

Private Linus T.J. Ryan in a pensive mood awaiting his return to New Zealand. Photograph taken in Manchester in February 1919. (Anne Smyth).

The Gravenstafel (Passchendaele) Memorial to New Zealand soldiers in Belgium. An unknown monument to the majority of New Zealanders. (Steve Douglas).

One of the few memorials commemorating the Passchendaele battle in New Zealand. This one is at Christchurch's Central Railway Station. (Timothy Lucock).

survived to return home. We are able to gauge the extent of this terrible family tragedy through the letters of Mrs Ellen (Nellie) Knight, which have survived and are housed at the Alexander Turnbull Library.

A letter written to George, the second son, shortly after the boys had enlisted reveals Mrs Knight's sense of duty, her fears, and her perhaps naive hope that the family's dreams would not be interrupted by the war. She wrote:

> I tried to write last night. I had to tell Dad I could not face it alone. I had a good blub and feel better. Of course I knew we could not hope to keep out of it, nor did I want to as I told the others, if you were needed and you felt you ought to go, it will be very hard to part with any of you and I dare say it will mean all three, but I am ready to do my duty always, as you are to do yours . . . The land won't be much use to us if you boys are not there to work it but please God you may not be wanted or if you are you will be spared to come back 'hero's' and take up your work again and we can all do the things we have planned together to make a lovely garden home.[49]

Both Herbert, the youngest of the brothers who went away, and George joined 2 Otago Infantry Battalion and served at Gallipoli. There Herbert was killed early in the campaign by a sniper. Mrs Knight's loss and sense of helplessness is revealed in another letter to George:

> He did not get long to do his little bit, I would have felt happier, could he have had a chance to shoot a few more goals, but perhaps he did something worth his brave young life. I prayed so hard that you might both come back to me, but it is part of God's great plan and we must bear it, but it is a hard task to be the mother of soldiers . . . We feel so helpless here, there is nothing to do but weep and I try not to.[50]

George Knight survived Gallipoli and served with his battalion in France. He took part in the Somme battles and started to rise through the military ranks. A natural leader with ability and charm, he seemed to influence all around him, as many letters written to Mrs Knight testify.

In March 1917, George was promoted to the rank of sergeant and went to complete his officer training. He returned to the Otago Battalion as a 2nd lieutenant in June 1917. 2 Otago was allocated a key role in the 12 October attack at Passchendaele. The young, newly promoted George found himself leading a company up Bellevue Spur, where he and the men who remained tried to get beyond the impenetrable wire they found there. The task proved impossible, and George was cut down by a burst of machine gun fire only feet from the enemy positions. His body was never recovered.

After George's death Mrs Knight received many letters of sympathy. One of his fellow soldiers wrote to her:

> Believe me lady he was a NZer through and through and a boy that any parents can be proud of. He was as good a soldier as ever left New Zealand.[51]

Another soldier described George as 'brave and fearless' and as the 'best officer' in the battalion.[52]

From George's battalion commander came a very special letter:

> I cannot speak too highly of him: he was killed on October 12th while leading his company of which he was in command, both he and the other two officers were killed and a large number of his men: they did magnificent work and you must be proud of him.

Describing how George's company commander had been seriously wounded at the start of the battle, the colonel explained: 'I had such confidence in your boy that I at once put him in Command and most nobly he carried out his duty on that terrible morning.' The colonel also stated that all the men had equal confidence in George, and, in an unusual admission, added:

> Personally I have lost a great friend as he had endeared himself to us all. A splendid example of a soldier and a Gentleman.[53]

This letter clearly meant a great deal to Mrs Knight, as she copied it out in full as if hanging on to every word. At the top she wrote:

> Copy of letter which I can justly be proud of and put by with my other treasures.[54]

In another unusual measure at George's popularity, Mrs Knight also received a letter of sympathy from Brigadier Braithwaite, the commanding officer of 2 New Zealand Infantry Brigade.

Describing George's record of service as 'a brilliant one', Braithwaite wrote:

> I am well aware that no words of mine can be of the slightest comfort to you and yours at such a time, but although a stranger to you, I would like to tell you how much I feel for you in your great sorrow.

While trying to comfort Mrs Knight, the brigadier added something that probably had the opposite effect:

> The 2nd Brigade and especially the 2nd Otago Battalion suffered grievous losses that morning and experienced desperate fighting under the most intense machine gun fire.

Braithwaite then told Mrs Knight how her son had led his company very bravely and had died only yards from the enemy.[55]

One is to left to wonder how many other George Knights perished in the two attacks at Passchendaele and throughout the course of the war. For Nellie Knight the suffering was far from over. In 1918 her eldest son William (Douglas), serving in the Auckland Infantry Battalion, was killed in France during the great advances made by the New Zealand Division in the second half of that year. His last letter to the family at home arrived after the news of his death and was never opened. Nellie Knight's dreams of 'a lovely garden home' were dealt the severest blow by the Great War.

Yet there was a further 'bitter blow' to come.[56] The youngest of the children, Maurice (Marty), a masters graduate of Canterbury University with a doctorate from London University, while serving as an officer in a British anti-aircraft battery in the Punjab, contracted malaria and died in 1944, only weeks before he was due to return to New Zealand. War certainly destroyed a large part of this family, and we can only guess how Nellie Knight, who died in 1966 aged 94, suffered because of it.

Nellie Knight's case is certainly not unique. Mrs Mary Ann Newlove of Takaka, near Nelson, suffered similar agonies when the casualty figures from Passchendaele reached New Zealand. Three of her sons had enlisted in 1916. One, Leonard, was killed on 4 October. The other two boys, Edwin and Leslie, were killed on 12 October. Not one of the Newlove boys has a known grave, their names being recorded on the New Zealand Memorial to the Missing at Tyne Cot. All words are inadequate to describe the extent of this family's suffering.

Chaplain G.H. Gavin, who spent most of 12 October 1917 assisting a medical officer in dressing the stumps of a man with both legs shot away at the knee — 'the most distressing case I have ever seen' — devoted the following days to writing to the families of the deceased. He received numerous replies and noted that the families back in New Zealand 'are so grateful for the least news one can give them of their lost sons and brothers'.[57] Nearly every New Zealand family was affected by Passchendaele, or knew someone who was. By now New Zealanders knew first-hand the maiming, death or uncertain fate of loved ones that had become the terrible price of the war. The heady days of 1914, with their innocent illusions of glory, had long gone. In October 1917, New Zealanders 'did not need to be told that the angel of death had passed over the land: they had heard the beating of its wings'.[58] With the passage of time, the reasons for going to war faded from memory, but the loneliness and heartache never did. The sense of loss endured. The pain of the losing of loved ones was all the greater for the fact that the ultimate separation occurred at such a distance, with families isolated from the events that caused it. Denied the rituals that usually accompany death — the funeral, the church service, the mourners, a grave with a headstone that could be visited and tended — no sense of closure accompanied the loss. Empty places around family dinner tables could never be filled and were a permanent reminder that life would never be the same again. The Great War created a huge chasm between then and now.

The suffering did not end in 1917 or with the end of the war. The distinguished Australian historian, Professor Sir Ernest Scott, believed the Great War had a lasting impact on Australia and Australians, cutting 'deep furrows' in the political and social fabric of society that would still be evident in one hundred years time.[59] The disaster of Passchendaele cut equally 'deep furrows' in the political and social fabric of New Zealand, especially through the experiences of those who had been through the fires of Passchendaele and survived. Lieutenant Colonel C.H. Weston, wounded on 4 October and graded PU (Permanently Unfit) as a result, certainly believed the war left an imprint on him. He reflected when packing his neatly pressed uniform away for good: 'Will Time then set to work with his iron, to smooth out the furrow made on my brain by the war?'[60] Whether Time ever did or could remove the deep furrow from Weston's brain will remain an unanswered question. For many New Zealand soldiers, the furrow made by war lasted a lifetime and was never erased.

Stanley Herbert, wounded at Messines, admitted he was an emotional wreck coming back from the war. He even burnt his discharge papers because he was 'full up with war'. What saved Herbert was a good marriage that lasted sixty-one years. Without his wife Herbert would have been a lost soul and a victim of his war experience:

> I would have been just a hobo. Because I was a hobo. Because I had learnt many things too young. I was a good boy and a good worker. But she [his wife Beatrice] made me . . . My wife got the war out of my mind.[61]

The suffering was not confined to war veterans. Jeremy Rees, reflecting on the death of a great-uncle at Passchendaele eighty years later, recalled:

> Back home his death was devastating. His mother lost two sons in the war, a third died soon after. Some times her pain burst forth. She would cry at the dining table, weeping and railing against the injustice of war.[62]

Many returned soldiers were not as lucky as Stanley Herbert in being rescued by a good marriage. A section in Robin Hyde's Nor the Years Condemn reveals much about the cost of the war, and Passchendaele in particular, to New Zealand:

> Those [men] that came back from the war had ventured over the hills somewhere, restless, trying for adventure; or they had picked up chest trouble at the front, or worse. You could get engaged, triumphantly, to a good-looking, fine-faced returned man, give trousseau parties and indulge in the pride of showing your silk and semi-silk things to your girl friends. Then, perhaps on the eve of the wedding, there would be an incoherent note, a policeman around in the morning, and an inquest on a man who had put a bullet through his head. Somebody would explain that he had been badly shell-shocked at Ypres, badly gassed. Poor old Jack, everybody said. Yes, but nobody thought, in the same degree, poor young Laura or Mavis.[63]

Jack was a victim of Passchendaele, but so were Mavis and Laura, their parents, Jack's parents and the community where these various tragedies unfolded. As the New Zealand writer John Mulgan, a casualty of the next war, testified: 'We had never . . . outgrown the shadow of that earlier war . . . We felt the tragic waste and splendour of this first Great War, and grew up in the waste land that it produced.'[64] For many New Zealanders, the 'scars of war' would never heal.

In many ways the mistrust, suspicion, hostility, almost contempt, that New Zealand has demonstrated in the past towards its military can be traced back to the disaster of 12 October 1917. According to A.J.P. Taylor, the Somme battle 'set the picture by which future generations saw the First World War: brave helpless soldiers; blundering obstinate generals; nothing achieved'.[65] For New Zealand, though, relative latecomers to the Somme battle, the Passchendaele attack of 12 October dominates public memory of the western front, even though few New Zealanders are familiar with its details. Certainly one veteran of the war believed the Passchendaele disaster awakened New Zealanders to the dreadful reality of total war, and that all the 'wild enthusiasm' for the war in New Zealand ended when the long casualty lists from the Passchendaele battles finally reached here.[66] The stark reality of war hit home with a crushing blow, and New Zealanders, deeply hurt by the massive casualties, looked for ways to vent their anger and turned against anything military.

The New Zealand army still lives with this legacy of Passchendaele. Those who doubt the existence of a deep-seated hostility towards the military need only read Oliver Duff's account of how military personnel were viewed during the interwar years to realise how widespread it was. Duff wrote in 1941: 'No one was so ridiculous in those days, so derided and so despised, as the man who ventured out in uniform.'[67] This attitude has persisted throughout most of this century, and it was not until the late 1970s that the New Zealand army permitted its soldiers posted to Auckland and Wellington to appear in public in their uniforms. Even then old attitudes died slowly. One senior officer who retired from service in 1997 recalled how, when he first appeared in uniform in Auckland's Queen Street, he was spat on by a member of the public who would not have given him a second glance had he been dressed in plain clothing. 'We all felt besieged all the time,' he recalled.[68]

The negative attitude of many New Zealanders towards their soldiers, fuelled by the experience of Vietnam, has continued to this day. Those in uniform, especially officers, are derided by many New Zealanders as unthinking, uncaring militarists who might send 'brave, helpless soldiers' to their deaths without giving it a second thought. As with most stereotypes — this one derived from the experience at Passchendaele in 1917 — it is wide of the mark.

In New Zealand, memories of the Great War have been repressed for eighty years. No detailed, popular history of the New Zealand experience in the Great War has been written, unlike the twelve volumes of the Australian official history. In his volume on the Australian home front, Professor Scott wrote that the Great War was an ordeal unlike any other that Australia had faced and that it was 'a stirring and straining run of experience which required to be studied and recorded'.[69] This is equally true for New Zealand, but New Zealanders have barely scratched the surface in studying their Great War experience. Why is this so? There is probably no definitive answer, but three possible reasons spring to mind.

The first is that the men who returned from Passchendaele and other battles like it were unable to talk about their experiences for some time, and when that time finally came, towards the end of their lives, few people seemed prepared to listen. Many participants felt extremely unwilling to talk about experiences that were mostly brutal, painful and horrific and which they wanted to leave far behind them. One veteran succinctly expressed this reluctance:

> There was a lot of things that happened that I would like to forget. I didn't tell my mother, I didn't tell my family.[70]

Vic Martin, a sniper with the Otago Regiment who was himself wounded in the arm at Passchendaele by an enemy sniper, saw a friend's face shot away by a sniper's hollow-point bullet. His friend was standing alongside him, yet Martin paid little attention to the incident at the time: 'In war time, there is no effect. You are looking out for number one, aren't you?' But after the war the image of his friend's shattered face haunted Vic Martin, who often thought of him. He remained unable to talk about it even to those closest to him: 'You couldn't explain it . . . It was a big mistake . . . They should never have sent us over, not under the conditions . . . It was over as far I was concerned . . . I just wanted to forget about it.'[71] Unfortunately, such an experience burns itself deep into an individual's memory and those affected cannot easily dismiss it, as Vic Martin found out during his lifetime.

John A. Lee, returned soldier, writer and maverick Labour MP, described the reluctance to discuss the war in his autobiographical novel:

> Looking at those glittering crosses, he had realized that the front, the suffering out of which this wreckage had stumbled to die, was beyond description, something men could know, something men could feel, something men could talk about only to those who had known and felt.[72]

Even on those occasions when veterans did get together, such as Anzac Day or reunions, their memories were selective. On such occasions rarely was there talk of the pain and suffering endured, or of the death and destruction that are a part of war.

In his influential work on the Great War and the modern memory of it, Professor Paul Fussell astutely noted:

> But even if those at home had wanted to know the realities of war, they couldn't have without experiencing them: its conditions were too novel, its industrialised ghastliness too unprecedented. The war would have been simply unbelievable. From the very beginning a fissure was opening between the Army and civilians.[73]

A Passchendaele veteran reflected this attitude when he stated: 'A terrible thing war, isn't it? You've got to be there to understand it.'[74] Another, when asked why he had been unable to talk of his experiences, reinforced this view:

> I just didn't bother. I didn't lock it away. It was there but you just didn't bother. How can you explain to a civilian that has never seen anything like that, what it was actually like?[75]

Writing home just after the Passchendaele attacks Bert Stokes almost started to explain what he had been through, but caught himself just in time:

> This is war, grim warfare, and some of the sights I've witnessed have hit me very hard, various things have taken place right under my nose that I'll never forget, a chap has to have a stern heart and a strong

nerve. But we won't say any more of these things, there's a cheerful side to all our experiences, so let's look at that side.[76]

The second reason why New Zealand has not examined its war experience is, as Jock Phillips has written, the overwhelming image of the New Zealand soldier. This image, a powerful social force, is that of a 'hard man' — physically tough but also 'emotionally hard as a man who will never admit to pain or fear or weakness'.[77] Most New Zealand soldiers of this century have believed it their duty not to inflict their personal pain upon others. The pain must be borne in silence and no one speaks of it. But in most cases, the silence does not indicate all is well; far from it. The silence is that of an unrelenting personal despair.

Most psychologists agree that repression of unfavourable memories is very unhealthy for individuals, and in post-1918 New Zealand it seems to have occurred on a vast scale. There are four individual responses to a traumatic experience. They are:

1. Mild reaction to stress: a slight reaction occurs but natural coping mechanisms take over.
2. Memory shutdown: a physiological response in the subconscious or deeper.
3. Conscious suppression: the individual makes a deliberate effort to suppress the memory.
4. Mental and/or physical breakdown.[78]

For the majority of New Zealanders returning from the war, the response to experiences like Passchendaele was either 2 or 3 — a deliberate or subconscious attempt to forget. Few New Zealand soldiers fell into categories 1 and 4.

There are, however, significant behavioural outcomes associated with memory suppression and shutdown. In increasing order of severity, these can include slight maladjustment, being mildly dysfunctional, mental illnesses such as mood and/or sleep disorder and compulsive behaviour, post-traumatic stress disorder, physical illnesses, relationship problems, social, economic and work problems, survivor's guilt, suicidal tendencies and suicide itself. Most New Zealand soldiers who returned from the Great War experienced some kind of adverse reaction. In the main, though, this ranged from being slightly maladjusted to experiencing considerable guilt for having survived.

Widespread memory repression also affects the development, maturity and health of a nation. If not dealt with openly through public policy or some form of national healing process, the end result is collective guilt, denial, the suppression and distortion of the nation's history and the damaging of the nation's social institutions — all consequences borne by New Zealand after the Great War.

The third explanation for New Zealand's unfamiliarity with the Great War, one particularly relevant to Passchendaele, has to do with the country's attitude to its military past. Canada's experience of Passchendaele, because of the Canadian Corps' success there, has become part of the national mythology of Canada as a nation of supersoldiers, that country's version of the Australian 'digger' legend. New Zealanders, by comparison, uncomfortable when talking about military successes, have tended to focus on heroic failures, when success came so tantalising close but never materialised. This certainly applies to the three actions on which, according to Michael King, New Zealanders have 'dwelt most considerably in retrospect': the actions at Gallipoli, in Crete and at Monte Cassino.[79] Neither of the New Zealand attacks at Passchendaele in October 1917 falls into this category. The first was an outstanding success, described by the German records as 'a black day' for their army. The second was such an abject failure it was best forgotten, and never spoken of. Both attacks are recorded only on the silent war memorials where the name Passchendaele undoubtedly puzzles many who read it. The New Zealand experience of Passchendaele deserves much better than this. It should become at least as well known as Gallipoli, the only battle of the Great War to occupy a prominent place in the imagination of most New Zealanders. The battles at Passchendaele — the textbook success and the bloody failure — rate as highly as any of New Zealand's military encounters in their significance to the nation.

In his official history of the Australian home front during the Great War, Sir Ernest Scott regarded the conflict as a pivotal event in Australian national life.[80] He believed this because of the terrific losses associated with the war (nearly 60,000 dead) and the social upheaval and economic dislocation which followed its conclusion. Many other Australian historians agree with Scott's assessment. For

New Zealand, with its own civil war in the 19th century and its heavy commitment to the Second World War, it is difficult to make this claim about the Great War. There is little doubt, however, that the Great War deeply affected New Zealand in ways we haven't yet begun to understand. The losses of men were as proportionately high as Australia's, and New Zealand suffered equally from postwar dislocation. Life for all New Zealanders could not turn back to 1914. Too much blood had been shed and too much pain, often borne in silence, endured. The shadow of death had fallen across the land and it would remain for some time to come. And Passchendaele lies at the heart of this experience.

From a population of slightly more than one million people, New Zealand suffered some 17,000 killed during the war and another 41,000 wounded. New Zealand's casualty rate was 59 per cent of those who served, second only to that of Australia (65 per cent) in the British Empire. This was an enormous price to pay. The significance of Passchendaele, New Zealand's one great military failure in Belgium, can be measured when one considers that 6 per cent of New Zealand's total casualties occurred in just one morning of action on 12 October 1917. This day of tragedy has to be ranked as the very worst in New Zealand's path towards nationhood.

Conclusion

In October 1917 there were compelling strategic reasons for continuing the Flanders campaign. These included the state of the French army coupled with problems on the Italian front culminating in the disaster of Caporetto at the end of the month. Caporetto would necessitate sending the most able army commander, Plumer, to the Italian front in November. The total domination of the German army on the eastern front meant the Flanders region was one of the few places where the Allies could pin down and seriously damage the German army. On every other front the Germans were winning the war, and there was only one army on the western front capable of mounting a large-scale offensive in the second half of the year. An American army study of the campaign completed in 1922 concluded that, for the reasons mentioned above, 'to let the new British conscript armies sit in the trenches and lose the offensive spirit would have been a blunder'.[1]

Many of the senior commanders, therefore, felt they had no alternative but to continue attacking the Germans in 1917 no matter what the conditions. The tragedy that occurred at Passchendaele had a sense of inevitability about it. Major General Sir Charles Harington:

> I have knelt in Tyne Cot Cemetery below Passchendaele on that hallowed ground, the most beautiful and sacred place I know in this world. I have prayed in that cemetery oppressed with fear lest even one of those gallant comrades should have lost his life owing to any fault or neglect on the part of myself and the Second Army Staff. It is a fearsome responsibility to have been the one who signed and issued all the Second Army orders for those operations. All I can truthfully say is that we did our utmost. We could not have done more. History must give its verdict.[2]

This view was not shared by those at the receiving end of those orders. One soldier summarised their opinions in his response to a historian's questioning:

> Question: Just to come back to Passchendaele. Looking back at it, do you think that the attack could ever have succeeded?
> Answer: Is there ever any success? Is there any success when you throw men's lives away like that? I'm not answering your question, but I'm posing another one.[3]

While there was indeed a strategic imperative to mount a large-scale operation on the western front, there was considerable flexibility in the way it could have been executed. There was no reason to keep plugging away at the Germans in the same area and in the same old manner, especially when this had failed as dismally as it had on 9 October. A principle of war is not to reinforce or repeat failure, as this will only compound the scale of the disaster that inevitably results. General Ludendorff wrote an accurate description of the British methods of attack after 4 October:

> The enemy charged like a wild bull against the iron wall which kept him from our submarine bases. He threw his weight against Houthulst Forest, Poelcapelle, Passchendaele . . . He dented it in many places, and it seemed as if he must knock it down. But it held, although a faint tremour ran through its foundations.[4]

Rather than learning from the first charge at the iron gate that this type of attack hurt very much, and despite having adopted new tactics in 1916–17, the British commanders failed to adapt and innovate. They seemed lost for new ideas after 4 October. Instead, it would be the Germans who came up with the next major innovation of the war in their spring offensive of 1918, and it caught the British armies completely by surprise.

It is obvious in hindsight, as it was to many of the junior and senior commanders at the time, that the attack of 12 October should never have gone ahead. Certainly there was considerable doubt about the viability of the operation in the minds of General Russell and his brigadiers. That these commanders did not express their doubts more forcefully and allowed the attack to continue is an indictment of the military system of the time. The attacks at Passchendaele after 4 October were not based on detailed analysis and accurate intelligence.

Rather, they rested on little more than wishful thinking, on 'hoping for the best' when all the available evidence suggested overwhelmingly such hope would prove vain and cost lives.

Two senior American army officers have recently written: 'Hope is not a method.'[5] Hope should never be a substitute for sound, realistic planning based on accurate intelligence; that is, a substitute for a proper appreciation process. Such a process was clearly lacking for the attack of 12 October 1917.

A New Zealander who took part in the attack on 4 October, and in the massive recovery effort following the disaster of 12 October, encapsulated the infantry soldier's experience many years later:

> An ordinary infantryman at Passchendaele was a pretty dumb beast. That's how he's treated you see. He was only gun fodder and when all is said . . . that's what I feel. We were pretty dumb beasts you see, or we wouldn't have been thrown into that sort of warfare, because it was hopeless before you started. We all knew that. We all felt it couldn't [succeed] . . . But you'd go on, you know, if you could, and if it was possible to get through the wire, they would have got through the wire all right. Fellas did try to get through, crawled under it and did all sorts of things to get through, but you'd get shot as soon as you stopped.[6]

Certainly the men forced to attack knew they had been given an impossible task. That they still tried to do it regardless of the cost was an abuse of their trust.

New Zealand commanders in coalition wars now have the authority, and, one hopes, the moral courage, to say 'No!' to operations they consider too risky for troops under their command. It is their paramount duty as national commanders to do so. This was the rather painful lesson Major General Bernard Freyberg had to learn after the débâcles of Greece and Crete in the next world war.

New Zealand commanders are now also expected to demonstrate inventiveness, and are required to complete a complex course of military education that provides them with the analytical skills required to achieve their objectives at a minimal cost to young New Zealand lives. If we take any lesson from the tragedy of Passchendaele, this one is fundamental. Given the right training and junior leadership, New Zealand's soldiers are superb, with 'a reputation as the best soldiers in the world in the twentieth century', according to John Keegan.[7] But this should not be taken as a licence to squander them in futile frontal assaults. The days of ordering New Zealand soldiers to do the impossible should be long gone.

It is a tragedy that the events of Passchendaele are largely unknown to the majority of New Zealanders. As a nation we have inherited a reluctance to explore fully our war experiences, and thus we emulate those silent soldiers of the Great War. Consequently, what should have been an unforgettable experience has all but disappeared from our collective memory. What citizen of the United States of America, for example, would not know of the events surrounding the Alamo, Valley Forge, Gettysburg or Omaha Beach? New Zealand's military history is a vital part of the nation's past and has affected countless New Zealanders and their families. Yet it is a part of the nation's heritage that is all too often forgotten. That so few New Zealanders know anything about the battle of Passchendaele, New Zealand's worst-ever disaster, only emphasises how much we have forgotten.

Writing eighty years after the battle, one New Zealander did remember, and reflected on the sacrifice his great-uncle made on 4 October 1917:

> He was no hero, my great-uncle. But I admire his courage. He kept going amid the slaughter and the mud. Other armies mutinied or fell apart . . . At Passchendaele, Arthur Brown and his fellows did the hard yards, yard by sodden yard. That's courage of a kind. It's something to hold on to 80 years later.[8]

It certainly is.

ENDNOTES

Introduction
1   J. Laffin, Guide to Australian Battlefields of the Western Front 1916–1918, Sydney, 1992, p. 51.
2   Sir Philip Gibbs, The Realities of War, quoted in J. Terraine, The Road to Passchendaele, London, 1977, p. xix.
3   J. Terraine, The Western Front 1914–18, London, 1964, p. 153.
4   Diary of W.K. Wilson, Accession No. 9402314, Kippenberger Military Archive and Research Library, Army Museum, Waiouru.
5   Quoted in D. Winter, Haig's Command. A Reassessment, London, 1991, pp. 108–9.
6   Nicholas Boyack, Behind the Lines. The Lives of New Zealand Soldiers in the First World War, Wellington, 1989, p. 78.
7   Jay Winter and Blaine Baggett, 1914–18. The Great War and the Shaping of the 20th Century, London, 1996, p. 195.

Chapter 1
1   P. Fussell, The Great War and Modern Memory, London, 1975, p. 36.
2   Major General J.F.C. Fuller, Introduction, in Leon Wolff, In Flanders Fields. The 1917 Campaign, London, 1958, p. xi.
3   T. Wilson, The Myriad Faces of War, Oxford, 1986, p. 458.
4   Quoted in General Sir Charles Harington, Plumer of Messines, London, 1935, p. 109.
5   George A.B. Dewar and J.H. Boraston, Sir Douglas Haig's Command December 19, 1915, to November 11, 1918, London, 1922, p. 340.
6   Dewar and Boraston, p. 340.
7   W.S. Churchill, The World Crisis 1916–1918 Part II, London, 1927, p. 331.
8   Linus T.J. Ryan, 'A Brief Record of my Three Years in Khaki', p. 128, unpublished manuscript, property of Smyth family, Hamilton.
9   Fussell, p. 49.
10 D. Winter, Haig's Command, London, 1991, p. 168.
11 Colonel Repington, quoted in J. Terraine, The Road to Passchendaele, p. 61.
12 Marshal von Hindenburg, Out of My Life, London, 1920, pp. 288–9.
13 For an account of this learning process see P. Griffith, Battle Tactics of the Western Front. The British Army's Art of Attack 1916–18, London, 1994.
14 Haig's Diary, 10 May 1917, Terraine Papers, quoted in Terraine, Road to Passchendaele, p. 91.
15 Wilson, p. 468.
16 Dewar and Boraston, p. 359.
17 Haig's Diary, 2 August 1917, Terraine Papers, quoted in Terraine, Road to Passchendaele, p. 217.
18 General Ludendorff, My War Memories 1914–1918 Vol II, London, 1920, p. 480.

19 C. Falls, The First World War, London, 1960, p. 283.
20 Wilson, p. 462.
21 Ludendorff, p. 489.
22 Harington, p. 87.
23 Harington, p. 88.
24 Wilson, p. 474.
25 Ludendorff, p. 488.
26 Terraine, The Western Front, p. 172.
27 Ludendorff, p. 488.
28 Ludendorff, p. 288.
29 Record of Conference held at Second Army HQ, CASSEL at 11 am 2 October 1917, OAD 645, WA 11/4 Box 3, Item 14 Future Operations of Second Army, National Archives of New Zealand, Head Office, Wellington.
30 Birdwood to Allen, 28 September 1917, Papers of Sir James Allen, J Box 9a Correspondence with Mr Massey, Birdwood and Russell, National Archives of New Zealand, Head Office, Wellington.
31 Fussell, p. 12.
32 Major General J.F.C. Fuller, Introduction, in Leon Wolff, In Flanders Fields. The 1917 Campaign, London, 1958, p. xiii.
33 Ludendorff, p. 476.
34 Birdwood to James Allen, 28 September 1917, Allen Papers, File 9a Correspondence with Mr Massey, Birdwood and Russell, National Archives of New Zealand, Head Office, Wellington.
35 C. Pugsley, 'The New Zealand Division at Passchendaele', p. 274, in Liddle, Peter H. (ed) Passchendaele in Perspective. The Third Battle of Ypres, London, 1997.
36 Ludendorff, p. 488.

Chapter 2
1   Linus T.J. Ryan, 'A Brief Record of my Three Years in Khaki', pp. 118–19.
2   Diary of Gunner Bert Stokes, 8601028 Kippenberger Military Archive and Research Library, Army Museum, Waiouru.
3   A.E. Byrne, Official History of the Otago Regiment, N.Z.E.F. in the Great War 1914–1918, Second Edition, Dunedin, n.d., p. 202.
4   Diary of Brigadier Sir Herbert Hart, 28 September 1917, Kippenberger Military Archive and Research Library, Army Museum, Waiouru.
5   Linus T.J. Ryan, p. 35.
6   Leonard Hart to Mother, Father and Connie, letter, 19 October 1917, MS Papers 2157, Alexander Turnbull Library, Wellington.
7   A. Stratton, 'Recollections of the First World War 1916–18 in France after Gallipoli', MS Papers 3823, Alexander Turnbull Library, Wellington.
8   C.H. Weston, Three Years With the New Zealanders, London, n.d., p. 227.
9   George McLaren, letter to Tina, 28 September 1917, Letters to family, MS Papers 6535-4, Alexander Turnbull Library, Wellington.
10 War Diary General Staff of II Anzac Corps, WA 11/1 War Diary General Staff 2nd A & NZ Army Corps 1-7-17 – 31-12-17, National Archives of New Zealand, Head Office, Wellington.
11 Diary of Brigadier Sir Herbert Hart, Kippenberger Military Archive and Research Library, Army Museum, Waiouru.
12 WA 50/1 War Diary HQ NZ Divisional Artillery October 1917, National Archives of New Zealand, Head Office, Wellington.
13 J.H. Luxford, With the Machine Gunners in France and Palestine, Auckland, n.d., pp. 86–8, 88–9.
14 War Diary of 2nd Auckland Bn, WA 72/1, National Archives of New Zealand, Head

Office, Wellington.

15 General Sir Andrew Andrew Russell, diary, 2 October 1917, The Russell Saga, Vol III World War I 1915–1919, Alexander Turnbull Library, Wellington.

16 Edward Wright, 'The Smashing Victory of Broodseinde', in H.W. Wilson (ed), The Great War, Part 182, Week ending February 9, 1918, London, p. 514.

17 Weston, p. 221.

18 Luxford, p. 88.

19 A.D. Carbery, The New Zealand Medical Service in the Great War 1914–18, Auckland, 1924, p. 332.

20 Report on Operations Carried Out by 1st NZ Infantry Brigade 30 Sept–6 Oct, National Archives of New Zealand, Head Office, Wellington.

21 War Diary 1st Auckland Battalion, WA 71/1, National Archives of New Zealand, Head Office, Wellington.

22 Henry Ashton (Harry) Highet, oral testimony, OH AB 478, Oral History Centre, Alexander Turnbull Library, Wellington.

23 Burton, Auckland Regiment, p. 173.

24 Report on Operations Carried Out by 1st NZ Infantry Brigade 30 Sept–6 October 1917, National Archives of New Zealand, Head Office, Wellington.

25 Linus T.J. Ryan, p. 134.

26 Diary of Pte R. Hamley, 3 October 1917, Kippenberger Military Archive and Research Library, Army Museum, Waiouru.

27 Diary of Brigadier Sir Herbert Hart, Kippenberger Military Archive and Research Library, Army Museum, Waiouru.

28 O.E. Burton, The Silent Division. New Zealanders at the Front: 1914–1919, Sydney, 1935, p. 240.

29 Stewart Callaghan, letter to Tot and Willie, 9 October 1917, MS Papers 5004, Alexander Turnbull Library, Wellington.

30 Gordon Kirkpatrick Neill, oral testimony, OH AB 503-1, Oral History Centre, Alexander Turnbull Library, Wellington.

31 Capt F.S. Varnham, Folder 2, Diary Entry 4 Oct 1917, MS Papers 4303, Alexander Turnbull Library, Wellington.

32 W.H. Cunningham, C.A.L. Treadwell, J. S. Hanna, The Wellington Regiment N.Z.E.F. 1914–1919, Wellington, 1928, p. 217.

33 Sidney George Stanfield, oral testimony, OH AB 516/1, Oral History Centre, Alexander Turnbull Library, Wellington.

34 Weston, p. 228.

35 War Diary of 2nd Auckland Bn 1–5 Oct 1917, WA 72/1, National Archives of New Zealand, Head Office, Wellington.

36 War Diary General Staff of II Anzac Corps, WA 11/1 War Diary General Staff 2nd A & NZ Army Corps 1-7-17–31-12-17, National Archives of New Zealand, Head Office, Wellington.

37 Malcolm Beaven to Mother and Father, letter, 7 October 1917, MB 195, Box 83, MacMillan Brown Library, Canterbury University.

38 See Diary of Capt E.H. Northcroft, 3 Battery, NZFA, 9300 995 Kippenberger Military Archive and Library, Army Museum, Waiouru.

39 Luxford, p. 88.

40 Report on Operations Carried Out by 1st NZ Infantry Brigade 30 Sept–6 Oct 1917, National Archives of New Zealand, Head Office, Wellington.

41 Narrative of Events For Operations Undertaken on October 4th 1917, BM 455 8 Oct 1917, Hart Papers, Kippenberger Military Archive and Library, Army Museum, Waiouru.

42 H. Stewart, The New Zealand Division 1916–1919, Auckland, 1921, p. 271.

43 Walter Curruthers to family, letter, 9 Oct 1917, MS Papers 4107, Alexander Turnbull Library, Wellington.

44 Diary of Gunner Bert Stokes, 8601028 Kippenberger Military Archive and Library, Army Museum, Waiouru.

45 Narrative by G.H. Gavin, 3 Jan 1918, WA 10/3 Box 1 ZMR 1/1/3 Chaplain' Reports, National Archives of New Zealand, Head Office, Wellington.

46 Weston, p. 234.

47 Weston, p. 235.

48 Linus T.J. Ryan, p. 138.

49 Linus T.J. Ryan, p. 138.

50 German Official Account, quoted in Terraine, The Road to Passchendaele, p. 281.

51 From the history of the 92nd Regiment, 20th Division, quoted in N. Cave, Ypres. Passchendaele. The Fight for the Village, London, 1997, p. 99.

52 C.E.W. Bean, The Official History of Australia in the War of 1914–1918. Volume IV The AIF in France: 1917, Sydney, Angus and Robertson, 1933, p. 875.

53 Wolff, p. 194.

54 Diary of W.K. Wilson, 9402314 Kippenberger Military Archive and Research Library, Army Museum, Waiouru.

55 Godley to Allen, letter, 7 October 1917, WA 252/4 Letters of Colonel Sir James Allen and General Sir Alexander Godley Jan–Dec 1917, National Archives of New Zealand, Head Office, Wellington.

56 Monash to Rosenhain, quoted in G. Serle, John Monash. A Biography, Melbourne, 1982, p. 296.

57 Diary of H.S. Muschamps, 4 October 1917, 9102219 Kippenberger Military Archive and Research Library, Army Museum, Waiouru.

58 Diary of Gunner Bert Stokes, written November 1917, 8601028 Kippenberger Military Archive and Research Library, Army Museum, Waiouru.

59 Diary of Cpl H. Green, 4 October 1917, Kippenberger Military Archive and Research Library, Army Museum, Waiouru.

60 Leonard Hart to Mother, Father and Connie, letter, 19 October 1917, MS Papers 2157, Alexander Turnbull Library, Wellington.

61 Terraine, The Western Front, p. 173.

62 General Sir Andrew Andrew Russell, diary, 4 October 1917, The Russell Saga, Vol III World War I 1914–1919, Alexander Turnbull Library, Wellington.

63 Russell to Allen, 4 October 1917, Papers of Sir James Allen, Box 9a Correspondence with Mr Massey, Birdwood and Russell, National Archives of New Zealand, Head Office, Wellington.

64 Diary of Brigadier Sir Herbert Hart, Kippenberger Military Archive and Research Library, Army Museum, Waiouru.

65 Peter Howden to Mrs Rhoda Howden, letter, 6 October 1917, Folder 4, MS Papers 1504, P. Howden, Alexander Turnbull Library, Wellington.

66 Dominion, 6 and 8 October 1917.

67 Press, 5 and 8 October 1917.

68 Dominion, 8 October 1917.

69 Malcolm Beaven to Mother and Father, letter, 7 October 1917, MB 195, Box 83, MacMillan Brown Library, Canterbury University.

70 Peter Howden to Mrs Rhoda Howden, letter, 6 October 1917, Folder 4, MS Papers 1504, P. Howden, Alexander Turnbull Library, Wellington.

71 New Zealand Herald, 8 October 1917.

Chapter 3

1 Lieut K.E. Luke to his family, letter, 7 October 1917, MS Papers 6027, Alexander Turnbull Library, Wellington.

2 J.E. Edmonds, Military Operations in France and Belgium 1917, Vol II, London, 1948, p. 327.

3   Charles to Alice Ivory, letter, 14 October 1917, Ivory, Alice Maud, ARC 1991.54 Canterbury Museum.
4   HQ NZ Div Engineers War Diary Oct 1917, 6 October 1917, WA 60/1, National Archives Of New Zealand, Head Office, Wellington.
5   War Diary NZ Pioneer Battalion Oct 1917, WA 97/1, National Archives Of New Zealand, Head Office, Wellington.
6   War Diary NZ Pioneer Battalion Oct 1917, WA 97/1, National Archives Of New Zealand, Head Office, Wellington.
7   Captain S.D. Rogers to Harold Rogers, letter, 30 September 1917, MS Papers 5553 Letters to Stanley Dick Rogers. (The date indicates when the letter was started and it covers the whole month of October 1917.)
8   Captain S.D. Rogers to Harold Rogers, letter, 30 September 1917, MS Papers 5553 Letters to Stanley Dick Rogers, Alexander Turnbull Library, Wellington.
9   Ernest Henry Looms, diary, 6 October 1917, 1998.222, Kippenberger Military Archive and Research Library, Army Museum, Waiouru.
10 Malcolm Beaven to Mother and Father, letter, 7 October 1917, MB 195, Box 83, MacMillan Brown Library, Canterbury University.
11 C.E.W. Bean, Official History of Australia in the War of 1914–18. Vol IV The AIF in France 1917, Sydney, 1933, p. 881.
12 Harington, p. 111.
13 Haig Diary, quoted in Terraine, The Road to Passchendaele, p. 287.
14 Bean, p. 883.
15 Bean, p. 884.
16 Wilson, p. 479.
17 Lieut C.F. Sharland, 8 October 1917, quoted in Wilson, p. 479.
18 Quoted in Wolff, p. 208.
19 Edmonds, p. 331.
20 Captain S.D. Rogers to Harold Rogers, letter, 30 September 1917, MS Papers 5553 Letters of Stanley Dick Rogers, Alexander Turnbull Library, Wellington.
21 Linus T.J. Ryan, p. 143.
22 William Roy Robson, Diary Entries from 11 Oct 1917, MS Papers 3834, Alexander Turnbull Library, Wellington.
23 Bean, p. 901.
24 General Sir Andrew Andrew Russell, diary, 9 October 1917, The Russell Saga, Vol III World War I 1914–1919, Alexander Turnbull Library, Wellington.
25 Quoted in Wolff, p. 226.
26 Quoted in Wolff, p. 226.
27 Edmonds, p. 342.

Chapter 4
1   Diary of Harold Sinclair Muschamps, 11 Oct 1917, 9102219 Kippenberger Military Archive and Research Library, Army Museum, Waiouru.
2   Diary of Cpl Edward Duthie, 10 Oct 1917, 9402342 Kippenberger Military Archive and Research Library, Army Museum, Waiouru.
3   Vincent Jervis, Diary 10 October 1917, MS Papers 2241, Alexander Turnbull Library, Wellington.
4   Luxford, p. 100.
5   Peter Howden to Rhoda Howden, letter, 14 October 1917, MS Papers 1504, P. Howden, Alexander Turnbull Library, Wellington.
6   Percy Williams, A New Zealanders's Diary. Gallipoli and France 1915–1917, Christchurch, 1998, p. 265.
7   Mr Bright Williams, ex 3rd Bn, NZRB, interview, Havelock North, 27 March 1998.
8   Haig's Diary, Terraine papers, quoted in Terraine, The Road to Passchendaele, pp. 297–8.

9   Dewar and Boraston, p. 379.
10 Remarks Capt L. J. Taylor (OC, B Coy 3 Bn), WA 20/5 Item 36 Passchendaele Offensive, National Archives Of New Zealand, Head Office, Wellington.
11 Quoted in Stewart, p. 292.
12 Luxford, p. 92.
13 Luxford, p. 93.
14 General Sir Andrew Andrew Russell, diary, 11 October 1917, The Russell Saga, Vol III World War I 1914–1919, Alexander Turnbull Library, Wellington.
15 Robert Vincent Closey, oral testimony, OH0006/11 Tape 4, Oral History Centre, Alexander Turnbull Library, Wellington.
16 Experiences of Gunner Alfred Thomas Stratton, 35467 Kippenberger Military Archive and Research Library, Army Museum, Waiouru.
17 Diary of Brigadier Sir Herbert Hart, 12 Oct 1917, Kippenberger Military Archive and Research Library, Army Museum, Waiouru.
18 Captain S.D. Rogers to Harold Rogers, letter, 30 September 1917, MS Papers 5553 Letters of Stanley Dick Rogers, Alexander Turnbull Library, Wellington.
19 Edmonds, p. 328.
20 Bean, p. 907–8.
21 Malcolm Beaven to Mother and Father, letter, 4 November 1917, MB 195, Box 83, MacMillan Brown Library, Canterbury University.
22 A.E. Byrne, p. 213.
23 Percy Williams, p. 265.
24 Patrol under Sgt Mjr R.C. Travis, Intelligence Reports 8:05 pm, 11 Oct 1917, WA 76/1 War Diary HQ 2nd NZIB, National Archives Of New Zealand, Head Office, Wellington.
25 A.E. Byrne, p. 211.
26 Quoted in R. Prior and T. Wilson, Passchendaele. The Untold Story, London, 1996, p. 57.
27 W.S. Austin, The Official History of the New Zealand Rifle Brigade, Wellington, 1924, p. 229.
28 Austin, p. 230.
29 A.E. Byrne, p. 210.
30 Mr Bright Williams, interview.
31 Report on Operations 11–14 October 1917, (Written by CO Lt Col Owen Mead), War Diary 2 Cant Bn, WA 78/1 National Archives Of New Zealand, Head Office, Wellington.
32 Leonard Hart to Mother, Father and Connie, letter, 19 October 1917, MS Papers 2157, Alexander Turnbull Library, Wellington.
33 James Harold Vincent Martin, oral testimony, OH AB 496, Oral History Centre, Alexander Turnbull Library, Wellington.
34 A.E. Byrne, p. 215.
35 D. Ferguson, The History of the Canterbury Regiment, N.Z.E.F. 1914–1919, Auckland, 1921, p. 197.
36 NZ Div Narrative of operations for Passchendaele Attack Oct 12 1917, GOC NZ Div 3 Nov 1917, WA 20/3 Box 12, Item 151/42 Operations Somme/Ypres October 1917– February 1918 General Reports, National Archives Of New Zealand, Head Office, Wellington.
37 Stewart, p. 282.
38 Quoted in O. Burton, The Silent Division. New Zealanders at the Front: 1914–1919, Sydney, 1935, p. 246.
39 Mr Bright Williams, interview.
40 Austin, p. 238.
41 Stewart, p. 285.
42 Leonard M. Hart to Mother, Father and Connie, letter, 19 October 1917, Folder 2, MS

Papers 2157, Leonard M. Hart, Alexander Turnbull Library, Wellington. This letter, one of the best primary sources on the attack of 12 October, is some 42 pages long as Leonard Hart unburdens himself to his family. In order to avoid the Army censors the letter was posted from the United Kingdom.

43 Private Ernest H. Langford, Diary entry 12 Oct 1917, MS Papers 2242, Alexander Turnbull Library, Wellington.

44 Gerald Craig Beattie, oral testimony, MSC 2540, Oral History Centre, Alexander Turnbull Library, Wellington.

45 James Frederick Blakemore, oral testimony, OH AB 453, Oral History Centre, Alexander Turnbull Library, Wellington.

46 Diary of N.C. Rowe, 12 Oct 1917, 9301005 Kippenberger Military Archive and Research Library, Army Museum, Waiouru.

47 Henry Ashton (Harry) Highet to The Senior Officer, 1st Canterbury Regiment, letter, n.d., in oral testimony, OH AB 478, Oral History Centre, Alexander Turnbull Library, Wellington.

48 Percy Williams, p. 266.

49 Percy Williams, p. 266–7.

50 Charlie Lawrence, oral testimony, OH AB 489, Oral History Centre, Alexander Turnbull Library, Wellington.

51 Leonard Leary Reminiscences, MS Papers 4022 Alexander Turnbull Library, Wellington.

52 Ferguson, p. 198.

53 David Albert Grant to Leslie, letter, 36 October 1917, MS Papers 542, Alexander Turnbull Library, Wellington.

54 Vincent Jervis, Diary 12 October 1917, MS Papers 2241, Alexander Turnbull Library, Wellington.

55 Vincent Jervis, Diary 12 October 1917, MS Papers 2241, Alexander Turnbull Library, Wellington.

56 Leslie Frederick Harris, oral testimony, OH AB 476, Oral History Centre, Alexander Turnbull Library, Wellington.

57 Vincent Jervis, Diary 12 October 1917, MS Papers 2241, Alexander Turnbull Library, Wellington.

58 Diary of Cpl Harold Green, 12 Oct 1917, 18926 Kippenberger Military Archive and Research Library, Army Museum, Waiouru.

59 Mr Bright Williams, interview.

60 Report of 2nd Lt M.G. Luxford, Int Off, 3rd Bn, 3 NZRB 17/10/17, WA 20/5 Item 36 Passchendaele Offensive, National Archives Of New Zealand, Head Office, Wellington.

61 George Brunton, oral testimony, MSC 2579, Oral History Centre, Alexander Turnbull Library, Wellington.

62 Diary of Cpl Edward Duthie, 12 Oct 1917, 9402342 Kippenberger Military Archive and Research Library, Army Museum, Waiouru.

63 Cpl A.D. (Decie) Bridge, letter to wife, 19 October 1917, MS Papers 4689, Folder 3, Bridge File, Alexander Turnbull Library, Wellington.

64 Mr Bright Williams, interview.

65 Serle, p. 298.

66 Carbery, p. 348.

67 Percy Williams, p. 268.

68 Figures for the KIA and DOW are from New Zealand and World War One, Roll of Honour, 1917. http://freepages.genealogy.rootsweb.com. New Zealand historians owe Christine Clement of Te Puke an enormous debt of gratitude for compiling this database. These figures have also been confirmed by Andrew Macdonald's research.

69 J. Philips, N. Boyack and E.P. Malone, The Great Adventure, Wellington, 1988, p. 3.

70 Report on Operations 10–20 October 1917, WA 76/1 War Diary HQ 2nd NZIB, National Archives Of New Zealand, Head Office, Wellington.

71 Report on Operations 11–14 October 1917, (Written by CO Lt Col Owen Mead), WA 78/1 War Diary 2 Cant Bn, National Archives Of New Zealand, Head Office, Wellington.

72 A.E. Byrne, p. 220.

73 Major Richardson's Papers, WA 250/8, National Archives Of New Zealand, Head Office, Wellington.

74 Report on Operations 10–20 October 1917, War Diary HQ 2nd NZIB, WA 76/1, National Archives Of New Zealand, Head Office, Wellington.

75 Austin, p. 244.

76 General Sir Andrew Andrew Russell, diary, 12 October 1917, The Russell Saga, Vol III World War I 1914–1919, Alexander Turnbull Library, Wellington.

77 Henry Ashton (Harry) Highet to The Senior Officer, 1st Canterbury Regiment, letter, n.d., in oral testimony, OH AB 478, Oral History Centre, Alexander Turnbull Library, Wellington.

78 Translation of Captured Message from 29 Infantry Regiment (2nd Battalion) on 12 October 1917, Current Papers Lt Cory Wright, Intelligence Enemy Back Lines Disposition of Troops, WA 21/2 Box 1 Item 4, National Archives Of New Zealand, Head Office, Wellington.

79 Prior to the German attack in the Battle of the Metz on 9 June 1918, for example, German POWs indicated to the French that an attack was imminent while a German deserter revealed the exact date and time of the planned attack. See J. H. Johnson, 1918. The Unexpected Victory, London, 1997, p. 77.

80 Report on Operations 10–20 October 1917, War Diary HQ 2nd NZIB, WA 76/1, National Archives Of New Zealand, Head Office, Wellington.

81 II Anzac Intelligence Summary to 8 pm 13 October 1917, Passchendaele Offensive, WA 20/5 Item 36, National Archives Of New Zealand, Head Office, Wellington.

82 Edward Wright, 'The Conquest of Poelcappelle and the Reverse of Passchendaele', in H. W. Wilson (ed), The Great War, Part 183, Week ending February 16, 1918, London, p. 537.

83 New Zealand Herald, 16 October 1917.

84 Leslie Frederick Harris, oral testimony, OH AB 476, Oral History Centre, Alexander Turnbull Library, Wellington.

85 Godley to Allen, Letter, 16 Oct 1917, WA 252/4 Letters of Colonel Sir James Allen and General Sir Alexander Godley Jan–Dec 1917, National Archives Of New Zealand, Head Office, Wellington.

86 See Christopher Pugsley, Te Hokowhitu A Tu. The Maori Pioneer Battalion in the First World War, Auckland, 1995.

87 Quoted in Pugsley, Maori Pioneer Battalion, p. 67.

88 General Sir Andrew Andrew Russell, diary, 14 October 1917, The Russell Saga, Vol III World War I 1914–1919, Alexander Turnbull Library, Wellington.

89 Vincent Jervis, Diary 14 October 1917, MS Papers 2241, Alexander Turnbull Library, Wellington.

90 George Brunton, oral testimony, MSC 2579, Oral History Centre, Alexander Turnbull Library, Wellington.

91 Linus T.J. Ryan, p. 144.

92 J.H. Luxford, p. 99.

93 Gordon Kirkpatrick Neill, oral testimony, OH AB 503-1, Oral History Centre, Alexander Turnbull Library, Wellington.

94 Gordon Kirkpatrick Neill, oral testimony, OH AB 503-1, Oral History Centre, Alexander Turnbull Library, Wellington.

95 Sidney George Stanfield, oral testimony, OH AB 516/1, Oral History Centre, Alexander Turnbull Library, Wellington.

96 A.E. Byrne, p. 224.
97 A. Stratton, 'Recollections', MS Papers 3823, Alexander Turnbull Library, Wellington.
98 Sidney George Stanfield, oral testimony, OH AB 516/1, Oral History Centre, Alexander Turnbull Library, Wellington.
99 Linus T.J. Ryan, p. 152.
100 Sister A.E. Shadforth, quoted in Jan Bassett, Guns and Brooches. Australian Army Nursing from the Boer War to the Gulf War, Melbourne, 1992, p. 65.
101 Private Ernest H. Langford, Diary entry 12 Oct 1917, MS Papers 2242, Alexander Turnbull Library, Wellington.
102 General Sir Andrew Andrew Russell, diary, 16 October 1917, The Russell Saga, Vol III World War I 1914–1919, Alexander Turnbull Library, Wellington.
103 General Sir Andrew Andrew Russell, diary, 9 November 1917, The Russell Saga, Vol III World War I 1914–1919, Alexander Turnbull Library, Wellington.
104 Russell to Allen, 7 November 1917, Papers of Sir James Allen, Allen, J Box 9a Correspondence with Mr Massey, Birdwood and Russell, National Archives Of New Zealand, Head Office, Wellington.
105 Allen to Russell, 29 January 1918, Papers of Sir James Allen, Allen, J Box 9a Correspondence with Mr Massey, Birdwood and Russell, National Archives Of New Zealand, Head Office, Wellington.
106 Russell to Allen, 3 April 1918, Papers of Sir James Allen, Allen, J Box 9a Correspondence with Mr Massey, Birdwood and Russell, National Archives Of New Zealand, Head Office, Wellington.
107 A.E. Byrne, p. 228.
108 Wilson Diary, 14 Oct 1917, 9402314 Kippenberger Military Archive and Research Library, Army Museum, Waiouru.
109 Godley to Allen, letter, 16 Oct 1917, Letters of Colonel Sir James Allen and General Sir Alexander Godley Jan–Dec 1917, WA 252/4, National Archives Of New Zealand, Head Office, Wellington.
110 Godley to Wigram, letter, 14 Oct 1917, Godley Papers, WA 252/14 (Micro Z 5083), National Archives Of New Zealand, Head Office, Wellington.
111 Wigram to Godley, letter, 16 Oct 1917, Godley Papers, WA 252/14 (Micro Z 5083), National Archives Of New Zealand, Head Office, Wellington.
112 Godley to Allen, letter, 16 Oct 1917, Letters of Colonel Sir James Allen and General Sir Alexander Godley Jan–Dec 1917, WA 252/4, National Archives Of New Zealand, Head Office, Wellington.
113 Captain S.D. Rogers to Harold Rogers, letter, 30 September 1917, MS Papers 5553 Letters of Stanley Dick Rogers, Alexander Turnbull Library, Wellington.
114 NZ Div Narrative of operations for Passchendaele Attack Oct 12 1917, GOC NZ Div 3 Nov 1917, Operations Somme/Ypres October 1917–February 1918 General Reports, WA 20/3 Box 12, Item 151/42, National Archives Of New Zealand, Head Office, Wellington.
115 2nd Lt M.G. Laxford, Intelligence Officer 3rd Bn 3 NZRB 17/10/17 Passchendaele Offensive 12 October 1916 [sic], National Archives Of New Zealand, Head Office, Wellington.
116 Diary of Brigadier Sir Herbert Hart, 12 Oct 1917, Kippenberger Military Archive and Research Library, Army Museum, Waiouru.
117 Report on Operations Carried out by 3rd NZ (Rifle) Brigade 9 October–14 October 1917, National Archives Of New Zealand, Head Office, Wellington.
118 Linus T.J. Ryan, p. 143.
119 Bean, p. 921.
120 Prior and Wilson, p. 169.
121 Edward Wright, 'The Conquest of Poelcappelle and the Reverse of Passchendaele', in H.W. Wilson (ed), The Great War, Part 183, Week ending February 16, 1918, London,

p. 538.

122 Dominion, 15 October 1917.
123 Dominion, 16 October 1917.
124 New Zealand Herald, 15 October 1917.
125 Wilson Diary, 15 Oct 1917, 9402314 Kippenberger Military Archive and Research Library, Army Museum, Waiouru.

Chapter 5
1 Haig Diary, 13 October 1917, quoted in Terraine, The Road to Passchendaele, pp. 301–2.
2 Bean, p. 376.
3 Ludendorff, p. 491.
4 Ludendorff, p. 512.
5 Ludendorff, p. 497.
6 Sir Philip Gibbs, quoted in Terraine, The Road to Passchendaele, p. 341.
7 Malcolm Beaven to Mother and Father, letter, 4 November 1917, MB 195, Box 83, MacMillan Brown Library, Canterbury University.
8 Wolff, p. 2.
9 L.M. Inglis, letter 26 October 1917, Folder 5 MS Papers 421, Inglis Papers, Alexander Turnbull Library, Wellington.
10 George McLaren, letters to Tina, 1 November 1917 and 20 December 1917, MS Papers 6536-1, Alexander Turnbull Library, Wellington.
11 Edmonds, p. 330.
12 Burton, The Auckland Regiment, p. 180.
13 Stewart, p. 290.
14 R.W. Toomath, Diary, 13 Oct 1917, MS Papers 2301, Alexander Turnbull Library, Wellington.
15 Comments by Lt Gen Freyberg, VC, Second Libyan Campaign 1941, Vol 1, Correspondence Libya, WA II Series 11 No. 5, National Archives Of New Zealand, Head Office, Wellington.
16 Bert Stokes, letter to Mum and Dad, 6 November 1917, MS Papers 4683, Folder 7, Alexander Turnbull Library, Wellington.
17 Diary of J.C. Heseltine, 4 November 1917, MSX Papers 4338, Alexander Turnbull Library, Wellington.
18 Recollections of General Russell's Aid (Colonel G.F. Gambrill), MS Papers 1619, Folder 215, Alexander Turnbull Library, Wellington.
19 Sidney George Stanfield, oral testimony, OH AB 516/1, Oral History Centre, Alexander Turnbull Library, Wellington.
20 Luxford, p. 95.
21 General Sir Andrew Andrew Russell, diary, 9 November 1917, The Russell Saga, Vol III World War I 1914–1919, Alexander Turnbull Library, Wellington.
22 Burton, Silent Division, p. 253.
23 F.J. (Gwynne) Potts, letter to Queenie, 24 October 1917, MS Papers 4302, Folder 4, Alexander Turnbull Library, Wellington.
24 Report of No. 1 NZ General Hospital Brockenhurst, England, WA 4/1 Item 1, New Zealand Hospitals 1914–18, National Archives Of New Zealand, Head Office, Wellington.
25 Boyack, p. 78.
26 J.F.C. Fuller, The Decisive Battles of the Western World and their influence upon history, Volume III, London, 1956, p. 272.
27 Boyack, p. 79.
28 Haig Diary, 13 October 1917, quoted in Terraine, The Road to Passchendaele, pp. 302–3.

29 Charlie Lawrence, oral testimony, OH AB 489, Oral History Centre, Alexander Turnbull Library, Wellington.
30 Gerald Craig Beattie, oral testimony, MSC 2540, Oral History Centre, Alexander Turnbull Library, Wellington.
31 General Sir Andrew Andrew Russell, diary, 5 October 1917, The Russell Saga, Vol III World War I 1914–1919, Alexander Turnbull Library, Wellington.
32 Recollections of General Russell's Aid (Colonel G.F. Gambrill), MS Papers 1619, Folder 215, Alexander Turnbull Library, Wellington.
33 Harington, p. 130.
34 Fred Majdalany, Cassino. Portrait of a Battle, London, 1957, p. 193.
35 Major General Russell to James Allen (NZ Minister of Defence), 7 November 1917, Allen Papers, National Archives Of New Zealand, Head Office, Wellington.
36 Gunner Thomas Ward, Diary, 1997.1829, Kippenberger Military Archive and Research Library, Army Museum, Waiouru.
37 Leonard Hart to Mother, Father and Connie, letter, 19 October 1917, MS Papers 2157, Alexander Turnbull Library, Wellington.
38 Gunner A. Stratton, 'Recollections', MS Papers 3823, Alexander Turnbull Library, Wellington.
39 Leonard Hart, letter, 19 Oct 1917, MS Papers 2157, Alexander Turnbull Library, Wellington.
40 Leonard Leary Reminiscences, MS Papers 4022, Alexander Turnbull Library, Wellington.
41 Gordon Kirkpatrick Neill, oral testimony, OH AB 503-1, Oral History Centre, Alexander Turnbull Library, Wellington.
42 Sir Edward Beddinton-Behrens, Daily Telegraph, 7 July 1967, quoted in Terraine, Road to Passchendaele, p. xx.
43 Mr Bright Williams, interview.
44 Robert Vincent Closey, oral testimony, OH0006/11 Tape 4, Oral History Centre, Alexander Turnbull Library, Wellington.
45 Russell to Allen, 7 November 1917, Papers of Sir James Allen, Allen, J Box 9a Correspondence with Mr Massey, Birdwood and Russell, National Archives Of New Zealand, Head Office, Wellington.
46 New Zealand Parliamentary Debates, Vol. 181, October 11 to November 1, 1917, Wellington, 1917, p. 742.
47 Jay Winter and Blaine Baggett, 1914–18 The Great War and the Shaping of the 20th Century, London, 1996, p. 15.
48 W.C. Smith to Mrs C.M. Smith, letter, 23 September 1917, MS Papers 2352 W.C. Smith, Alexander Turnbull Library, Wellington.
49 Mrs N. Knight, letter to Georgie, n.d., MS Papers 5548 File 10, Alexander Turnbull Library, Wellington.
50 Mrs N. Knight, letter to My Dear Boy, n.d., MS Papers 5548 File 10, Alexander Turnbull Library, Wellington.
51 F.W. Hamill to Mrs N. Knight, letter, 31 October 1917, MS Papers 5548 File 11, Alexander Turnbull Library, Wellington.
52 Stuart Varnhauss to Mrs N. Knight, letter, 15 October 1917, MS Papers 5548 File 11, Alexander Turnbull Library, Wellington.
53 Lt Col G.S. Smith to Mrs N. Knight, letter, 18 October 1917, MS Papers 5548 File 11, Alexander Turnbull Library, Wellington.
54 Copy of Lt Col G.S. Smith's letter to Mrs N. Knight, 18 October 1917, MS Papers 5548 File 11, Alexander Turnbull Library, Wellington.
55 Brigadier W.G. Braithwaite to Mrs N. Knight, letter, 4 November 1917, MS Papers 5548 File 11, Alexander Turnbull Library, Wellington.
56 Nancy Croad, My Dear Home: The letters of three Knight brothers who gave their lives

during World War I, Auckland, 1995, p. 5.

57 Narrative by G.H. Gavin, 3 Jan 1918, WA 10/3 Box 1 ZMR 1/1/3 Chaplain' Reports, National Archives Of New Zealand, Head Office, Wellington.

58 Quoted in M. King, New Zealanders at War, Auckland, 1981, p. 167.

59 Sir Ernest Scott, Australian During the War, Sydney, 1936, p. 864.

60 Weston, p. 233.

61 Stanley Frederick Herbert, oral testimony, OH AB 482, Oral History Centre, Alexander Turnbull Library, Wellington.

62 'They did the hard yards — yard by sodden yard', Jeremy Rees, Central Leader, date unknown.

63 Robin Hyde, Nor the Years Condemn, New Women's Press Edition, 1986, p. 118.

64 John Mulgan, Report on Experience, Auckland, 1947, p. 33.

65 A.J.P. Taylor, The First World War. An Illustrated History, Harmondsworth, 1966, p. 140.

66 Sidney George Stanfield, oral testimony, OH AB 516/1, Oral History Centre, Alexander Turnbull Library, Wellington.

67 Oliver Duff, New Zealand Now, Wellington, 1941, p. 108.

68 Name withheld by request, interview, 20 April 1999.

69 Scott, p. viii.

70 Stanley Frederick Herbert, oral testimony, OH AB 482, Oral History Centre, Alexander Turnbull Library, Wellington.

71 James Harold Vincent Martin, oral testimony, OH AB 496, Oral History Centre, Alexander Turnbull Library, Wellington.

72 J.A. Lee, Civilian into Soldier, London, 1963, p. 44.

73 Fussell, p. 87.

74 Charlie Lawrence, oral testimony, OH AB 489, Oral History Centre, Alexander Turnbull Library, Wellington.

75 Mr Bright Williams, interview.

76 Bert Stokes, letter to Mum and Dad, 14 October 1917, MS Papers 4683, Folder 6, Alexander Turnbull Library, Wellington.

77 J. Phillips, A Man's Country? The image of the Pakeha male – a history, Auckland, 1987, p. 212.

78 From work undertaken by Dr James Conner. See also D. Grossman, On Killing: The psychological cost of learning to kill in war and society, Boston, 1995.

79 Michael King, New Zealanders at War, Auckland, 1918, p. 1.

80 Scott, p. 858.

Conclusion

1 Major R.E. Beebe, 'Course at the Army War College, Command, Problem No. 1 — The Principles of War', US Army War College Curriculum Archives 227-53, US Army Military History Institute, Carlisle, Pennsylvania.

2 Harington, p. 112.

3 Gordon Kirkpatrick Neill, oral testimony, OH AB 503-1, Oral History Centre, Alexander Turnbull Library, Wellington.

4 Ludendorff, p. 492.

5 Gordon R. Sullivan and Michael V. Harper, Hope is Not a Method, New York, 1996, p. 229.

6 Sidney George Stanfield, oral testimony, OH AB 516/1, Oral History Centre, Alexander Turnbull Library, Wellington.

7 J. Keegan, The First World War, London, 1998, p. 262.

8 'They did the hard yards — yard by sodden yard', Jeremy Rees, Central Leader, date unknown.

Appendix

THE FALLEN

As a tribute to the New Zealanders who fell at Passchendaele, whose sacrifice, with that of others in the Great War, helped preserve the rights and freedoms we now take for granted, we offer here details of those whose names are recorded together. The range in age and life experiences of these New Zealanders is incredibly varied, and indicates that a large slice of New Zealand society as it was at the turn of the century remains buried beneath the Flanders' soil. If the words 'Lest We Forget' are to have any meaning, the names of the fallen, and the battles in which they fell, should be remembered. May the memory of their deeds live on and never be forgotten.

The following names are on the Memorial to the Missing at Tyne Cot Cemetery, Zonnebeke, West-Vlaanderen. The memorial bears the names of almost 1,200 New Zealanders who fell in the Passchendaele battles and whose bodies were never recovered. The number at the end of each entry refers to the panel on which the name appears. (From the database of the Commonwealth War Graves Commission.)

ABBOTT, Rifleman, GEORGE, 41461. 1st Bn 3rd NZ Rifle Brigade. Killed in action 12 October 1917. Husband of Mrs M. Abbott, of 15 High St, Petone, Wellington. 8.

ACKHURST, Second Lieutenant, GEORGE, 18207. 1st Bn Wellington Regiment, NZEF. Killed in action 4 October 1917. Husband of Eusebia Margaret Ackhurst, of 63 Collingwood St, Hamilton. 6.

ADAMSON, Private, ALEXANDER JAMES, 37959. 17th Coy 2nd Bn Wellington Regiment, NZEF. Killed in action 4 October 1917. Age 30. Son of Alexander Adamson, of Ormondville, Hawke's Bay, Napier. 6.

AFFLECK, Private, HENRY DANIEL BLANE, 24527. 1st Bn Canterbury Regiment, NZEF. Killed in action 14 October 1917. Age 25. Son of James and Annie Affleck, of Glentunnel, Canterbury. 2.

AISHER, Private, FRANCIS JOSEPH, 40098. 2nd Bn Otago Regiment, NZEF. Killed in action 12 October 1917. Age 21. Son of Frederick and Rose Mary Aisher, of 60 Grey St, Palmerston North, Wellington. 4.

AITCHISON, Private, FRANCIS WILLIAM DOUGLAS, 39510. 9th Coy 1st Bn Wellington Regiment, NZEF. Killed in action 22 October 1917. Son of Mrs Isabella

Aitchison, of Methven, Canterbury. 6.

AITKEN, Private, ARTHUR HEATHER, 34304. 6th (Hauraki) Coy 2nd Bn Auckland Regiment, NZEF. Killed in action 4 October 1917. Age 33. Son of Alexander and Isaline Elsie Elizabeth Aitken, of 'Kereone', Morrinsville, Hamilton. 1.

ALLAN, Private, ROBERT BREACHIN, 29203. 3rd Bn Canterbury Regiment, NZEF. Died of wounds 17 October 1917. Son of Mr and Mrs John Allan, of 237 Papanui Rd, St Albans, Christchurch. 2.

ALLAN, Private, WILLIAM, 38925. 1st Bn Canterbury Regiment, NZEF. 12 October 1917. Age 33. Son of William Allan, of Dunphail, Morayshire, Scotland. 2.

ALLARDICE, Private, HENRY JOCELYN, 30500. 3rd Bn Wellington Regiment, NZEF. Killed in action 4 October 1917. Age 20. Son of James and Agnes Allardice, of Dannevirke, Napier. 6.

ALLEN, Private, STANLEY, 42007. 17th Coy 3rd Bn Wellington Regiment, NZEF. Killed in action 4 October 1917. Age 23. Son of William Rodda Allen and Mary Allen. 6.

ALLISON, Private, ERIC CHARLES, 27431. 8th Coy 2nd Bn Otago Regiment, NZEF. Killed in action 12 October 1917. Son of H. and W. Allison, of 73 Mary St, Invercargill. 4.

ALLISON, Lance Corporal, JOHN, 27425. 4th Coy 1st Bn Otago Regiment, NZEF. Killed in action 12 October 1917. Age 23. Son of Arthur and Isabella Allison, of 'Clover Lea', Drummond, Invercargill. 4.

AMYES, Private, ALFRED CUTHBERT, 27191. No. 2 Coy 2nd Bn Canterbury Regiment, NZEF. Killed in action 12 October 1917. Age 33. Son of Alfred and Elizabeth Anne Amyes, of Motukaika Cave, South Canterbury. 2.

ANDERSEN, Rifleman, NEILS, 22914. A Coy 3rd Bn 3rd NZ Rifle Brigade. Killed in action 12 October 1917. Age 34. Son of Jens and Amalie Andersen, of Norsewood, Napier. 8.

ANDERSON, Rifleman, ALBERT ROBERT JOHN, 11/1629. J Coy 2nd Bn 3rd NZ Rifle Brigade. Killed in action 12 October 1917. Age 25. Son of John and Georgina Anderson, of 155 Owen St, Wellington. 8.

ANDERSON, Corporal, DAVID, 28574. 3rd Bn attd 4th Light Trench Mortar Bty Auckland Regiment, NZEF. Killed in action 4–5 October 1917. Age 41. Son of the late David and Mary Anderson, of Franklin, Waikato, New Zealand; husband of Eva Clarice Anderson, of 'Crosslea', Symonds St, Onehunga, Auckland. Native of Fife, Scotland. 1.

ANDERSON, Private, HERBERT JOHN LANCELOT, 30335. 3rd Bn Wellington Regiment, NZEF. Killed in action 4 October 1917. Age 26. Son of David and the late Charlotte Mary Anderson. Native of Taranaki. 6.

ANDERSON, Private, JOHN, 43936. 2nd Bn Canterbury Regiment, NZEF. Killed in action 12 October 1917. Age 22. Son of Williarn and Catherine Anderson, of Lyalldale, St Andrew's. 2.

ANDERSON, Private, THOMAS RAMSEY, 35153. 3rd Bn Wellington Regiment, NZEF. Killed in action 4 October 1917. Son of Mr and Mrs H.R. Anderson, of 203 Charles St, Hastings, Napier. 6.

APPELBE, Private, ALBERT, 35233. 1st Bn Auckland Regiment, NZEF. Killed in action 4 October 1917. Son of Charles G. Appelbe, of Marton, Wellington. Native of Otago. 1.

APTED, Private, ALBERT, 10/3828. 1st Bn Wellington Regiment, NZEF. Killed in action 4 October 1917. Son of Mrs Emma Apted, of Neerim, Gippsland, Victoria, Australia. 6.

ARMSTRONG, Private, BENJAMIN, 27156. 3rd Bn Canterbury Regiment, NZEF. Killed in action 4 October 1917. Age 27. Son of John and Sarah Armstrong, of 21A Campbell St, Palmerston North. Native of Otaki. 2.

ARMSTRONG, Corporal, THOMAS, 25/932. 3rd Bn Canterbury Regiment, NZEF, formerly 3rd NZ Rifle Brigade. Killed in action 19 October 1917. Age 23. Son of Robert and Minnie Armstrong, of Wakanui Rd, Ashburton. 2.

ARNABOLDI, Private, PHILIP GEORGE, 52358. E Coy 3rd Bn Wellington Regiment, NZEF. Killed in action 15 October 1917. Age 20. Son of William Joseph and Rebecca Anne Arnaboldi, of Panmure, Auckland. Native of Glen Murray, Waikato, Hamilton. 6.

ARNOLD, Private, FREDERICK SAMUEL, 25430. No. 1 Coy NZ Machine Gun Corps. Killed in action 4 October 1917. Age 22. Son of Elizabeth Arnold, of 36 Beech Rd, Millbrook, Southampton, England, and the late Walter Amold. Emigrated to New South Wales, then to New Zealand. 9.

ASH, Private, HENRY EDWIN, 33274. 3rd Bn Wellington Regiment, NZEF. Killed in action 4 October 1917. Age 21. Son of Thomas and Elizabeth Ash (née Bezar), of 76C Adelaide Rd, Newtown, Wellington. Native of Rotherhithe, London, England. 6.

ASHBY, Private, GLADSTONE FREDERICK, 14366. 1st Bn Auckland Regiment, NZEF. Killed in action 22 October 1917. Age 23. Son of Ellen Ashby, of 66 Custom St West, Auckland. 1.

ASTRIDGE, Corporal, WILLIAM GEORGE, 24/1331. 2nd Bn 3rd NZ Rifle Brigade. Killed in action 12 October 1917. Age 30. Son of George and Sarah Astridge, of Queen St, Levin, Wellington. 7.

ATKINSON, Private, CLARENCE CLIFFORD, 23/1541. 2nd Bn Auckland Regiment, NZEF. Killed in action 4 October 1917. Son of Mr and Mrs G.R. Atkinson, of Mangatete, Awanui North, Auckland. 1.

ATKINSON, Private, EDWARD GEORGE, 26761. NZ Machine Gun Corps. Killed in action 12 October 1917. Age 26. Son of John Craston Atkinson and Hannah Sophia Atkinson, of 'Haeremai', 23 Royal Terrace, Mount Albert, Auckland. 9.

ATKINSON, Private, HUBERT HATTERSLEY, 24124. 1st Bn Canterbury Regiment, NZEF. Killed in action 2 October 1917. Age 27. Son of Thomas and Mary Jane Atkinson, of Sheffield, Canterbury. 2.

AUTRIDGE, Rifleman, CHARLES, 40271. 2nd Bn 3rd NZ Rifle Brigade. Killed in action 12 October 1917. Son of Mrs M. Autridge, of Richmond St, Thames. 8.

BAILES, Private, THOMAS THOMSON, 11225. 2nd Bn Otago Regiment, NZEF. Killed in action 12 October 1917. Age 36. Son of John Philip and Mary Bailes, of 155 Main Rd, Ravensboume, Dunedin. Native of North East Valley, Dunedin. 4.

BAILEY, Private, STANLEY, 29206. 3rd Bn Canterbury Regiment, NZEF. Killed in action 12 October 1917. Son of Mr and Mrs G. Bailey, of 21 Dilworth St, Riccarton. Christchurch. 2.

BAILLIE, Private, THOMAS DOUGLAS, 34325. 3rd Bn Auckland Regiment, NZEF. Killed in action 4 October 1917. Husband of the late Alice Baillie, of Otorohanga, Hamilton. 1.

BAIRD, Private, DAVID, 40862. 1st Bn Otago Regiment, NZEF. Killed in action 12 October 1917. Husband of Mrs J. Baird, of 72 Newton Rd, Auckland. 4.

BAIRD, Private, JOHN, 39144. 1st Bn Otago Regiment, NZEF. Killed in action 12 October 1917. Age 22. Son of William and Isabella Baird, of Benmore, Southland, Invercargill. Native of Otapiri Gorge, Southland. 4.

BAKER, Corporal, EDWIN THOMAS, 20080. 3rd Bn 3rd NZ Rifle Brigade. Killed in action 12 October 1917. Age 35. Son of Mr R.W. and Mrs E.E. Baker, of 32 Seafield Rd, St Lawrence, Ramsgate, England. 7.

BAKER, Private, FREDERICK GEORGE, 5/513A. 1st Bn Wellington Regiment, NZEF. Killed in action 21 October 1917. Son of Mrs E. Baker, of 330 Liverpool St, Hobart, Tasmania. 6.

BAKER, Private, GEORGE, 34317. 3rd Bn Auckland Regiment, NZEF. Died of wounds 4 October 1917. Son of Mrs R. Brown (formerly Baker), of 7 Fenton St., Stratford, New Plymouth. 1.

BAKER, Rifleman, JOHN RAPHAEL, 24804. 2nd Bn 3rd NZ Rifle Brigade. Killed in action 12 October 1917. Age 34. Son of John Stamner Baker and Katie Baker, of 5 Park View, Victoria Rd, Cork, Ireland. 8.

BAKER, Private, WILLIAM TORODE, 44692. 1st Bn Auckland Regiment, NZEF. Killed in action 4 October 1917. Age 20. Son of Williain T. and Alice C. Baker, of Station Rd, Otahuhu, Auckland. 1.

BALDWIN, Private, STANLEY HERBERT, 33812. 1st Bn Auckland Regiment, NZEF. Killed in action 21 October 1917. Son of Mr and Mrs Eber Baldwin, of Kirikopuni, Northern Wairoa, Auckland. 1.

BALL, Private, LINTON, 24/1589. 2nd Bn Auckland Regiment, NZEF. Killed in action 4 October 1917. Son of Mr and Mrs C.W. Ball, of Matakohe, Kaipara, Auckland. 1.

BALLAGH, Private, SAMUEL, 24125. 1st Bn Canterbury Regiment, NZEF. 12 October 1917. Age 34. Son of William and Margaret Ballagh, of 'Glenview', Ligoniel, Belfast, Ireland. 2.

BALSILLIE, Lance Corporal, WILLIAM JOHN, 39934. 2nd Bn Otago Regiment, NZEF. Killed in action 12 October 1917. Age 31. Only son of John and Annie Balsillie, of 10 Massey St, Palmerston North, Wellington. 4.

BANKS, Serjeant, SAMUEL WILLIAM MOSEBURY, 6/3965. 1st Bn Canterbury Regiment, NZEF. Killed in action 12 October 1917. Age 25. Son of Elizabeth Esther Banks, of 64 Eton St, Ashburton East, and the late Samuel John Banks. 2.

BARBER, Private, THEOPHILUS, G/2045. 2nd Bn Otago Regiment, NZEF. Killed in action 12 October 1917. Age 22. Son of Stephen and Margaret Alice Barber, of 42 Richmond St, South Dunedin. 4.

BARCLAY, Private, WALTER WADDELL, 39145. 1st Bn Otago Regiment, NZEF. Killed in action 12 October 1917. Age 35. Son of the late Lawrence and Marion Barclay. Native of Dunrobin, Otago. 4.

BARKER, Rifleman, THOMAS EDGAR, 44960. B Coy 1st Bn 3rd NZ Rifle Brigade. Killed in action 12 October 1917. Age 24. Son of Simon Henry Barker (ex-Bandmaster, RN) and Elizabeth Barker, of 40 Blaenanty Groes Rd, Cwmbach, Aberdare, South Wales. Born at The Old Barracks, Warwick, England. 8.

BARNETT, Private, ERNEST EDGAR, 30161. 3rd Bn Otago Regiment, NZEF. Killed in action 4 October 1917. Son of Mrs N. Barnett, of 98 Waimea St, Nelson. 4.

BARRETT, Private, JOHN, 36535. 3rd Bn Auckland Regiment, NZEF. Killed in action 4 October 1917. Son of Mrs E. Barrett, of Chapman St, St. Kilda, Dunedin. 1.

BARRON, Rifleman, PETER, 25/1658. A Coy 4th Bn 3rd NZ Rifle Brigade. Killed in action 12 October 1917. Age 30. Son of Peter and Margaret Barron, of Toko St, Rotorua, Hamilton. Native of Keith, Scotland. 8

BARRY, Private, GERALD, 24126. 1st Bn Canterbury Regiment, NZEF. Killed in action 12 October 1917. Brother of A.H. Barry, of Kialla East, Shepparton, Victoria, Australia. 2.

BARRY, Rifleman, JOHN PATRICK, 38482. 2nd Bn 3rd NZ Rifle Brigade. Killed in action 12 October 1917. Age 22. Son of Sarah Barry, of 19 Haiston Rd, Mount Eden, Auckland, and the late Garrett John Barry. 8.

BARTON, Private, PERCY GEORGE, 30732. North Auckland Coy 1st Bn Auckland Regiment, NZEF. Killed in action 4 October 1917. Age 21. Son of George Frederick and Flora Barton, of Norwood Rd, Bayswater, Auckland. 1.

BATES, Private, CLINTON MILLER, 13587. 2nd Bn Otago Regiment, NZEF. Killed in action 12 October 1917. Age 22. Son of the Rev. John James and Caroline Bates, of 'The Manse', Sheffield, Canterbury. Native of Lyttelton, Christchurch. 4.

BATES, Private, ERNEST JOHN, 3/165. NZ Medical Corps. Died of wounds 4 October 1917. Son of Mrs E. Bates, of 1 Abbey St, Newton, Auckland. 9.

BATTY, Lance Corporal, WILLIAM, 6/2392. 1st Bn Canterbury Regiment, NZEF. Killed in action 12 October 1917. Age 22. Son of Wilkinson and Theresa N. Batty, of 34 Douglas St, Ponsonby, Auckland. Also served at Gallipoli. 2.

BEAL, Private, JAMES EDWARD, 10297. 3rd Bn Otago Regiment, NZEF. Killed in action 4 October 1917. Age 21. Son of Henry and Thirza Beal, of Beach St, Waikouaiti, Dunedin. 4.

BEAMAN, Private, JOHN THOMAS, 5/1191A. No. 5 Coy NZ Machine Gun Corps. Killed in action 11 October 1917. Age 23. Son of Annie Moore (formerly Beaman), of 214A Cuba St, Wellington and the late John Thomas Bearnan. Native of Greymouth. 9.

BEAN, Private, JOHN, 49587. 3rd Bn Canterbury Regiment, NZEF. Killed in action 18 October 1917. Age 26. Son of Thomas and Caroline Bean, of Hook, Waimate. 2.

BEATTIE, Private, JOHN, 34794. 3rd Bn Otago Regiment, NZEF. Killed in action 4 October 1917. Age 29. Son of Robert and Isabella Beattie, of Ngapuna, Central Otago. 4

BEAUMONT, Private, ALFRED GORDON ROI, 28653. 1st Bn Auckland Regiment, NZEF. Killed in action 4 October 1917. Son of Mrs M. Beaumont, of 36 Strand Arcade, Auckland. 1.

BEAUMONT, Lance Serjeant, EDWARD HAROLD, 24127. 2nd Bn Canterbury Regiment, NZEF. Killed in action 12 October 1917. Age 21. Son of William David and Emma Jane Beaumont, of Ruapuna, Ashburton. Native of Temuka. 2.

BECK, Serjeant, MATTHIAS, M M, 10/2855. 1st Bn Wellington Regiment, NZEF. Killed in action 4 October 1917. Age 30. Son of Matthew Petersen Beck. 6.

BECKETT, Rifleman, CYRIL DONALD, 24/2150. 2nd Bn 3rd NZ Rifle Brigade. Killed in action 12 October 1917. Age 22. Son of William and Jane Beckett, of Frasertown, Napier. 8.

BECROFT, Rifleman, WILLIAM CLIFFORD, 10988. 1st Bn 3rd NZ Rifle Brigade. Killed in action 12 October 1917. Age 28. Son of Lewis Philip Becroft and Eliza Becroft, of Belmont Avenue, Mount Albert, Auckland. 8.

BEDFORD, Private, ERNEST JOHN, 34011. Canterbury Regiment, NZEF. 12th October 1917. 2.

BEEBY, Private, THOMAS, 14559. 1st Bn Otago Regiment, NZEF. Killed in action 12 October 1917. Age 27. Son of Joseph and Elizabeth Beeby, of Gateshead, England. 4.

BELL, Private, PERCY, 26773. 1st Bn Auckland Regiment, NZEF. 4 October 1917. Age 32. Son of John and Alice Bell, of 1 Kingsway, Waterloo, Liverpool, England. 1.

BELTON, Rifleman, EDWARD LANCELOT, 22930. A Coy 2nd Bn 3rd NZ Rifle Brigade. Killed in action 12 October 1917. Age 24. Son of William and Elizabeth Ann Belton. Native of Brookside, Canterbury. 8.

BENBOW, Private, PERCY JAMES, 38256. No. 1 Coy 1st Bn Canterbury Regiment, NZEF. Killed in action 12 October 1917. Age 28. Son of James and Alice Benbow, of Bankside, Canterbury. 2.

BENFELL, Private, FRANK, 40867. 1st Bn Otago Regiment, NZEF. Killed in action 12 October 1917. Husband of Mrs A.E. Benfell, of 7 Frame St, North East Valley, Dunedin. 4.

BENNETT, Private, ALFRED WILLIAM, 27834. 2nd Bn Otago Regiment, NZEF. Killed in action 12 October 1917. Husband of Hilda Bennett, of 3 Fitzherbert St, Petone, Wellington. 4.

BENNETT, Second Lieutenant, EDWIN BOLTON, 24326. 2nd Bn 3rd NZ Rifle Brigade. Killed in action 12 October 1917. Age 22. Son of Arthur Edwin and Rebecca Bennett, of Palmerston North. 7.

BENNETT, Second Lieutenant, JOSEPH LLEWELLYN, 21142. 2nd Bn 3rd NZ Rifle Brigade. Killed in action 12 October 1917. Age 24. Son of Frances and Katherine Bennett, of Waerenga Rd, Otaki, Wellington. 7.

BERN, Private, JAMES ROSS, 29352. 3rd Bn Wellington Regiment, NZEF. Killed in action 4 October 1917. Son of Mr and Mrs Joseph Bern, of Tamahere, Waikato, Hamilton. 6.

BERRY, Rifleman, JOHN ALBERT, 27767. 2nd Bn 3rd NZ Rifle Brigade. Killed in action 12 October 1917. Age 26. Son of George and Agnes Berry, of Russell Flat, Canterbury. 8.

BIGGS, Private, BERTIE, 11619. 2nd Bn Wellington Regiment, NZEF. Killed in action 4 October 1917. Brother of David Biggs, of Drayton, Ontario, Canada. 6.

BILLING, Private, PERCY HARRY, 27205. 2nd Bn Canterbury Regiment, NZEF. Killed in action 12 October 1917. Son of the late George Billing. 2.

BIRD, Private, FRANK, 8/2406. 5th Coy 1st Bn Otago Regiment, NZEF. Killed in action 10 October 1917. Age 19. Son of Frank and Bertha Bird, of Ohaupo Rd, Hamilton, New Zealand. Native of Manchester, England. 4.

BIRSS, Second Lieutenant, ALEXANDER CECIL, 26/52. 2nd Bn 3rd NZ Rifle Brigade. Killed in action 12 October 1917. Son of Mr and Mrs Alex. W. Birss, of Hamilton. 7.

BISHOP, Second Lieutenant, JOHN JOSEPH, Mentioned in Despatches, 23294. 4th Coy 1st Bn Otago Regiment, NZEF. Killed in action 12 October 1917. Age 24. Son of John Joseph and Emily Bishop, of 'Dunvegan', Titirangi, Auckland. 3.

BISMAN, Private, CHARLES, 28960. 3rd Bn Canterbury Regiment, NZEF. Killed in action 4 October 1917. Age 21. Son of Annie Jane Bisman, of 55 Hawdon St, Sydenham, Christchurch, and the late Charles Bisman. 2.

BISSET, Private, GORDON, 39150. Otago Regiment, NZEF. Killed in action 1 October 1917. Son of Jessie Bisset, of Wangaloa, Kaitangata, Dunedin. 4.

BJERMQUIST, Lance Serjeant, CHARLES HENRY, 28612. 3rd Bn Wellington

Regiment, NZEF. Killed in action 4 October 1917. Age 43. Son of Henry Bjermquist; husband of Selina Louie Bjermquist, of 74 Russell Terrace, Wellington. Served in the South African Campaign. 6.

BLACK, Private, DUNCAN ARCHIE, 28851. 3rd Bn Canterbury Regiment, NZEF. Killed in action 19 October 1917. Husband of Mrs E. Black, of Methven, Canterbury. 2.

BLACKETT, Private, PIERRIE LUDWIG, 32430. 3rd Bn Canterbury Regiment, NZEF. Killed in action 4 October 1917. Age 23. Son of Andrew Benton Blackett and Frederikke Marie Blackett, of Rolleston, Canterbury. Native of Rangiora, Canterbury. 2.

BLAKE, Private, HAROLD DAVID, 26377. No. 5 Coy NZ Machine Gun Corps. Killed in action 12 October 1917. Son of Mrs M. Blake, of St Andrew's Rd, Epsham, Auckland. 9.

BLAKER, Private, CLEMENT, 12/1556. NZ Medical Corps. 12 October 1917. 9.

BLAKIE, Private, HENRY WALTER, 40871. 2nd Bn Otago Regiment, NZEF. Killed in action 12 October 1917. Age 33. Son of Mr and Mrs William Blakie, of Ryal Bush, Southland, Invercargill. 4.

BLUNDEN, Private, LEONARD WALTER, 28576. 3rd Bn Canterbury Regiment, NZEF. Killed in action 4 October 1917. Son of Reginald and Alice Blunden, of Bennett's, North Canterbury. 2.

BOLSTAD, Private, JOHN ARNOLD, 45630. 1st Bn Wellington Regiment, NZEF. Killed in action 4 October 1917. Son of Mrs E.M. Bolstad, of Pahiatua, Wellington. 6.

BOLTON, Private, HAROLD WILSON, 27842. 2nd Bn Otago Regiment, NZEF. Killed in action 12 October 1917. Son of John Bolton, of 'Ru Belle', Springfield Avenue, Punchbowl Sydney, Australia, and the late C. Bolton. 4.

BOLTON, Private, PHILIP LESLIE ALFRED, 31010. No. 2 Coy NZ Machine Gun Corps. Killed in action 4 October 1917. Age 21. Son of Granville Edward William and Georgina Bolton, of 9 Seddon Rd, Hamilton West, Waikato, New Zealand. Native of Addlestone, Surrey, England. 9.

BOND, Private, ERNI, 44680. 2nd Bn Auckland Regiment, NZEF. Killed in action 4 October 1917. Age 21. Son of Ernie and Alice Bond, of 51 Remuera Rd, Auckland. 1.

BOUCHER, Sapper, EDGAR WOODWARD, 4/1736. Signal Coy NZ Engineers. Killed in action 12 October 1917. Age 24. Son of Ernest Woodward Boucher and Anna A. Boucher, of Tarewa, Rotorua. Also served at Samoa and in Egypt. 1.

BOUCHER, Lance Corporal, FRANK, 7/819. 2nd Bn Canterbury Regiment, NZEF. Killed in action 12 October 1917. Son of Mr and Mrs J.W. Boucher, of Methven, Canterbury. 2.

BOUGHTON, Private, CLEMENT ROBERT, 36545. 4th Coy 3rd Bn Otago Regiment, NZEF. Killed in action 17 October 1917. Age 21. Son of Elizabeth Boughton, of 109 Arthur St, Dunedin, and the late Clement Boughton. 4.

BOULTON, Private, LAWRENCE WILLIAM, 39940. No. 1 Coy NZ Machine Gun Corps. Killed in action 12 October 1917. Age 21. Son of Joel and Elizabeth Boulton, of Weraroa, Levin, Wellington. 9.

BOVEY, Private, WILLIAM STEED, 45974. 1st Bn Canterbury Regiment, NZEF. Killed in action 12 October 1917. Brother of George Bovey, of 151 Waimia St, Nelson. 2.

BOWERS, Private, CHARLES WILLIAM, 37963. 1st Bn Wellington Regiment,

NZEF. Killed in action 17 October 1917. Son of G.W. and M.J. Bowers. of Myrtle St, Lower Hutt, Wellington. 6.

BOWLER, Captain, DANIEL CORNEILIUS, M C, 14025. 2nd Bn 3rd NZ Rifle Brigade. Killed in action 12 October 1917. Husband of Mrs A. Bowler, of Davis St, Hastings, Napier. 7.

BOYD, Serjeant, ARTHUR ALEXANDER, 241355. 2nd Bn 3rd NZ Rifle Brigade. Killed in action 12 October 1917. Age 23. Son of Alexander and Lucy Jane Boyd, of Rosedale, Kaikoura, Christchurch. 7.

BOYD, Corporal, LESLIE HANIBAL, 23/1001. 1st Bn 3rd NZ Rifle Brigade. Killed in action 12 October 1917. Age 22. Son of William John and Louisa Lyne Boyd, of 22 Main St, Napier. 7.

BOYD, Private, RICHARD, 42781. 3rd Bn Canterbury Regiment, NZEF. Killed in action 4 October 1917. Son of Mrs David Boyd, of Kaikoura, Marlborough; husband of Mrs C. Palmer (formerly Boyd), of Te Matai Rd, Te Puke, Bay of Plenty. 2.

BOYLE, Serjeant, JAMES MCKENZIE, M M, 24331. 1 Oth Coy 2nd Bn Otago Regiment, NZEF. Killed in action 12 October 1917. Age 34. Son of James and Mary Stuart Boyle; husband of Frances Arbon (formerly Boyle), of 164 Jackson St, Petone; Wellington, New Zealand. Native of New South Wales, Australia. Served in the South African Campaign. 3.

BRADFORD, Private, HENRY ANDREW, 813188. No. 1 Coy NZ Machine Gun Corps. Killed in action 12 October 1917. Age 37. Son of Thomas and Amelia Bradford, of 66 Eton St, Hampstead, Ashburton, Christchurch. 9.

BREEN, Private, JOHN, 8/3498. 2nd Bn Otago Regiment, NZEF. Killed in action 1 October 1917. Son of Mr and Mrs Thomas Breen, of 2 Farnham St, Parnell, Auckland. 4.

BRENAN, Corporal, ERROL LYNDON, 1212920. 6th (Hauraki) Coy 1st Bn Auckland Regiment, NZEF. Killed in action 4 October 1917. Age 23. Son of Joseph and Amy Frederica Brenan, of Paeroa, Thames. 1.

BRENNAN, Rifleman, JOHN, 32808. 2nd Bn 3rd NZ Rifle Brigade. Killed in action 12 October 1917. Brother of Mrs Margaret Trewern, of Wellington. 8.

BRICKDALE, Private, JOHN BANCEL, 1211899. 1st Bn Auckland Regiment, NZEF. Killed in action 4 October 1917. Age 23. Son of Charlotte P. E. Brickdale, of Harding St, Greytown, Natal, South Africa, and the late Comdr. E.F. Brickdale. Also served at Gallipoli. 1.

BRIDGE, Rifleman, WILLIAM HENRY, 31110. C Coy. 2nd Bn 3rd NZ Rifle Brigade. Killed in action 12 October 1917. Age 23. Son of William Henry and Alice Gertrude Bridge, of 31 Disraeli St, Mount Eden, Auckland. 8.

BROADMORE, Rifleman, LEONARD FRENCH, 30340. 1st Bn 3rd NZ Rifle Brigade. Died of wounds 12 October 1917. Age 33. Son of Frederick and Sarah Broadmore, of Inglewood, Taranaki; husband of Emmalene Broadmore, of 27 Williamson's Avenue, Grey Lynn, Auckland. 8.

BROOK, Private, LAWRENCE DART, 11212. 1st Bn Otago Regiment, NZEF. Killed in action 12 October 1917. Age 20. Son of G. and F.J.W. Brook, of 129 Kimbolton Rd, Feilding, Wellington. Native of Lawrence, Dunedin. 4.

BROOKS, Rifleman, JAMES CHARLES, 47114. 3rd Bn 3rd NZ Rifle Brigade. Killed in action 12 October 1917. Son of Mr and Mrs James Brooks, of Lilydale, Tasmania. 8.

BROSNAN, Private, ARTHUR WILLIAM, 45060. 2nd Bn Otago Regiment, NZEF.

Killed in action 12 October 1917. Age 31. Son of James and Elizabeth Brosnan, of Exeter St, Mataura, Southland, Invercargill; husband of Sophie L. Brosnan, of 196 Gloucester St, Christchurch. 4.

BROUGH, Private, JULIAN PETER, 30339. 3rd Bn Wellington Regiment, NZEF. Killed in action 4 October 1917. Age 21. Son of Alexander and Harriet Brough, of Kakahi. Hamilton. 6.

BROUGHAN, Private, ARTHUR WILLIAM, 35494. 1st Bn Canterbury Regiment, NZEF. Killed in action 12 October 1917. Age 23. Son of William and Julia Broughan, of Tua Marina, Marlborough. 2.

BROWN, Private, DAVID BURTON, 10/2083. 1st Bn Wellington Regiment, NZEF. Killed in action 4 October 1917. Age 22. Son of John and Jessie Brown, of Burton, Vogeltown, New Plymouth. Native of Mangorei, Taranaki. 6.

BROWN, Private, DAVID HAROLD BINNS, 23962. No. 1 Coy NZ Machine Gun Corps. Killed in action 4 October 1917. Age 22. Son of Frederick William and Ellen Brown, of Shaddock St, Auckland. 9.

BROWN, Corporal, KENNETH ROBSON, 33809. 3rd Bn Auckland Regiment, NZEF. Accidentally killed 16 October 1917. Age 28. Son of Henry and Catherine Brown, of 2 Green Lane, Remuera, Auckland. Native of Pakiri, Auckland. 1.

BROWN, Private, WILLIAM ALEXANDER, 22184. 2nd Bn Otago Regiment, NZEF. Killed in action 12 October 1917. Age 34. Son of Catherine Meek Hastie Brown, of 363 Cargill Rd, South Dunedin, and the late John Brown. 4.

BROWN, Private, WILLIAM JAMES LAURIE, 23511. D Coy 1st Bn Otago Regiment, NZEF. Killed in action 1 October 1917. Age 26. Son of William and Rebekah Brown. Native of Oraki, Southland, Invercargill. 4.

BROWNE, Private, PERCY WILFRED, 42274. A Coy 1st Bn Auckland Regiment, NZEF. Killed in action 4 October 1917. Age 31. Son of the late Edward and Eliza Browne; husband of Agnes Neil Browne, of Argyle St, Avondale, Auckland. 1.

BRYAN-BROWN, Chaplain 4th Class, the REV. GUY SPENCER, 41286. NZ Chaplains' Dept. 4 October 1917. Age 32. Son of Grace Margaret Bryan-Brown, of Lydgate, Boar's Hill, Oxford, England, and the late Rev. Willoughby Bryan-Brown. 9.

BRYDEN, Rifleman, THOMAS JAMES, 45341. 4th Bn 3rd NZ Rifle Brigade. Killed in action 12 October 1917. Brother of David Bryden, of 3 Richmond Avenue, Grey Lynn, Auckland. 8.

BUCKLEY, Private, BENJAMIN ALFRED, 47310. 1st Bn Canterbury Regiment, NZEF. Killed in action 12 October 1917. Age 45. Son of Benjamin Alfred and Elizabeth Josephine Buckley, of Hook, Waimate, South Canterbury. Native of Timaru, South Canterbury. 2.

BULMAN, Private, JOHN, 10312. 2nd Bn Otago Regiment, NZEF. Killed in action 12 October 1917. Son of Mrs G.A. Brown (formerly Bulman), of 313 North Rd, Gladstone, Invercargill. 4.

BURGESS, Rifleman, GEORGE BRUCKSHAW, 32294. 2nd Bn 3rd NZ Rifle Brigade. Killed in action 12 October 1917. Age 28. Son of Richard Henry and Bessie Ferguson Burgess, of Staveley, Christchurch. 8.

BURKE, Private, ISAAC EDWARD, 46168. 1st Bn Canterbury Regiment, NZEF. Killed in action 12 October 1917. Son of the late Antonia Palatchie. 2.

BURNETT, Private, HAROLD JOHN, 13418. 3rd Bn Auckland Regiment, NZEF. Killed in action 4 October 1917. Age 20. Son of Emma Louisa Burnett, of Murumuru Raetihi, and the late J.H. Burnett. Also served with N.Z. Cyclist Corps. 1.

BURNETT, Private, PERCY JAMES, 42034. E Coy 1st Bn Auckland Regiment, NZEF. Killed in action 4 October 1917. Age 31. Son of William Johnson Burnett and Frances Burnett, of Ngaruawahia, Auckland. 1.

BURNSIDE, Private, GEOFFREY HERBERT, 42279. 6th (Hauraki) Coy 3rd Bn Auckland Regiment, NZEF. Killed in action 15 October 1917. Age 22. Son of David Parker Burnside and Lydia Elizabeth Octavia Burnside, of Ardmore, Papakura. 1.

BURR, Private, CHARLES WITTOX, 51553. 3rd Bn Auckland Regiment, NZEF. 16 October 1917. Age 32. Son of George and Jane Burr, of Headrooms, Lonmay, Aberdeenshire, Scotland. 1.

BURROWS, Private, HAROLD EDWARD, 14384. 16th (Waikato) Coy 1st Bn Auckland Regiment, NZEF. Killed in action 4 October 1917. Age 21. Son of Margaret Burrows, of Te Atatu, Henderson, Auckland, and the late John Burrows. 1.

BUTLER, Rifleman, THOMAS, 44251. 4th Bn 3rd NZ Rifle Brigade. Killed in action 12 October 1917. Age 41. Son of James and Annie Butler, of Settlement Rd, Papakura, Auckland. 8.

BUTTERWORTH, Private, JOHN THOMAS, 45068. 1st Bn Otago Regiment, NZEF. 3 October 1917. Age 24. Son of John and Elizabeth Butterworth, of Mid Cottage, Scotby, Carlisle, England. 4.

CALLAGHAN, Private, EDWARD, 37972. 1st Bn Wellington Regiment, NZEF. Killed in action 4 October 1917. Age 35. Son of the late John and Elizabeth Callaghan. Native of Cardrona, Otago. 6.

CAMERON, Lance Corporal, ALLAN, 8/2550. 1st Bn Otago Regiment, NZEF. 12 October 1917. Age 26. Son of Mrs Mary Cameron, of Church Side Cottage, Kilchoan, Argyll, Scotland. 4.

CAMERON, Lance Corporal, ANGUS, 8/3517. 2nd Bn Otago Regiment, NZEF. Killed in action 12 October 1917. Age 26. Son of Mary Frances Cameron, of Woodend, Awarua Plains, Southland, Invercargill, and the late Angus Cameron. Native of Edendale, Southland. 4.

CAMPBELL, Rifleman, ALLAN, 2311947. 1st Bn 3rd NZ Rifle Brigade. Killed in action 12 October 1917. Age 24. Son of Catherine and the late Patrick Campbell. Native of Ballarat, Victoria, Australia. 8.

CAMPBELL, Private, ARCHIBALD DONALD, 25671. 3rd (Auckland) Coy 1st Bn Auckland Regiment, NZEF. Killed in action 4 October 1917. Age 31. Son of Sarah Eliza Campbell, of 17 Collingwood St, Ponsonby, Auckland, and the late Angus Campbell. 1.

CAMPBELL, Serjeant, ERNEST GEORGE, 36771. 1st Bn Auckland Regiment, NZEF. Killed in action 4 October 1917. Age 25. Son of Robert and Clara Campbell, of Taupiri, Hamilton. 1.

CAMPBELL, Private, JOHN, 45073. 2nd Bn Otago Regiment, NZEF. Killed in action 12 October 1917. Son of Hugh and Jessie Campbell, of Wendon, Riversdale, Invercargill. 4.

CAMPBELL, Private, WILLIAM, 8/3204. 1st Bn Otago Regiment, NZEF. Killed in action 12 October 1917. Son of P. and A. Campbell, of Matata, Bay of Plenty. 4

CARMICHAEL, Private, JEOFFREYS, 42283. A Coy 1st Bn Auckland Regiment, NZEF. Killed in action 4 October 1917. Age 35. Son of William and Diana Carmichael. Native of Edinburgh, later of Fairfield, Liverpool, England. 1.

CARMODY, Private, JAMES, 33110. 1st Bn Wellington Regiment, NZEF. Killed in action 4 October 1917. Son of Mr and Mrs John Carmody, of 14 North St, Palmerston North, Wellington. 6.

CARMODY, Rifleman, WILLIAM, 35158. 3rd Bn 3rd NZ Rifle Brigade. Killed in action 12 October 1917. Son of Mr and Mrs John Carmody, of 14 North St, Palmerston North. 8.

CARNCROSS, Second Lieutenant, CYRIL CUTTEN, 39724. 1st Bn 3rd NZ Rifle Brigade. Killed in action 12 October 1917. Son of the Hon. W.C.F. Carncross of Eltham, New Plymouth. 7.

CARRUTHERS, Company Serjeant Major, WILLIAM THOMAS, 8/738. 1st Bn Otago Regiment, NZEF. Killed in action 12 October 1917. Son of Mrs M. Carruthers, of 23 Brunswick St, Dunedin. 3.

CARTER, Private, ALBERT BROOK, 33298. 3rd Wellington Regiment, NZEF. 4 October 1917. 6.

CASEY, Private, PATRICK, 36316. 3rd Bn Otago Regiment, NZEF. Killed in action 4 October 1917. Age 25. Son of Patrick and Ellen Casey, of Balfour, Southland, Invercargill. 4.

CASSIDY, Private, ARTHUR, 8/3207. 2nd Bn Otago Regiment, NZEF. Killed in action 1 October 1917. Son of Mrs J. Cassidy, of Money Staghan, Port Glenone, Co. Derry, Ireland. 4.

CASSIDY, Rifleman, PATRICK, 31814. 3rd Bn 3rd NZ Rifle Brigade. 12 October 1917. 8.

CATHRO, Private, DURHAM, 15135. 2nd Bn Otago Regiment, NZEF. Killed in action 12 October 1917. Son of William and M.C. Cathro, of Kokonga, Otago. 4.

CAVEN, Corporal, DAVID SINCLAIR, 22207. 2nd Bn Otago Regiment, NZEF. Killed in action 12 October 1917. Age 25. Son of Mary Caven, of Garlieston, Scotland. 3.

CHADWICK, Rifleman, NORMAN, 42285. 3rd Bn 3rd NZ Rifle Brigade. Killed in action 12 October 1917. Age 30. Son of Mr and Mrs Chadwick, of Hyde Bank Rd, New Mills, Stockport, England. 8.

CHALMERS, Private, ALEXANDER, 23973. 2nd Bn Otago Regiment, NZEF. Killed in action 12 October 1917. Son of the late William Chalmers, of Old Aberdeen, Scotland. 4.

CHAMBERS, Private, FREDERICK WILLIAM, 42287. 3rd Bn Auckland Regiment, NZEF. Died of wounds 17 October 1917. Age 22. Son of the late John and Mary Chambers. Native of Auckland. 1.

CHASE, Private, HERBERT, 8/1427. 1st Bn Otago Regiment, NZEF. 12 October 1917. Age 35. Son of Elizabeth Chase, of 13 London St, Paddington, London, England. 4.

CHISNALL, Private, JOHN, 33693. 3rd Bn Auckland Regiment, NZEF. Killed in action 4 October 1917. Son of Mr and Mrs W.H. Chisnall, of 21 Melrose St, Christchurch. 1.

CHOAT, Lance Corporal, SIDNEY WILLIAM, 23/1587. 16th (North Auckland) Coy 2nd Bn Auckland Regiment, NZEF. Killed in action 4 October 1917. Age 21. Son of James and Susannah Choat, of Puketona, Bay of Islands. 1.

CHUCK, Rifleman, GORDON HENRY, 12506. 4th Bn 3rd NZ Rifle Brigade. Killed in action 12 October 1917. Son of Mr and Mrs T.H. Chuck, of 32 Jolimond St, East Melbourne, Victoria, Australia. 8.

CLAFFEY, Private, PATRICK JOSEPH, 28323. 2nd Bn Wellington Regiment, NZEF.

4 October 1917. Age 33. Son of Patrick and Anne Claffey, of Connaught St, Birr, King's Co, Ireland. 6.

CLARIDGE, Private, ISAAC EDWARD, 24138. 1st Bn Canterbury Regiment, NZEF. Killed in action 12 October 1917. Son of Mr and Mrs Thomas Claridge, of Chapel Rd, Papanui, Christchurch. 2.

CLARK, Private, CHARLES WILLIAM, 8/3214. 2nd Bn Otago Regiment, NZEF. Killed in action 12 October 1917. Son of Mr and Mrs F. Clark, of Roslyn Bush, Southland, Invercargill. 4.

CLARK, Serjeant, EDWIN MICHELSON, 12/3920. A Coy 2nd Bn Auckland Regiment, NZEF. Died of wounds 4 October 1917. Age 21. Son of Harriet Clark, of 20 Herbert Rd, Mount Eden, Auckland, and the late George Clark. Native of Whakahara, Northern Wairoa. 1.

CLARK, Second Lieutenant, PERCY JOHN, Mentioned in Despatches, 23136. NZ Machine Gun Corps. Killed in action 11 October 1917. Age 23. Son of Edward Halcomb Clark and Caroline Louisa Clark, of 8 Phillip St, Linwood, Christchurch. Native of Whitfield, Dover, England. Also served in Egypt. 9.

CLARK, Private, WILLIAM, 44702. 1st Bn Auckland Regiment, NZEF. Killed in action 23 October 1917. Son of Mrs L. Clark, of Shaw St, Morningside, Auckland. 1.

CLARKE, Rifleman, WILLIAM WALTER, 45668. 4th Bn 3rd NZ Rifle Brigade. Killed in action 12 October 1917. Son of Mr and Mrs W. Clarke, of Hora Hora Rd, Whangarei, Auckland. 8.

CLEMENT, Private, MARK, 51005. B Coy 3rd Bn Wellington Regiment, NZEF. Killed in action 20 October 1917. Age 22. Son of Gus and Albertina Clement, of 48 Hutt Rd, Petone, Wellington. 6.

CLIFFORD, Private, LESLIE THOMAS JAMES, 33520. Ruahine Coy 3rd Bn Wellington Regiment, NZEF. Killed in action 4 October 1917. Age 23. Son of John James and Harriet Elizabeth A. Clifford, of Glenorchy, Tasmania. 6.

COATMAN, Second Lieutenant, ARTHUR SINDEL MEHRTENS, 8/25. 2nd Bn Otago Regiment, NZEF. Killed in action 12 October 1917. Age 24. Son of Joseph and Anna Coatman, of 67 Chelmer St, Oamaru. 3.

COBBE, Second Lieutenant, ERNEST, 25/262. 4th Bn 3rd NZ Rifle Brigade. Killed in action 12 October 1917. Age 30. Son of John G. and Frances A. Cobbe, of The Hill, Feilding, Wellington. 7.

COCHRANE, Private, JOHN ALEXANDER, 29738. 1st Bn Otago Regiment, NZEF. Killed in action 12 October 1917. Age 31. Husband of Janet Cochrane, of Ladbrooks, Christchurch. Native of Darvel, Ayrshire, Scotland. 4.

COCKBURN, Rifleman, ANDREW, 25813. 1st Bn 3rd NZ Rifle Brigade. 12 October 1917. 8.

COFFEY, Private, CHARLES EDWARD, 33695. 3rd Bn Canterbury Regiment, NZEF. Killed in action 4 October 1917. Son of Mr and Mrs Michael Coffey, of 128 Blights Rd, Papanui, Christchurch. 2.

COLE, Corporal, DAVID COATES, 21216. 2nd (Waikato) Coy 2nd Bn Auckland Regiment, NZEF. Killed in action 4 October 1917. Age 21. Son of David Graeme Cole and Minnie Cole, of 'Clontivem', Trafalgar St, Onehunga, Auckland. 1.

COLLINGS, Private, BERTRAM CHARLES, 39170. 15th (North Auckland) Coy 3rd Bn Auckland Regiment, NZEF. Killed in action 3 October 1917. Age 32. Son of Fredrick Arthur and Sarah Ann Collings, of 122 North St, Timaru. Native of Cromwell, Otago. 1.

COLLINS, Private, FRED ALBERT, 27468. 2nd Bn Otago Regiment, NZEF. Killed in action 12 October 1917. Age 24. Son of John and Alice Agusta Collins, of 227 Forbury Rd, St Clair, Dunedin. 4.

COLLINSON, Private, WILLIAM HENRY, 3/2835. NZ Medical Corps. Killed in action 12 October 1917. Age 36. Son of John Benjamin and Alice Maud Mary Collinson. Native of Brighton, England. 9.

CONNELL, Private, ALFRED HENRY, 29360. lst Bn Wellington Regiment, NZEF. Killed in action 4 October 1917. Son of Mrs M. Connell, of Matamata, Hamilton. 6.

COOK, Private, ARCHIE, 614223. 1st Bn Canterbury Regiment, NZEF. Killed in action 12 October 1917. Son of Mr and Mrs George Cook, of 236 St Asaph St, Christchurch. 2.

COOK, Private, JOHN SCOTT, 26/535. 3rd Bn Otago Regiment, NZEF. Killed in action 4 October 1917. Age 23. Son of David and Elizabeth Cook, of Hilderthorpe, Oamaru. Native of Owaka, Dunedin. 4.

COOKSON, Private, CLEMENT FRANK, 6/1494. 3rd Bn Canterbury Regiment, NZEF. Killed in action 18 October 1917. Son of Mr and Mrs Arthur Cookson, of Lincoln, Canterbury. 2.

COONEY, Rifleman, JAMES VINCENT, 32820. 3rd Bn 3rd NZ Rifle Brigade. Killed in action 12 October 1917. Son of Mrs M. Cooney, of 35 Reed St, Oamaru. 8.

CORBETT, Private, THOMAS HUGH LESLIE, 36319. 3rd Bn Canterbury Regiment, NZEF. Killed in action 4 October 1917. Age 24. Son of James and Sarah Jane Corbett, of 48 Winchester St, Merivale, Christchurch. Native of Canterbury. 2.

COSTER, Private, FRANK PORTEOUS, 27461. 2nd Bn Otago Regiment, NZEF. Killed in action 12 October 1917. Age 23. Son of Williain Gordon Coster and Maggie Auld Coster, of Waimauku, Auckland. Native of Winton, Southland, Invercargill. 4.

COULSON, Private, BERTIE, 22309. 2nd Bn Otago Regiment, NZEF. Killed in action 12 October 1917. Age 22. Son of Louisa Sarah Coulson, of Alexandra, Otago. 4.

COULTER, Private, ARTHUR, 9/1029. 2nd Bn Otago Regiment, NZEF. Killed in action 12 October 1917. Age 29. Son of William and Sarah Coulter, of Roxburgh, Otago. 4.

COUPER, Corporal, JAMES ROBERT, 1212253. 2nd Bn Auckland Regiment, NZEF. Killed in action 4 October 1917. Son of Mr and Mrs D. Couper, of 6 Le Cren St, Timaru. 1.

COWIE, Private, ALEXANDER GEORGE, 33833. A Coy 3rd Bn Auckland Regiment, NZEF. Killed in action 15 October 1917. Age 20. Son of William and Mary Cowie, of 9 Taenui Rd, Cheltenham, Devonport, Auckland. 1.

COX, Serjeant, BERNARD SHEFFIELD, 11591. 3rd Bn Canterbury Regiment, NZEF. Killed in action 4 October 1917. Brother of Cleeve Arthur Cox, of Te Awatea, Chatham Islands, South Pacific. 2.

COX, Private, JOHN, 29671. 1st Bn Auckland Regiment, NZEF. Killed in action 4 October 1917. Age 36. Son of George and Annie Cox, of 16 Caledonian Rd, Oamaru. 1.

CRABB, Private, ALEXANDER, 22314. 2nd Bn Otago Regiment, NZEF. 12 October 1917. Age 22. Son of James and Eliza I.A. Crabb, of 'Thrum's', Maitland St, Leven, Fife, Scotland. 4.

CRABBE, Private, JAMES, 813224. 2nd Bn Otago Regiment, NZEF. Killed in action 12 October 1917. Son of Mr and Mrs J. Crabbe, of Bannockburn, Otago. 4.

CRAIG, Lance Corporal, ALEXANDER DEMPSTER, 8/1958. 1st Bn Otago Regiment, NZEF. Killed in action 12 October 1917. Brother of W.E. Craig, of Puketapu, Palmerston South. 4.

CRAWFORD, Private, ROBERT, 40193. 2nd Bn Canterbury Regiment, NZEF. 12 October 1917. Age 44. Son of the late Mathew Crawford. 2.

CREANEY, Private, MARK OWEN, 12974. 1st Bn Wellington Regiment, NZEF. Killed in action 4 October 1917. 7.

CREE, Private, JAMES, 40891. 10th Coy 1st Bn Otago Regiment, NZEF. Killed in action 12 October 1917. Age 37. Son of James and Margaret Cree, of Otekaieke, Oamaru. 4.

CRESSWELL, Rifleman, GORDON HALLAM, 32507. 3rd Bn 3rd NZ Rifle Brigade. Killed in action 12 October 1917. Age 20. Son of Thomas Richard and Sarah Reese Cresswell, of Wellington. Native of Wanganui. 8.

CRESSWELL, Rifleman, JACK TENNYSON, 44258. H Coy 3rd Bn 3rd NZ Rifle Brigade. Killed in action 12 October 1917. Age 23. Son of Charles Marshall Cresswell and Eleanor Mary Cresswell, of Wanganui. 8.

CRICHTON, Private, HENRY, 45075. 2nd Bn Otago Regiment, NZEF. Killed in action 12 October 1917. Son of Mr and Mrs H. Crichton, of Ellis Rd, South Invercargill. 4.

CRIMMINS, Private, JOHN PATRICK, 6/1502. 1st Bn Canterbury Regiment, NZEF. Killed in action 12 October 1917. Son of Mr and Mrs M. Crimmins, of Moana, Greymouth. 2.

CRONIN, Rifleman, MICHAEL, 14232. 1st Bn 3rd NZ Rifle Brigade. Killed in action 12 October 1917. Son of Mr and Mrs M. Cronin, of Pukekohe Hill, Pukekohe, Auckland. 8.

CROSS, Private, ERNEST CLARENCE, 46558. 1st Bn Canterbury Regiment, NZEF. Killed in action 12 October 1917. Age 24. Son of Charles and Mary Cross, of Matipo St, Lower Riccarton, Christchurch; husband of Florrie Cross. 2.

CROWE, Corporal, ADAM, 8/1723. 1st Bn Otago Regiment, NZEF. Killed in action 12 October 1917. Son of the late Mrs N. Crowe, of Napier. 3.

CRULLER, Rifleman, ARCHIBALD HENRI BASIL, 31401. 2nd Bn 3rd NZ Rifle Brigade. Killed in action 12 October 1917. Age 22. Son of William Rufus Cruller and Annie Kathrine Cruller, of Keri Keri, Auckland. Native of Kaeo, North Auckland. 8.

CRUTCHLEY, Private, JOHN CLARENCE, 36566. 3rd Bn Otago Regiment, NZEF. Killed in action 4 October 1917. Son of Mr and Mrs J. Crutchley, of 392 North Rd, North East Valley, Dunedin. 4.

CULPITT, Private, HENRY WILLIAM, 21665. 12th (Nelson) Coy 2nd Bn Canterbury Regiment, NZEF. Killed in action 12 October 1917. Age 31. Son of Alice Culpitt, of 45 Roderick Rd, Hampstead, London, England, and the late Henry Culpitt. 2.

CUMING, Private, REGINALD ADDINGTON, 32436. 1st Bn Canterbury Regiment, NZEF. Killed in action 12 October 1917. Age 32. Son of William and Eliza A. Cuming, of 17 Bealey St, St. Albans, Christchurch. 2.

CUNNINGHAM, Private, WILLIAM JOSEPH, 11422. NZ Medical Corps. Killed in action 12 October 1917. Son of Mr and Mrs T. Cunningham, of 9th Avenue, Cameron Rd, Tauranga, Thames. 9.

CURNICK, Private, JAMES, 6/3292. 1st Bn Canterbury Regiment, NZEF. Killed in action 12 October 1917. Age 29. Brother of Mrs Ada King, of Waikuku, North Canterbury. 2.

CURRIE, Corporal, WALTER, 10/3870. 3rd Bn Wellington Regiment, NZEF. Killed in action 4 October 1917. Age 31. 6.

CURRY, Private, ALBERT BERT, 31231. 2nd Bn Wellington Regiment, NZEF. Died of wounds 17 October 1917. Age 21. Son of James and Harriett Curry, of Ross St, Woodville, Wellington. 7.

CURRY, Private, JOHN HUGH, 45834. C Coy lst Bn Canterbury Regiment, NZEF. Killed in action 12 October 1917. Age 20. Son of Ada Curry, of 376 Cashel St, Christchurch, and the late Arthur Curry. Native of Wellington. 2.

CURTIS, Rifleman, GEORGE, 39183. 4th Bn 3rd NZ Rifle Brigade. Killed in action 12 October 1917. Son of Mr P. Curtis, of Melrose, Waiareka Junction, Oamaru. 8.

DALE, Rifleman, ROBERT JOSEPH, 41073. 3rd Bn 3rd NZ Rifle Brigade. Killed in action 1 October 1917. Age 26. Son of Kezia Dale, of Clyde Terrace, Kaitangata, Dunedin. 8.

DALLEY, Private, REGINALD WHITMAN, 24/2571. 2nd Bn Canterbury Regiment, NZEF. Killed in action 12 October 1917. Age 21. Son of Joseph and Edith Jane Dalley, of 108 Oxford St, Ashburton. 2.

DALY, Private, MARTIN, 44997. 1st Bn Canterbury Regiment, NZEF. Killed in action 12 October 1917. Age 26. Son of the late Martin George and Helena Daly. Native of Akarao, New Zealand. 2.

DANN, Private, JOHN, 12147. 2nd Bn Auckland Regiment, NZEF. Killed in action 4 October 1917. Son of A.J. and A. Dann, of 113 St Albans St, St. Albans, Christchurch. 1.

DAVEY, Lance Corporal, DANIEL, 23/113. A Coy 1st Bn 3rd NZ Rifle Brigade. Killed in action 12 October 1917. Age 26. Son of John and Ellen Davey, of Broomfield, Papakaio, Oamaru, Otago, New Zealand; husband of Nellie Florence Vernon (formerly Davey), of 30A Pinner Rd, Oxhey, Watford, England. 8.

DAVIDSON, Private, LOGAN LEONARD, 31663. NZ Medical Corps. Killed in action 12 October 1917. Son of Mr and Mrs J.A. Davidson, of Devonport, Auckland. 9.

DAVIS, Private, ARTHUR HERBERT, 40907. 1st Bn Otago Regiment, NZEF. Killed in action 12 October 1917. Son of Henry Charles Davis, of Dunedin. 4.

DAVIS, Lance Corporal, LEONARD SYDNEY, 34339. 3rd Bn Auckland Regiment, NZEF. Killed in action 4 October 1917. Son of Thomas and A. Davis, of Alexandra St, Te Awamutu, Hamilton. 1.

DAVIS, Private, PERCY CHARLES, 8/3235. 1st Bn Otago Regiment, NZEF. Killed in action 12 October 1917. Age 25. Son of Walter John and Harriet Elinor Davis, of Havelock North, Hawke's Bay, Napier. Native of Hastings, Hawke's Bay. 4

DAVIS, Private, RICHARD GEORGE, 12990. 2nd Bn Otago Regiment, NZEF. Killed in action 3–4 October 1917. Age 29. Son of Sarah Davis, of 56 Anglesea St, Ponsonby, Auckland, and the late Richard Alfred Davis. Native of Kamo, Auckland. 4.

DAVIS, Private, THOMAS, 8/746. 1st Bn Otago Regiment, NZEF. Killed in action 12 October 1917. Brother of Mr F.H. Davis, of 4 Eastown Rd, Wanganui East. 4.

DAWSON, Rifleman, JOHN HENRY, 42633. 3rd Bn 3rd NZ Rifle Brigade. Killed in action 12 October 1917. Son of Herbert Henry and Margaret A. Dawson, of Kennington, Invercargill. 8.

DAWSON, Private, SAMUEL JAMES, 20309. 2nd Bn Wellington Regiment, NZEF. Killed in action 4 October 1917. Age 22. Son of Samuel and Mary Dawson, of Third

St, Lansdowne, Masterton, Wellington. Previously wounded at the Battle of the Somme, 1916. 7.

De SPONG, Private, THOMAS PEARSE NASH, 27472. 2nd Bn Otago Regiment, NZEF. Killed in action 12 October 1917. Son of Mr and Mrs Thomas Nash De Spong, of 63 Wallace St, Roslyn, Dunedin. 4.

DEANS, Second Lieutenant, ALEXANDER, 27693. 3rd Bn Canterbury Regiment, NZEF. Killed in action 4 October 1917. Age 26. Son of Catherine Edith Deans, of Riccarton, Christchurch, and the late John Deans; husband of Norah Deans, of Morven, Waddington, Christchurch. Native of Canterbury. 2.

DEARSLY, Private, WALTER, 51579. 2nd Bn Auckland Regiment, NZEF. Killed in action 4 October 1917. Age 25. Son of Annie Boenicke (formerly Dearsly), of 165 Karangahape Rd, Auckland, and the late Thomas Dearsly. Also served in Egypt. 1.

DEBENHAM, Private, HENRY EDWARD, 29230. 13th Coy 1st Bn Canterbury Regiment, NZEF. Killed in action 12 October 1917. Age 28. Son of H.E. and M.E. Debenham, of Bright St, Cobden, Greymouth. Native of Kumara. 2.

DELANEY, Rifleman, GEORGE IRVIN, 31403. 3rd Bn 3rd NZ Rifle Brigade. Killed in action 12 October 1917. Son of Mr and Mrs Thomas Delaney, of Tapuhi, Hukerenui, Auckland. 8.

DENNEHY, Private, THOMAS, 46565. 1st Bn Canterbury Regiment, NZEF. Killed in action 12 October 1917. Son of the late Michael Frederick and Margaret Josephine Dennehy, of North St, Timaru. 2.

DENNISTON, Rifleman, JAMES ARCHIBALD, 24115. A Coy 2nd Bn 3rd NZ Rifle Brigade. Killed in action 12 October 1917. Age 19. Son of Robert and Jane Denniston, of 15 Mary St, Port Chalmers, Dunedin. Also served in Egypt. 8.

DENSHIRE, Corporal, CHARLES DE CHAIR, 14195. 2nd Bn Otago Regiment, NZEF. Killed in action 12 October 1917. Age 35. Son of Fannie Denshire, of 22 Jackson Rd, Fendalton, Christchurch, and the late William Banks Denshire. Native of Ashburton, Christchurch. 3.

DERBY, Private, JOHN WILLIAM, 41507. 2nd Bn Canterbury Regiment, NZEF. Killed in action 12 October 1917. Son of Mr and Mrs George Henry Derby, of Piriaka, Hamilton. 2.

DEVANEY, Private, THOMAS MICHAEL, 312723. NZ Medical Corps. Killed in action 12 October 1917. Brother of Imelda Devaney, of Hokitika, Greymouth. 9.

DEVEREUX, Private, JOHN PATRICK, 14956. 2nd Bn Canterbury Regiment, NZEF. Killed in action 12 October 1917. Age 28. Son of Marion Devereux, of 41 Murphy St, Wellington, and the late John Devereux. 2.

DEWAR, Private, LESLIE HASTIE, 33036. 1st Bn Otago Regiment, NZEF. Killed in action 12 October 1917. Age 19. Son of Margaret Dewar, of 12 Bellevue St, Roslyn, Dunedin, and the late Stewart Dewar. Native of Queenstown, Invercargill. 4.

DEWAR, Lance Corporal, WILLIAM, 26067. 4th Bn 3rd NZ Rifle Brigade. 12 October 1917. 8.

DICKEY, Second Lieutenant, CECIL VERNON, 26/26. 3rd Bn NZ Rifle Brigade. Killed in action 12 October 1917. Son of Mr and Mrs William F. Dickey, of 79 Bryndwyr Rd, Fendalton, Christchurch. 7.

DICKSON, Private, HENRY LESLIE, 34823. 3rd Bn Otago Regiment, NZEF. Killed in action 4 October 1917. Son of Mr and Mrs John Dickson, of Kuri Bush, Otago. 4.

DINSDALE, Private, CHARLES, 14404. 2nd Bn Canterbury Regiment, NZEF. 12 October 1917. Age 22. Son of George and Mary Dinsdale. 2.

DINSDALE, Private, JOSEPH, 12/1613. 1st Bn Auckland Regiment, NZEF. 4 October 1917. Age 31. Brother of Robert Dinsdale, of 3 Railway Cottages, Stillington Junction, Ferry Hill, Co Durham, England. 1.

DIX, Rifleman, GERALD, 47997. 2nd Bn 3rd NZ Rifle Brigade. Killed in action 12 October 1917. Son of Mr and Mrs A.P. Dix, of St Andrew's, Timaru. 8.

DIXON, Lance Corporal, THOMAS HAROLD, 6/3299. 1st Bn Canterbury Regiment, NZEF. Killed in action 12 October 1917. Age 21. Son of Gilbert and Mary Hannah Dixon, of 85 Lyttelton St, Spreydon, Christchurch. 2.

DOAK, Private, SAMUEL WILLIAM, 44578. 1st Bn Canterbury Regiment, NZEF. Killed in action 12 October 1917. Son of J.G. and A. Doak, of Fernside, North Canterbury. 2.

DODDS, Private, HAROLD BINNIE, 23475. 1st Bn Otago Regiment, NZEF. Killed in action 12 October 1917. Age 24. Son of Nicholas and Christine Isabel Dodds, of George St, Port Chalmers, Dunedin. 4.

DODDS, Private, JOHN ROBERTSON, 8/2898. 10th Coy 1st Bn Otago Regiment, NZEF. Killed in action 12 October 1917. Age 32. Son of the late Alexander and Isabella Dodds. Native of Goodwood, Otago. 4.

DODUNSKI, Private, PAUL, 28109. 2nd Bn Wellington Regiment, NZEF. Killed in action 4 October 1917. Age 31. Son of Mickl and Catharine Dodunski, of Broadway, South Stratford, New Plymouth. 7.

DOIG, Corporal, JAMES, 32788. 2nd Bn Wellington Regiment, NZEF. Killed in action 4 October 1917. Age 39. Son of the late William and Elizabeth Doig, of Papakaio, Oamaru; husband of Agnes S. Doig, of Greta St, Oamaru. 6.

DONEHUE, Private, ALBERT THOMAS, 14079. 2nd Bn Canterbury Regiment, NZEF. Killed in action 12 October 1917. Son of Mr and Mrs S. Donehue, of Dergholm, Casterton, Victoria, Australia. 2.

DONOVAN, Corporal, DANIEL JOSEPH, 33023. 3rd Bn Auckland Regiment, NZEF. Killed in action 4 October 1917. Father of Daniel John Donovan, of Mount Eden, Auckland. 1.

DORAN, Private, FREDERICK AUGUSTUS, 51020. 3rd Bn Wellington Regiment, NZEF. Killed in action 20 October 1917. Son of Mrs M.J. Doran, of Capleston, Westland, Greymouth. 7.

DORRICOTT, Rifleman, WILLIAM, 41315. 1st Bn 3rd NZ Rifle Brigade. Killed in action 12 October 1917. Son of Mrs Ruth Dorricott, of Hobsonville, Auckland. 8.

DOUGLAS, Rifleman, WILLIAM KENNETH, 25/612. 3rd Bn 3rd NZ Rifle Brigade. Killed in action 12 October 1917. Age 25. Son of the late William Douglas and E. Douglas, of Gore, Invercargill. 8.

DOW, Rifleman, JOHN WILLIAM, 32831. 4th Bn 3rd NZ Rifle Brigade. Killed in action 12 October 1917. Age 29. Son of Elizabeth Dow, of Woodside, West Taieri, Dunedin, and the late Peter Dow. 8.

DOWNES, Rifleman, WALTER, 36430. 2nd Bn 3rd NZ Rifle Brigade. Killed in action 12 October 1917. Age 19. Son of Thomas and Grace Downes, of Waitati, Dunedin. 8.

DOWNS, Rifleman, CHARLES HENRY, 20508. 2nd Bn 3rd NZ Rifle Brigade. Killed in action 12 October 1917. Son of Mr and Mrs C. Downs, of Marton Junction, Wanganui. 8.

DOYLE, Private, JOHN, 42307. 1st Bn Auckland Regiment, NZEF. Killed in action 4 October 1917. Husband of Mrs L.M. Doyle, of King St, Pukekohe, Auckland. 1.

DOYLE, Rifleman, JAMES, 38136. 1st Bn 3rd NZ Rifle Brigade. Killed in action 12 October 1917. Brother of Mr M. Doyle, of South Loburn, Canterbury. 8.

DOYLE, Private, PHILIP EDMUND, 41512. F Coy 3rd Bn Canterbury Regiment, NZEF. Died of wounds 20 October 1917. Age 24. Son of William Henry and Mary Eveline Doyle, of Chamberlain Rd, Johnsonville, Wellington. 2.

DRABBLE, Private, WILLIAM THOMAS HENRY, 29234. 13th (North Canterbury and Westland) Coy 2nd Bn Canterbury Regiment, NZEF. Killed in action 12 October 1917. Age 22. Son of Thomas Henry and Mary Drabble, of Cookson St, Kaiapoi, Canterbury. 2

DRUMMEY, Private, JAMES, 42308. 1st Auckland Regiment, NZEF. Killed in action 4 October 1917. 1.

DRUMMOND, Serjeant, ALFRED ERNEST, 12/2687. 1st Bn Auckland Regiment, NZEF. Killed in action 4 October 1917. Son of Mr and Mrs Robert Drummond, of Willow St, Te Papapa, Onehunga, Auckland. 1.

Du VALL, Corporal, VERNER HENRY, 32510. 1st Bn Canterbury Regiment, NZEF. Killed in action 12 October 1917. Age 30. Son of Mrs Mary E. Harrison (formerly Du Vall), of 248 Highgate, Maori Hill, Dunedin, and the late Mr H.W. Du Vall. Native of Auckland. 2.

DUDFIELD, Rifleman, ARTHUR JOHN SCOBIE, 45346. 2nd Bn 3rd NZ Rifle Brigade. Killed in action 12 October 1917. Age 20. Son of Alice Dudfield, of 12 Carr St, North East Valley, Dunedin, and the late Harry Dudfield. 8.

DUFFILL, Private, GEORGE, 10/626. 1st Bn Wellington Regiment, NZEF. Killed in action 4 October 1917. Brother of John A. Duffill, of Argyle St, Hawera, Taranaki. 7.

DUNN, Private, ALLAN, 24/1032. 3rd Bn Wellington Regiment, NZEF. Killed in action 4 October 1917. Son of Mr and Mrs R. Dunn, of Shag Point, Otago. 7.

DUPEYRON, Rifleman, CHARLES LOUIS, 24/1033. 2nd Bn 3rd NZ Rifle Brigade. Killed in action 12 October 1917. Son of Mr and Mrs L. Dupeyron, of St Saviour's, Guernsey, Channel Islands. 8.

EASTWELL, Private, JAMES HENRY, 27476. 2nd Bn Otago Regiment, NZEF. Killed in action 12 October 1917. Age 37. Son of Edward and Mary Ann Eastwell, of Rose Vale, Swan Creek, Warwick, Queensland. 4.

EATON, Private, THOMAS, 32150. 1st Bn Canterbury Regiment, NZEF. Killed in action 12 October 1917. Son of Ernest and Sarah Eaton, of Tepapakuku, Dannevirke. 2.

ECKFORD, Serjeant, GEORGE, 15153. 3rd Bn Otago Regiment, NZEF. 4 October 1917. Age 26. Son of John and E. Moss Eckford, of 16 Trinity Crescent, Edinburgh, Scotland. 3.

EDEN, Private, JOHN, 29754. D Coy 2nd Bn Otago Regiment, NZEF. Killed in action 12 October 1917. Age 21. Son of Miranda Throp (formerly Eden), of 276 Castle St, Dunedin, New Zealand. Native of England. 4.

EDMONSTON, Private, HENRY, 42485. D Coy 2nd Bn Otago Regiment, NZEF. Killed in action 12 October 1917. Age 27. Son of John and Margaret Edmonston, of Moeraki, Hillgrove, Otago. 4.

EDMUNDS, Private, CHARLES LIONEL, 33859. 3rd Bn Auckland Regiment, NZEF. Killed in action 4 October 1917. Husband of Mrs N.I. Edmunds, of 115 Franklin Rd, Ponsonby, Auckland. 1.

EIFFE, Private, JOHN KENNETH, 44461. 3rd Bn Wellington Regiment, NZEF.

Killed in action 4 October 1917. Age 21. Son of Simon and Mary Eiffe, of Adelaide St, Petone, Wellington, New Zealand. Native of Australia. 7.

ELLERY, Lance Corporal, SILAS GEORGE, 17772. D Coy 3rd Bn 3rd NZ Rifle Brigade. Killed in action 12 October 1917. Age 26. Son of Silas and Beatrice Ellery, of Belfield, Timaru. 8.

ELLIOTT, Private, WILLIAM, 3/891. 4th Field Amb NZ Medical Corps. Killed in action 12 October 1917. Age 23. Son of Mr and Mrs William Elliott, of Frankton Junction, Hamilton, New Zealand. Native of Longframlington, Northumberland, England. Also served at Gallipoli and in Egypt. 9.

ELLIS, Second Lieutenant, EDWIN GEORGE, 25992. 2nd Bn Auckland Regiment, NZEF. Killed in action 4 October 1917. Age 28. Son of Richard Henry and Cecelia Ellis, of Tararu, Thames. 1.

ELLIS, Lance Corporal, HERBERT, 24149. 1st Bn Canterbury Regiment, NZEF. Died of wounds 12 October 1917. Age 35. Son of Arthur and Elizabeth Ellis, of Fernside, Canterbury. 2.

ELLIS, Private, HERBERT HORACE, 27252. 1st Bn Canterbury Regiment, NZEF. Killed in action 12 October 1917. Age 26. Son of William and Susan Celia Ellis, of 79 Olliviers Rd, Linwood, Christchurch. 2.

ELLIS, Rifleman, PETER, 41078. 3rd Bn 3rd NZ Rifle Brigade. Killed in action 12 October 1917. Age 21. Son of Peter and Margaret Ellis, of Wairio, Invercargill. 8.

ELMBRANCH, Private, JOHN FREDERICK, 42312. lst Bn Auckland Regiment, NZEF. Killed in action 4 October 1917. Son of Mrs A. Elmbranch, of 103 Franklin Rd, Auckland. 1.

ESPIE, Private, WILLIAM CAMPBELL, M M and bar, G/924. 2nd Bn Otago Regiment, NZEF. Killed in action 12 October 1917. Brother of John H.K. Espie, of York Plains, Tasmania. 4.

EVANS, Private, FREDERICK LESLIE, 28995. 3rd Bn Canterbury Regiment, NZEF. Killed in action 18 October 1917. Son of Mr and Mrs John Evans, of 41 Disraeli St, Christchurch. 2.

EVENDEN, Private, WILLIAM SANDFORD, 32643. 1st Bn Otago Regiment, NZEF. Killed in action 12 October 1917. Age 20. Son of Walter Henry and Maria Annie Evenden, of Kumara, Westland, Greymouth. 4.

EVERS-SWINDELL, Private, ERNEST FREDERICK, 10/2597. 1st Bn Wellington Regiment, NZEF. Killed in action 4 October 1917. Age 22. Son of Wilfred and Alice Evers-Swindell, of 'The Towers', Burleigh Stroud, Glos, England. 7.

EVERTON, Rifleman, CYRIL FREDERICK LIONEL, 40107. 2nd Bn 3rd NZ Rifle Brigade. Killed in action 12 October 1917. Age 21. Son of Frederick Charles and Dora Everton, of New Windsor Rd, Avondale, Auckland; husband of Sybil Everton. Native of Featherston, Wellington. 8.

EYRES, Lance Corporal, FRANK GEORGE, 22610. 2nd Bn 3rd NZ Rifle Brigade. Killed in action 12 October 1917. Age 25. Son of John Alfred and Annie Eyres, of 22 Queen St, Petone, Wellington, New Zealand. Native of Upper Stratton, Swindon, England. 8.

FAIR, Private, RICHARD ALEXANDER, 33531. 3rd Bn Wellington Regiment, NZEF. Killed in action 4 October 1917. Son of Mr and Mrs T.R. Fair, of Ringarooma, Tasmania. 7.

FAIRWEATHER, Rifleman, JOHN, 32836. 4th Bn 3rd NZ Rifle Brigade. 12 October

1917. Age 30. Son of the late James Fairweather. Native of Monaltrie, Turriff, Scotland. 8.

FARMER, Private, REUBEN ARTHUR, 23817. 2nd Bn Wellington Regiment, NZEF. Killed in action 4 October 1917. Brother of Mr T. Farmer, of Main St, Greytown, Wellington. 7.

FARMER, Rifleman, WILLIAM PERCY, 45374. 3rd Bn 3rd NZ Rifle Brigade. Killed in action 12 October 1917. Son of Mrs J.W. Farmer, of Waikino, Upper Thames. 8.

FARRELL, Private, WILLIAM FRANCIS, 5/1483A. 3rd Bn Wellington Regiment, NZEF. Killed in action 20 October 1917. Son of Mr and Mrs R. Farrell, of Tattons Rd, Papanui, Christchurch. 7.

FAULKNER, Rifleman, CHARLES EDGAR GEORGE, 39039. 2nd Bn 3rd NZ Rifle Brigade. Killed in action 12 October 1917. Age 26. Son of Samuel and Bertha Faulkner, of 180 Edgeware Rd, St Albans, Christchurch. 8.

FAULKNER, Private, ERNEST, 51710. 1st Bn Auckland Regiment, NZEF. Killed in action 20 October 1917. Husband of Lucy Beatrice Faulkner, of Birkenhead, Auckland. 1.

FAULL, Private, WILLIAM THOMAS, 24/417. 3rd Bn Otago Regiment, NZEF. Killed in action 17 October 1917. Age 24. Son of Mrs F.A. Foreman (formerly Faull), of Ward St, Dannevirke, Hawke's Bay, Napier, and the late William J. Faull. Native of Kaponga, Taranaki. 4.

FERGUSON, Private, DAVID, 39788. 1st Bn Wellington Regiment, NZEF. Killed in action 24 October 1917. Age 34. Son of Hugh A. Ferguson, of 'Glenside', Dundonald, Co Down, Ireland. 7.

FERGUSON, Serjeant, JOHN, 241138. 2nd Bn 3rd NZ Rifle Brigade. Killed in action 12 October 1917. Brother of Mr D. Ferguson, of Warrington, Dunedin. 7.

FIFE, Private, WILLIAM JOHN, 46573. lst Bn Canterbury Regiment, NZEF. Killed in action 12 October 1917. Son of William and Corona Fife, of 365 St Asaph St, Christchurch. 2.

FILL, Private, HENRY VANT, 39789. 5th Coy 1st Bn Wellington Regiment, NZEF. Killed in action 4 October 1917. Age 28. Son of Alfred and Susan Fill, of 82 Russell Terrace, Newtown, Wellington. 7.

FINCH, Private, DONALD MCNAUGHTON STUART, 32649. 1st Bn Otago Regiment, NZEF. Killed in action 12 October 1917. Age 33. Son of George and Jessie Finch, of Stirling, Otago. Native of Milton, Otago. 4.

FINDLAY, Rifleman, JAMES ARTHUR, 40922. 1st Bn 3rd NZ Rifle Brigade. Killed in action 12 October 1917. Age 34. Son of the late Thomas and Janet Findlay, of Invercargill. 8.

FINLAY, Private, GEORGE RAYMOND, 33532. 3rd Bn Wellington Regiment, NZEF. Killed in action 4 October 1917. Son of Mr and Mrs Matthew Finlay, of 'Broadholm', Puketaha, Hamilton. 7.

FINLAY, Private, JAMES, 26256. 2nd Bn Canterbury Regiment, NZEF. Killed in action 12 October 1917. Son of Mr and Mrs William Finlay, of 58 Avonhead Rd, Riccarton, Christchurch. 2.

FINLAYSON, Private, JOHN LAWRENCE, 28331. J Coy 1st Bn Auckland Regiment, NZEF. Killed in action 4 October 1917. Age 19. Son of William and Martha Finlayson, of Napier, Hawke's Bay. 1.

FINN, Private, WILLIAM FRANCIS, 45089. 1st Bn Otago Regiment, NZEF. Killed in action 10 October 1917. Son of Mr and Mrs Thomas Finn, of Wrey's Bush,

Southland, Invercargill. 4.

FINNERTY, Private, JOHN THOMAS, 42070. 1st Bn Auckland Regiment, NZEF. Killed in action 22 October 1917. Age 27. Husband of Jean Finnerty, of 'Rothesay', Tamahana St, Matamata, Hamilton. 1.

FITZGERALD, Private, CORNELIUS FRANCIS, 52402. 2nd Bn Wellington Regiment, NZEF. Killed in action 21 October 1917. Age 46. Son of John and Ann Fitzgerald, of Tuapeka Flat, Lawrence, Dunedin. 7.

FITZGERALD, Private, EDWARD BERNARD, 32648. 1st Bn Otago Regiment, NZEF. Killed in action 12 October 1917. Son of Margaret Fitzgerald, of Tuatapere, Southland, Invercargill. 4.

FITZGERALD, Private, JAMES, 17/56. 2nd Bn Otago Regiment, NZEF. Killed in action 12 October 1917. Age 26. Son of John and Johannah Fitzgerald, of Waimate, Timaru. 4.

FITZPATRICK, Private, EDWARD, 39203. 3rd Bn Otago Regiment, NZEF. Killed in action 4 October 1917. Age 24. Son of Daniel and Charlotte Fitzpatrick, of Arthur's Point Queenstown, Invercargill. 4.

FLANAGAN, Rifleman, JOSEPH, 34049. 4th Bn 3rd NZ Rifle Brigade. Killed in action 12 October 1917. Age 31. Son of the late Peter and Sarah Flanagan, of Litherland, Liverpool, England. 8.

FLANAGAN, Lance Corporal, JAMES FRANCIS, 14247. 1st Bn Auckland Regiment, NZEF. Killed in action 22 October 1917. Age 27. Son of James and Lizzie Flanagan, of Moneydara More, Annalong, Co Down, Ireland. 1.

FLANNERY, Rifleman, PETER, 45200. 2nd Bn 3rd NZ Rifle Brigade. Killed in action 12 October 1917. Son of Mr and Mrs Thomas Flannery, of Poolburn, Dunedin. 8.

FLINT, Private, HERBERT LANHAM, 42492. 2nd Bn Otago Regiment, NZEF. Killed in action 12 October 1917. Age 25. Son of the late Joseph Flint of Cardiff. Wales; husband of Mrs J.S. Hinton (formerly Flint) of Eamscieugh, Otago, New Zealand. Native of Ophir, Otago Central. 4.

FLOOD, Rifleman, THOMAS FREDERICK, 38516. 2nd Bn 3rd NZ Rifle Brigade. Killed in action 12 October 1917. Age 24. Son of Robert Patrick and Frances Louisa Flood, of Utakura, Hokianga, Auckland. Native of Rawene, Hokianga. 8.

FLYNN, Private, MICHAEL JOSEPH, 36857. 3rd Bn Otago Regiment, NZEF. Killed in action 17 October 1917. Brother of Mr C.P. Flynn, of Wrey's Bush, Southland, Invercargill. 4.

FODEN, Second Lieutenant, WILLIAM ROY, 23/1047. 12th (Nelson) Coy 2nd Bn Canterbury Regiment, NZEF. Killed in action 12 October 1917. Age 22. Son of Edward and Grace Eliza Foden, of Wilson St, Hawera, Taranaki. Also served in Egypt. 2.

FORDE, Private, NORMAN ARTHUR, 38679. 1st Bn Wellington Regiment, NZEF. Killed in action 3rd October 1917. Son of Mr and Mrs Frederick Hamilton Forde, of Auckland. 7.

FORWARD, Rifleman, CAREY, 39791. 4th Bn 3rd NZ Rifle Brigade. Killed in action 12 October 1917. Age 28. Son of George and Louisa Forward, of 5 Lucknow Place, Rye, Sussex, England. 8.

FOSTER, Lance Corporal, ALFRED WELLS, 613320. 1st Bn Canterbury Regiment, NZEF. Killed in action 12 October 1917. Age 26. Son of Rosetta Amelia Campion (formerly Foster), and stepson of Joseph Campion, of 67 North Parade, Richmond,

Christchurch. Native of Lyttelton. 2.

FOUNTAINE, Private, HENRY RICHARD, 28332. 1st Bn Auckland Regiment, NZEF. Killed in action 4 October 1917. Age 26. Son of Charles Albert and Charlotte Fountaine, of 23 Russell St, Westport, Greymouth. 1.

FOWLER, Private, DAVID, 45086. 1st Bn Otago Regiment, NZEF. Killed in action 12 October 1917. Son of Mrs M. Fowler, of Wendon, Southland, Invercargill. 4.

FRASER, Private, DAVID EDGAR, 31983. E Coy 1st Bn Auckland Regiment, NZEF. Killed in action 4 October 1917. Age 29. Son of Robert Fraser, of Marohemo, North Auckland. 1.

FRASER, Private, THOMAS, 29762. D Coy 3rd Bn Otago Regiment, NZEF. Killed in action 4 October 1917. Age 18. Only son of Thomas and Robina Fraser, of Cherry Farm, Katea, Otago, New Zealand. Native of Ellon, Aberdeenshire, Scotland. 4.

FREEMAN, Private, JOHN, 47418. 3rd Bn Wellington Regiment, NZEF. Killed in action 4 October 1917. Age 23. Son of Frederick George Freeman, of Tainui St, Ohakune, Wellington, and the late Sarah Freeman. Native of Wanganui. 7.

FRISBY, Private, EDWARD WILLIAM, 8/4127. 1st Bn Otago Regiment, NZEF. Killed in action 10 October 1917. Son of William Frisby, of Brown's, Southland, Invercargill, and the late Elizabeth Frisby. 4.

FULCHER, Serjeant, HARRY EDWARD, 12/2550. 2nd Bn Wellington Regiment, NZEF. Killed in action 4 October 1917. Age 22. Only son of Harry and Kate Fulcher, of Great South Rd, Papakura, Auckland. 6.

FUNNELL, Private, GEORGE WILLIAM, 9/1170. 2nd Bn Otago Regiment, NZEF. Killed in action 12 October 1917. Son of Mr and Mrs W. F. Funnell, of South St, Blenheim. 4.

GAIN, Private, THOMAS WILLIAM, 10/261 1. No. 2 Coy NZ Machine Gun Corps. Killed in action 3 October 1917. Son of Mr and Mrs G. Gain of Featherston, Wellington. 9.

GALBRAITH, Rifleman, JAMES CHRIS, 44637. 1st Bn 3rd NZ Rifle Brigade. Killed in action 12 October 1917. Son of Christopher and Flora Galbraith, of King Edward St, Dominion Rd, Auckland. 8.

GALLOWAY, Private, FREDERICK ANDREW, 42318. 2nd Bn Auckland Regiment, NZEF. Killed in action 4 October 1917. Son of Mr and Mrs Malcolm Galloway, of Station Rd, Papatoetoe, Auckland. 1.

GANDY, Lance Corporal, WILLIAM FRANCIS, 29387. 3rd Bn Wellington Regiment, NZEF. Killed in action 4 October 1917. Age 24. Son of Harry H. and Mary E. Gandy, of Almner's Farm, Lyne, Chertsey, England. 6.

GARRETT, Private, ERNEST, 29899. 2nd Bn Otago Regiment, NZEF. Killed in action 1 October 1917. Son of Mrs S. Garrett, of 48 Douglas St, St Kilda, Dunedin. 4.

GASON, Private, WILLIAM HENRY, 614248. 1st Bn Canterbury Regiment, NZEF. Killed in action 12 October 1917. Son of H.J.B. and Rose Gason, of Temuka, Timaru. 2.

GAVIN, Corporal, ARTHUR, 25696. 3rd Bn 3rd NZ Rifle Brigade. Killed in action 12 October 1917. Son of Mrs H. Gavin, of Nanaimo, British Columbia, Canada. 7.

GEANGE, Private, GEORGE ALFRED, 37805. 2nd Bn Canterbury Regiment, NZEF. Killed in action 12 October 1917. Son of Mrs Clara Geange, of Levin, Wellington. 2.

GEARY, Rifleman, FRANCIS, 42649. 3rd Bn 3rd NZ Rifle Brigade. Killed in action

12 October 1917. Brother of D. Geary, of Raetihi, Wanganui. 8.

GEARY, Private, THOMAS FRANCIS, 6/231. 12th (Nelson) Coy 1st Bn Canterbury Regiment, NZEF. Died of wounds 12 October 1917. Age 27. Son of Thomas and Clara Geary, of Wellington. 2.

GEDDES, Rifleman, ALEXANDER, 44970. 2nd Bn 3rd NZ Rifle Brigade. 12 October 1917. 8.

GENGE, Private, GUY, 32842. 3rd Bn Otago Regiment, NZEF. Killed in action 4 October 1917. Age 21. Son of Thomas and Jane Genge, of Wyndharn, Southland, Invercargill. 4.

GEORGE, Private, FRANK WALTER, 24425. 2nd Bn Wellington Regiment, NZEF. Killed in action 4 October 1917. Husband of Jane Kennelly (formerly George), of 25 Picton Avenue, Newtown, Wellington. 7.

GEORGE, Private, THOMAS, 6/4610. 2nd Bn Otago Regiment, NZEF. Killed in action 12 October 1917. Age 22. Son of James and Mary George, of Glenorchy, Lake Wakatipu, Invercargill. 4.

GIBSON, Private, CLARENCE HUGH, 29766. 8th Coy 2nd Bn Otago Regiment, NZEF. Killed in action 12 October 1917. Age 22. Son of Norman and Christina Gibson, of 12 Chelmsford St, Invercargill. 4.

GIBSON, Private, GEORGE JAMES WILSON, 42495. 3rd Bn Otago Regiment, NZEF. Killed in action 4 October 1917. Age 36. Son of Robert and Alice Gibson. Native of Mosgiel, Otago. 4.

GIBSON, Private, JAMES WILLIAM, 42496. D Coy 1st Bn Otago Regiment, NZEF. Killed in action 12 October 1917. Age 21. Son of Ellen M. Gibson, of Bannockburn, Otago, and the late James L. Gibson. 4.

GIBSON, Lieutenant, MCKENZIE, 6/635. 1st Bn Canterbury Regiment, NZEF. Killed in action 12 October 1917. Age 27. Son of the Rev. Mackenzie Gibson and Mary Coates Alice Gibson, of Hillbrow Cottage, Esher, Surrey, England. 2.

GILES, Private, WILLIAM HENRY, 33872. 3rd Bn Auckland Regiment, NZEF. Killed in action 4 October 1917. Son of Mr and Mrs J. Giles, of Oratia, Waikumete, Auckland. 1.

GILLETT, Captain, LAWRENCE HENRY, 12/1416. 3rd Bn Auckland Regiment, NZEF. Killed in action 2 October 1917. Son of Mr and Mrs Richard Gillett, of 'The Drive', Epsom, Auckland. 1.

GIRVIN, Rifleman, JOHN, 31122. 3rd Bn 3rd NZ Rifle Brigade. Killed in action 12 October 1917. Age 32. Son of William John Girvin, of Tapuhi, Hukerenui, Auckland. 8

GISBORNE, Private, HENRY, 25508. 1st Bn Wellington Regiment, NZEF. 4 October 1917. Age 34. Son of the late Oliver and Elizabeth Hannah Gisborne. 7.

GIVEN, Private, WILLIAM, 44468. 3rd Wellington Regiment, NZEF. 4 October 1917. 7.

GLEESON, Rifleman, FREDERICK HAROLD, 45688. 1st Bn 3rd NZ Rifle Brigade. Killed in action 12 October 1917. Age 24. Son of Frederick J. and Emily Gleeson, of Havelock North, Napier. Native of Greymouth. 8.

GLENNIE, Private, CHARLES, 47324. 1st Bn Canterbury Regiment, NZEF. Killed in action 12 October 1917. Age 35. Son of Charles and Helen Glennie, of Christchurch. 2.

GOGGIN, Corporal, JAMES, 23/1391. 1st Bn 3rd NZ Rifle Brigade. Killed in action

12 October 1917. Age 20. Son of James and Johannah Goggin, of Raumati, Dannevirke, Napier. 7.

GOLDSMITH, Lance Corporal, FREDERICK, 10341. 1st Bn Wellington Regiment, NZEF. Killed in action 22 October 1917. Son of Mr and Mrs Edwin Samuel Goldsmith, of 313 Whitaker St, Gisborne. 6.

GONLEY, Lance Corporal, DOMINIC, 26/561. 4th Bn 3rd NZ Rifle Brigade. Killed in action 12 October 1917. Age 23. Son of Patrick and M.A. Gonley, of 26 Church Hill, Sligo, Ireland. Educated at Rockwell College, Co Tipperary, and Ferinoy College, Co Cork. 8.

GOOD, Rifleman, MARTIN LEO, 25850. 2nd Bn 3rd NZ Rifle Brigade. Killed in action 12 October 1917. Age 23. Son of Martin and Margaret Good, of Mahoe St, Te Awamutu, Hamilton. Native of Sanson, Wellington. 8.

GOODALL, Corporal, JOHN ROBERT, 12/1959. 1st Bn Auckland Regiment, NZEF. Killed in action 4 October 1917. Son of Mr and Mrs A. Goodall, of Pin St, Raetihi, Wellington. 1.

GOODALL, Rifleman, ROBERT HEARTLY, 21818. 3rd Bn 3rd NZ Rifle Brigade. Killed in action 12 October 1917. Husband of Mrs H.G. Goodall, of 17 Whersteade Rd, Cashmere, Christchurch. 8.

GOODWIN, Private, WALTER EARL, IO/3889. 1st Bn Wellington Regiment, NZEF. Killed in action 4 October 1917. Age 21. Son of Charles James and Kate Isabella Goodwin. Native of Tuna, Midhurst, New Plymouth. 7.

GORDON, Serjeant, WILLIAM ELLIOT, M M, 2311646. 2nd Bn Otago Regiment, NZEF. Killed in action 12 October 1917. Age 31. Son of Douglas and Susannah Gordon, of 28 Abbotts Rd, Mount Eden, Auckland. 3.

GORDON-GLASSFORD, Rifleman, JAMES DOUGLAS, 26/445. 4th Bn 3rd NZ Rifle Brigade. Killed in action 12 October 1917. Age 21. Son of James and Mary Lucilla Gordon-Glassford, of 'Tawhera', Levin, Wellington. 8.

GORMACK, Private, ROBERT, 15162. 2nd Bn Otago Regiment, NZEF. Killed in action 12 October 1917. Age 31. Son of the late John and Mary Gormack. Native of Wairuna, Otago. 4.

GOUDIE, Private, JOHN CLAUDE BRISBANE, 29772. D Coy 1st Bn Otago Regiment, NZEF. Killed in action 12 October 1917. Age 24. Son of John and Rebecca Johnstone Goudie, of 8 Barclay St, North East Valley, Dunedin. 4.

GOULD, Private, JOHN EDWARD, 33539. E Coy 3rd Bn Wellington Regiment, NZEF. Killed in action 4 October 1917. Age 31. Son of Walter and Anna Gould, of Cheddar, England; husband of Mary Alice Gould, of 248 Manakau Rd, Newmarket, Auckland, New Zealand. 7.

GOW, Private, CHARLES, 34599. 3rd Bn Auckland Regiment, NZEF. Killed in action 4 October 1917. Age 21. Son of John Cowie Gow and Marjory Gow, of 48 Elizabeth St, Timaru. Native of Palmerston South. Assistant Scoutmaster, Timaru. 1.

GOWER, Private, ARTHUR, 29615. No. 1 Coy NZ Machine Gun Corps. 12 October 1917. Age 27. Son of Mr and Mrs H. Gower, of Watch Oak, Battle, Sussex, England. 9.

GOWLAND, Private, WILFRED, 28464. 9th Coy 1st Bn Wellington Regiment, NZEF. Killed in action 21 October 1917. Age 30. Son of John and Emily Gowland, of 85 Cobham St, Spreydon, Christchurch. Native of Yorkshire, England. 7.

GRADWELL, Private, ARTHUR ERNEST, 34054. 3rd Bn Canterbury Regiment, NZEF. Killed in action 17 October 1917. Age 29. Son of Frederick and Dinah Jane

Gradwell, of Karamu Rd, Hastings, Napier. Native of Hawke's Bay. 2.

GRAHAM, Lance Corporal, ALBERT EDWARD, 24/769. 2nd Bn 3rd NZ Rifle Brigade. Killed in action 12 October 1917. Son of Mr and Mrs William Graham, of Terrace St, Thames. 8.

GRANT, Private, HORACE, 813908. 1st Bn Otago Regiment, NZEF. 12 October 1917. Age 20. Son of John Henry and Isabel Grant, of 50 St Edward's Rd, Southsea, England. 4.

GRAY, Private, HUGH, 42499. 8th Coy 3rd Bn Otago Regiment, NZEF. Killed in action 4 October 1917. Age 34. Son of Hugh Gray, of 33 Frame St, North East Valley, Dunedin, and the late Mary Gray. 4.

GRAY, Rifleman, JEFFRY CHARLES WILLIAM, 26/1165. 4th Bn 3rd NZ Rifle Brigade. Killed in action 10 October 1917. Son of Frank Baidock Gray and Jane Gray, of Masterton, Wellington. 8.

GRAY, Rifleman, THOMAS, 44273. 3rd Bn 3rd NZ Rifle Brigade. Killed in action 12 October 1917. Age 28. Son of David and Elizabeth Gray, of 49 Howe St, Dunedin, New Zealand. Native of Friockheim, Forfar, Scotland. 8.

GRAY, Private, WILLIAM ALEXANDER, 13905. 1st Bn Otago Regiment, NZEF. Killed in action 12 October 1917. Son of Mr W. Gray, of 524 Battie St East, Glasgow, Scotland. 4.

GREEN, Second Lieutenant, JAMES LESLIE, 6/239. 2nd Bn Canterbury Regiment, NZEF. Died of wounds 12 October 1917. Son of Mr and Mrs Charles Green, of Pokororo, Nelson. 2.

GREEN, Rifleman, WALTER JOHN, 45334. 2nd Bn 3rd NZ Rifle Brigade. Killed in action 12 October 1917. Son of Mr and Mrs John Green, of Tokomaru Bay, Gisborne. 8.

GRIBBLE, Private, LEICESTER GORDON, 12/3031. 6th (Hauraki) Coy 2nd Bn Auckland Regiment, NZEF. Killed in action 4 October 1917. Age 24. Son of James and Emma Eleanor Cribble, of Bauff St, Mairtown, Whangarei. Native of Hawke's Bay. Also served in Egypt, 1915–1916. 1.

GRIFFIN, Private, JOHN, 39590. 1st Bn Canterbury Regiment, NZEF. Killed in action 12 October 1917. Husband of Mrs E.S. Oldham (formerly Griffin), of 12 Queen St, Westport. 2.

GRIFFIN, Rifleman, REGINALD JOHN, 18993. 4th Bn 3rd NZ Rifle Brigade. Killed in action 12th October 1917. Age 26. Son of the late Edward and Maria Griffin, of Reefton, Greymouth. 8.

GRIFFITHS, Private, ALFRED VIVIAN, 29393. 1st Bn Wellington Regiment, NZEF. Killed in action 21 October 1917. Son of Mrs A. Morton (formerly Griffiths), of Mount Roskill Rd, Three Kings, Auckland. 7.

GRIGOR, Private, JAMES WILLIAMSON, 28276. No. 3 Coy NZ Machine Gun Corps. 3 October 1917. Age 27. Son of Archibald Grigor, of 131 Caledonia Rd, South Side, Glasgow, Scotland. 9.

GROVES, Private, GEORGE, 8/3279. 2nd Bn Otago Regiment, NZEF. Killed in action 30 September 1917. Son of Mr and Mrs G. Groves, of 158 Ettrick St, Invercargill. 4.

GUDSELL, Private, JOHN THOMAS, 34667. 3rd Bn Canterbury Regiment, NZEF. Killed in action 4 October 1917. Age 26. Son of Robert and Marie Gudsell, of 146 Edgeware Rd, Christchurch. Native of Canterbury. 2.

GUINNESS, Second Lieutenant, ARTHUR GRATTAN, 51166. 2nd Bn 3rd NZ Rifle

Brigade. Killed in action 12 October 1917. Age 27. Son of E.R. and F.A. Guinness, of Timaru. 7.

GUINNESS, Private, CECIL GEORGE, 11463. 3rd Bn Auckland Regiment, NZEF. Killed in action 19 October 1917. Age 23. Son of Jessie Green (formerly Guinness), of Tauranga, Thames, and the late Frank Hart Guinness. Native of Dunedin. 1.

GUNN, Private, ROBERT, 45091. 2nd Bn Otago Regiment, NZEF. Killed in action 12 October 1917. Son of Mrs Jane Gunn, of 85 Picton Avenue, Lower Riccarton, Christchurch. 4.

GUY, Regimental Serjeant Major, ALBERT HECTOR, M S M, Mentioned in Despatches, 6/244. 1st Bn Canterbury Regiment, NZEF. Killed in action 12 October 1917. Age 27. Son of John Arliss Guy and Elizabeth Mouter Guy, of Ngatimoti, Nelson. 2.

HACKETT, Private, LAWRENCE, 45859. 3rd Bn Wellington Regiment, NZEF. Killed in action 4 October 1917. Son of Mrs C. Hackett, of Bute St, Aramoho, Wanganui. 7.

HADDRELL, Rifleman, SYDNEY HERBERT, 18656. 1st Bn 3rd NZ Rifle Brigade. Killed in action 12 October 1917. Age 35. Son of Walter Henry Haddrell, of Westown, New Plymouth, and the late Mary Ann Haddrell. Native of Bealey, Canterbury. 8.

HAHN, Private, LESLIE LEONARD, 47193. 1st Bn Auckland Regiment, NZEF. Killed in action 22 October 1917. Son of Gustay and Elizabeth Hahn, of Ahaura, Greymouth. 1.

HALFORD, Corporal, EDMUND WILLIAM, 36832. 2nd Bn Otago Regiment, NZEF. Killed in action 12 October 1917. Brother of Mr E.J. Halford, of 52 Stout St, Gisbome. 3.

HALL, Serjeant, ARTHUR THOMAS, 2312195. 3rd Bn Wellington Regiment, NZEF. Killed in action 4 October 1917. Age 34. Son of Archibald and Katherine Hall of Hill St, Wellington; husband of Jessie Catherine Hall, of 252 Somme Parade, Aramoho, Wanganui. 6.

HALL, Private, COLIN, 27500. 2nd Bn Otago Regiment, NZEF. Killed in action 12 October 1917. Age 20. Son of Margaret Hall, of Awarua Plains, Southland. Invercargill, and the late Thomas Hall. Native of Woodend, Southland. 4.

HALL, Private, GEORGE, 39802. 1st Bn Wellington Regiment, NZEF. Killed in action 4 October 1917. Son of Mrs C. Hall, of 10 Waitoa Rd, Haitaitai, Wellington. 7.

HALL, Rifleman, HARRY, 41084. 3rd Bn 3rd NZ Rifle Brigade. Killed in action 12 October 1917. Age 36. Son of the late Samuel and Catherine Hall, of Christchurch. 8.

HALL, Private, RICHARD, 40318. 2nd Bn Auckland Regiment, NZEF. 4 October 1917. Age 41. Son of the late George and Isabella Hall, of Wyresdale, Garstang, Lancs, England. 1.

HALLY, Private, JOHN BERTRAND, 27883. 2nd Bn Otago Regiment, NZEF. Killed in action 12 October 1917. Age 21. Son of Patrick and Ellen Hally, of 56 Gladstone Rd, Parnell, Auckland. Native of Dunedin. 4.

HAM, Rifleman, FREDERICK, 26/1613. 2nd Bn 3rd NZ Rifle Brigade. Killed in action 12 October 1917. Age 32. Son of Job and Mary Ham, of 3 Queen St, Wellington. 8.

HAMBLIN, Private, ERNEST JAMES, 42323. 3rd Bn Auckland Regiment, NZEF. Killed in action 4 October 1917. Son of Charles James and Alice Augusta Hamblin, of Victoria Rd, Avondale, Auckland. 1.

HAMILTON, Rifleman, JAMES HENRY, 39803. 2nd Bn 3rd NZ Rifle Brigade. 12

October 1917. Age 43. Son of the late Hugh and Margret Hamilton. 8.

HAMILTON Private, PERCY, 20998. 3rd Bn Auckland Regiment, NZEF. Killed in action 15 October 1917. Age 22. Son of John Kennedy Hamilton and Mary Honor Hamilton, of 21 Gordon Rd, Mount Eden, Auckland. Native of Whitianga. 1.

HAMPTON, Private, GEORGE JAMES, 8/3282. 8th Coy 1st Bn Otago Regiment, NZEF. Killed in action 12 October 1917. Age 43. Son of George James and Mary Hampton. Native of Dundry, Bristol, England. 4.

HANCOCK, Lance Corporal, SYDNEY FERRIDAY, 26/106. 4th Bn 3rd NZ Rifle Brigade. Killed in action 12 October 1917. Age 24. Son of Emma Hancock, of Stratford, Taranaki, and the late Peter Hancock. 8.

HANNA, Private, JAMES REYNOLDS, 24111. 1st Bn Canterbury Regiment, NZEF. Killed in action 12 October 1917. Age 20. Son of Joseph and Sarah Hanna, of 370 Worcester St, Christchurch, New Zealand. Native of Belfast, Ireland. 2.

HANNA, Rifleman, WILLIAM HENRY, 26611. 2nd Bn 3rd NZ Rifle Brigade. Killed in action 12 October 1917. Age 33. Son of William Henry and Rebecca Hanna, of Ireland. Native of Cork, Ireland. 8.

HANNAGAN, Private, FRANK, 24433. 2nd Bn Otago Regiment, NZEF. Killed in action 12 October 1917. Age 37. Son of John and Bridget Hannagan, of 97A Harrow St, Dunedin. 4.

HANSBY, Private, ALOYSIUS JOHN, 6/3726. 2nd Bn Canterbury Regiment, NZEF. Killed in action 12 October 1917. Son of Mr and Mrs William Hansby, of Westport. 2.

HANSEN, Corporal, CARL WALTER, M M, 10/12953. 1st Bn Wellington Regiment, NZEF. Killed in action 4 October 1917. Age 24. Son of Mr J. Hansen of 10 Domain St, Palmerston North, Wellington. Native of Waitara, New Plymouth. 6.

HANSEN, Private, JOHN, 46582. 2nd Bn Canterbury Regiment, NZEF. Died of wounds 12 October 1917. Age 20. Son of Peter and Catrina Hansen. Native of Canterbury. 3.

HANSEN, Private, WILFRED ROLAND, 25862. 3rd Bn Auckland Regiment, NZEF. Killed in action 4 October 1917. Son of Mr and Mrs E.C. Hansen, of Kaikohe, Bay of Islands. 1.

HANSON, Private, EDWARD, 8/920. 2nd Bn Otago Regiment, NZEF. Killed in action 12 October 1917. Son of Mr and Mrs J.G. Hanson, of Upper Riccarton, Christchurch. 4.

HARDING, Private, ARTHUR EDWARD, 6/3338. A Coy 1st Bn Canterbury Regiment, NZEF. Killed in action 12 October 1917. Age 21. Son of Elizabeth Harding, of 120 Huxley St, Sydenham, Christchurch, and the late Charles Harding. 3.

HARDING, Rifleman, GEORGE FREDERICK, 26612. 2nd Bn 3rd NZ Rifle Brigade. Killed in action 12 October 1917. Brother of Mrs G. Warren, of Okoroire Springs, Rotorua Line, Hamilton. 8.

HARDISTY, Private, AMOS ARTHUR, 37813. A Coy 1st Bn Otago Regiment, NZEF. Killed in action 12 October 1917. Age 44. Son of the late Amos and Hannah B. Hardisty, of Bannoldswick, England; husband of Elizabeth Cameron Hardisty, of 210 Featherston St, Palmerston North, Wellington, New Zealand. Native of Drax Abbey, Selby, England. 4.

HAROLD, Private, MICHAEL JOHN, 18219. No. 5 Coy NZ Machine Gun Corps. Killed in action 11 October 1917. Age 21. Son of David and Emily Harold, of Waimiro, Dannevirke, Napier. 9.

HARRIS, Private, CHARLES DAVEY, 33719. 3rd Bn Canterbury Regiment, NZEF.

Killed in action 4 October 1917. Age 28. Son of Charles and Emma Harris, of Omihi, North Canterbury. 3.

HARRIS, Private, JOHN, 40211. 1st Bn Canterbury Regiment, NZEF. Died of wounds 12 October 1917. Age 24. Son of John William and Elizabeth Harris, of Kaikoura, Marlborough. 3.

HARRIS, Private, JAMES, 10/2955. 1st Bn Wellington Regiment, NZEF. Killed in action 21 October 1917. Son of Mr and Mrs George Toyne Harris, of Whangarei, Auckland. 7.

HARRIS, Private, JAMES HENRY, 40210. 2nd Bn Canterbury Regiment, NZEF. Killed in action 12 October 1917. Son of John Henry and Mary Harris, of North East Harbour, Dunedin. 3.

HARRIS, Rifleman, LEONARD JOHN, 24451. 4th Bn 3rd NZ Rifle Brigade. Killed in action 12 October 1917. Age 22. Son of Alice Mary Harris, of 7 Main South Rd, Hillside, Dunedin, and the late John Harris. 8.

HARRIS, Private, WALTER, 41542. 1st Bn Otago Regiment, NZEF. Killed in action 12 October 1917. Son of Mr and Mrs D. Harris, of Pahautanui, Wellington. 4.

HART, Private, ROBERT JAMES, 8/2937. 1st Bn Otago Regiment, NZEF. Killed in action 12 October 1917. Son of Mr and Mrs Archibald Paul Hart, of 73 Dundas St, Dunedin. 4.

HARTNETT, Lance Corporal, CYRIL, 8/3618. 2nd Bn Otago Regiment, NZEF. Killed in action 12 October 1917. Son of Patrick and Mary Hartnett, of Deloraine, Tasmania. 4.

HARTSTONGE, Private, JOHN JOSEPH, 29779. 8th Coy 2nd Bn Otago Regiment, NZEF. Killed in action 12 October 1917. Age 22. Native of Dunedin. Son of James and Margaret Hartstonge 4.

HARVEY, Private, DAVID, 3/939. NZ Medical Corps. Killed in action 12 October 1917. Age 28. Son of John and Jane Harvey, of 'Rata', Wells St, Kingsland, Auckland. 9.

HASKELL, Rifleman, WILLIAM ALEX, 31126. J Coy 3rd Bn NZ Rifle Brigade. Died of wounds 12 October 1917. Age 20. Son of Alexander John and Eva Haskell, of New Lynn, Auckland. 8.

HASTIE, Corporal, JOEIN MALAM, 12/2728. 2nd Bn Auckland Regiment, NZEF. Killed in action 4 October 1917. Son of Mr and Mrs J. Hastie, of Te Awamutu, Hamilton. 1.

HATTE, Private, ALFRED HENRY, 23/1413. 3rd Bn Auckland Regiment, NZEF. Killed in action 19 October 1917. Son of the late James Rayson Hatte and Anne Hatte (née Kirkwood), of Ballygar, Co Galway, Ireland. 1.

HAWKE, Private, JOHN MARTIN, 49189. 8th Coy Ist Bn Otago Regiment, NZEF. Killed in action 12 October 1917. Age 33. Son of William and Frances Hawke, of Geraldine, South Canterbury; husband of Winifred Hawke, of Salcombe St, Kaitangata, Dunedin. 2.

HAWKES, Lance Corporal, HUBERT ALFRED, 12391. 3rd Bn Wellington Regiment, NZEF. 4 October 1917. Age 33. Son of Samuel and Margaret Hawkes, of Hungerford, England. 6.

HAWKES, Corporal, RICHARD NEVILLE, 8/1501. Otago Regiment, NZEF. Killed in action 12 October 1917. Age 20. Son of Christina Hawkes, of 60 Wilson St, Timaru, and the late R.N. Hawkes. Also served at Gallipoli. 3.

HAWKINS, Corporal, JAMES HAROLD, 12/1978. 3rd Coy 1st Bn Auckland

Regiment, NZEF. Killed in action 4 October 1917. Age 25. Son of John and Lucy Hawkins, of Waiorongomai, Thames. 1.

HAYCOCK, Private, LEWIS ROY GORDON, 11661. 2nd Bn Canterbury Regiment, NZEF. Killed in action 12 October 1917. Age 22. Son of George Stanfield Haycock and Emma C. Haycock, of Richmond, Nelson. Native of Hope, Nelson. 3.

HAYES, Private, ROBERT WILLIAM, 8/3622. 3rd Bn Otago Regiment, NZEF. Killed in action 18 October 1917. Age 23. Son of Richard and Joan Hayes, of 50 Seddon St, Aramoho, Wanganui. Native of Tasmania. 4.

HAYNES, Rifleman, THOMAS WILLIAM, 32849. 4th Bn 3rd NZ Rifle Brigade. Killed in action 12 October 1917. Age 25. Son of William and Jessie Pearcy Haynes, of Hook, South Canterbury. 8.

HEAL, Private, ALFRED GORDON, 14622. 1st Bn Wellington Regiment, NZEF. Killed in action 4 October 1917. Age 22. Son of Alfred and Mary Heal, of Te Tawa, Inglewood, Taranaki. 7.

HEALD, Lance Corporal, EDMUND JOHN, 24/1071. 2nd Bn Otago Regiment, NZEF. Killed in action 12 October 1917. Son of Mr and Mrs E.J. Heald, of Wrey's Bush, Invercargill. 4.

HENDERSON, Rifleman, CHARLES JOHN, 24/793. C Coy 2nd Bn 3rd NZ Rifle Brigade. Killed in action 12 October 1917. Age 27. Son of the late William and Margaret Henderson, of Lowburn, Dunedin. Native of Central Otago. 8.

HENDERSON, Private, FRANK ALLAN, 40565. 3rd (Auckland) Coy IS Bn Auckland Regiment, NZEF. Killed in action 23 October 1917. Age 21. Son of John George and Annie Marie Henderson, of 17 Gordon Rd, Mount Eden, Auckland. Native of Devonport, Auckland. 1.

HENDERSON, Rifleman, WILLIAM, 38530. 2nd Bn 3rd NZ Rifle Brigade. 12 October 1917. Age 30. Son of John and Charlotte Henderson, of Troal Norwick, Haroldswick, Lerwick, Shetland. 8.

HENERY, Private, ALBERT THOMAS COURTENAY, 43976. 2nd Bn Canterbury Regiment, NZEF. Killed in action 12 October 1917. Son of Mr and Mrs William James Henery, of 153 Riccarton Rd, Christchurch. 2.

HENNESSY, Private, JOHN, 23179. 1st Bn Canterbury Regiment, NZEF. Killed in action 12 October 1917. Age 23. Son of John and Mary Hennessy, of Waimangaroa, Greymouth. 3.

HENRY, Private, JOHN EDWARD, 5/786A. 2nd Bn Otago Regiment, NZEF. Killed in action 1 October 1917. Son of Mr and Mrs Reuben Henry, of 97 Teviot St, Invercargill. 4.

HENSON, Private, ERIC SHOLTO ROBERT, 41801. 2nd Bn Otago Regiment, NZEF. Killed in action 12 October 1917. Age 21. Son of Emma Ada Henson, of 'Beaumont', Feilding, Wellington, and the late John Henson. Native of [Sanson, Manawatu], Wellington. 4.

HERBERT, Private, ALEX DUNCAN, 39233. 2nd Bn Otago Regiment, NZEF. Killed in action 12 October 1917. Age 30. Son of William Herbert, of Milton, Otago, and the late Catherine Herbert; husband of Wilhelmina Gibbon Herbert, of Clinton, Otago. Native of Popotunoa, Otago. 4.

HERMAN, Private, WILLIAM, 36865. 3rd Bn Wellington Regiment, NZEF. Killed in action 4 October 1917. Son of Mr and Mrs E. Herman, of Bamfield St, Waikiwi, Invercargill. 7.

HETHERINGTON, Private, JOSEPH, 40947. 1st Bn Otago Regiment, NZEF. Killed in action 12 October 1917. Age 21. Son of Sarah Hetherington, of 402 Leith St, Dunedin, and the late John Hetherington. 4.

HEWAT, Corporal, ALEX STRONACH, 22211. 1st Bn Otago Regiment, NZEF. Killed in action 3 October 1917. Age 22. Son of E.C. and J.W. Hewat, of Havelock St, Riverton, Invercargill. 3.

HEYS, Private, JAMES HENRY, 23832. 3rd Bn Wellington Regiment, NZEF. 4 October 1917. Age 33. Son of Richard and Mary Heys. 7.

HICKEY, Private, JAMES JOSEPH, 8/2008. 8th Coy 1st Bn Otago Regiment, NZEF. Killed in action 12 October 1917. Age 28. Son of Mr and Mrs Henry Hickey, of 19 Helena St, Dunedin South. 4.

HIGGIE, Rifleman, MALCOLM, 28478. 2nd Bn 3rd NZ Rifle Brigade. Killed in action 12 October 1917. Son of Mrs E. Higgie, of Whiritoa, Wanganui. 8.

HIGGINS, Private, JOHN, 34859. 1st Bn Otago Regiment, NZEF. Died of wounds 16 October 1917. Brother of Miss J.F. Higgins, of Dunedin South. 4.

HIGHT, Rifleman, CECIL MORLAND, 15901. 3rd Bn 3rd NZ Rifle Brigade. Killed in action 12 October 1917. Age 22. Son of Albert and Mary Hight, of 27 High St, Timaru. 8.

HIGHT, Rifleman, LEONARD HENRY DIXON, 15902. 3rd Bn 3rd NZ Rifle Brigade. Killed in action 12 October 1917. Age 27. Son of Albert and Mary Hight, of 27 High St, Timaru. 8.

HILDRETH, Rifleman, DAVID, 41331. 1st Bn 3rd NZ Rifle Brigade. Killed in action 12 October 1917. Age 36. Son of John and Annie Hildreth, of Fernhill, Hastings, Napier. Native of Hawke's Bay. 8.

HILL, Rifleman, JOHN GEORGE, 14822. 2nd Bn 3rd NZ Rifle Brigade. Killed in action 12 October 1917. Son of Mr and Mrs George Hill, of Taikatu Rd, Auroa, Taranaki. 8.

HILL, Private, LISTON, 38699. 1st Bn Auckland Regiment, NZEF. Killed in action 4 October 1917. Age 21. Son of James and Janet Hill, of Hunua, Auckland. 1.

HILLIER, Serjeant, ARCHIBALD LIONEL, 14205. 2nd Bn 3rd NZ Rifle Brigade. Killed in action 12 October 1917. Husband of Georgina Isabella Hillier, of Mill Rd, Whangarei, Auckland. 7.

HODGSON, Private, SIDNEY BERTRAM, 39813. 3rd Bn Wellington Regiment, NZEF. Killed in action 4 October 1917. Age 26. Son of James Charles Hodgson, of New Brighton, Christchurch, New Zealand, and the late Katherine Hodgson; husband of Florence Hamilton Hodgson, of 13 Ngaio Rd, Kelburn, Wellington. Native of Berwick, Victoria, Australia. 7.

HODGSON, Lance Serjeant, THOMAS, 11283. D Coy 2nd Bn Otago Regiment, NZEF. Killed in action 12 October 1917. Age 30. Son of Jane Reid Crow (formerly Hodgson), of 14 Helena St, Dunedin, and the late Thomas Hodgson. 3.

HOLBECHE, Serjeant, VINCENT AEMILIAN, 28588. 3rd Bn Auckland Regiment, NZEF. Killed in action 18 October 1917. Husband of Alice Beatrice Holbeche, of Epsom, Auckland. 1.

HOLLOW, Lance Corporal, JAMES WALKER, 8/2012. 2nd Bn Otago Regiment, NZEF. Killed in action 12 October 1917. Age 23. Son of James and Isabella Hollow, of Yare St, Oamaru. Also served at Gallipoli. 4.

HOLM, Private, JOHN WILLIAM, 12/4014. 6th (Hauraki) Coy 1st Bn Auckland Regiment, NZEF. Killed in action 4 October 1917. Age 22. Eldest son of Wilfred E. and Sarah H. Holm, of 27 King George Avenue, Epsom, Auckland. 1.

HOOPER, Private, ROY BOLTON, 6/4061. 2nd Bn Canterbury Regiment, NZEF. Killed in action 12 October 1917. Age 25. Son of Francis and Rachel Mary Hooper, of Wakefield, Nelson. 3.

HOPKINS, Private, JOHN, 30225. 3rd Bn Canterbury Regiment, NZEF. Killed in action 12 October 1917. Brother of P. Hopkins, of Opunake, Taranaki. 3.

HORSCROFT, Private, CLARENCE ALEXANDER, 30803. 3rd Bn Auckland Regiment, NZEF. Killed in action 4 October 1917. Age 21. Son of Charles and Mary Ann Horscroft, of Church St West, Onehunga, Auckland. 1.

HORSFIELD, Private, JAMES KAY, 14986. 1st Bn Canterbury Regiment, NZEF. Killed in action 12 October 1917. Age 40. Son of Thomas Horsfield, of The Ridge, Knowle Hill, Evesham, England; husband of Alice Horsfield, of Alexander St, Bexley Rd, New Brighton, Christchurch, New Zealand. 3.

HOUGHTON, Corporal, HENRY PRYCE, 18804. No. 2 Coy NZ Machine Gun Corps. Killed in action 4 October 1917. Age 38. Son of Edward Pryce Houghton and Emma Margaret Houghton, of Dunedin. 9.

HOURSTON, Private, ARCHIBALD, 12/2741. 1st Bn Auckland Regiment, NZEF. Killed in action 4 October 1917. Age 33. Son of Robert and Margaret Hourston, of Quoybirstane, St Ola, Orkney, Scotland. 1.

HOWARD, Corporal, HAROLD, 10351. 2nd Bn Wellington Regiment, NZEF. Killed in action 4 October 1917. Son of Mr and Mrs Robert James Howard, of Pakowhai, Hawke's Bay, Napier. 6.

HOWE, Rifleman, THOMAS HENRY, 12183. D Coy. 1st Bn 3rd NZ Rifle Brigade. Killed in action 12 October 1917. Age 20. Son of Albert and Beatrice Ann Howe, of 50 Caledonian Rd, St Albans, Christchurch, New Zealand. Native of Callington, Cornwall, England. 8.

HOWELLS, Private, IRA JOHN, 31504. 1st Bn Canterbury Regiment, NZEF. 2 October 1917. Age 30. Son of John Henry Brown, of 74 North Rd, Ferndale (Rhondda), Glam, Wales. 3.

HUBBARD, Captain, ARTHUR CHARLES, M C, 14347. 16th (Waikato) Coy 2nd Bn Auckland Regiment, NZEF. Killed in action 4 October 1917. Age 45. Son of John Charles and Elizabeth Anne Hubbard, of Paeroa, Thames. 1.

HUBBARD, Private, RAYNAL EDWARD, 37817. No. 1 Coy 3rd Bn Canterbury Regiment, NZEF. Killed in action 4 October 1917. Son of Mrs M. Matthews (formerly Hubbard), of Julyean St, Shannon, Wellington. 3.

HUDSON, Private, GEORGE ALEXANDER, 35086. 3rd Bn Canterbury Regiment, NZEF. Killed in action 18 October 1917. Husband of Laurie Constance Hudson, of 144 Redruth Avenue, Spreydon, Christchurch. 3.

HUNTHRIES, Private, OSCAR EDWARD, 46187. 2nd Bn Canterbury Regiment, NZEF. Killed in action 12 October 1917. Age 25. Son of George Edward and Jessie Humphries, of Deep Creek, Marlborough. 3.

HUNTER, Rifleman, ALBERT HENRY, 22984. 4th Bn 3rd NZ Rifle Brigade. Killed in action 12 October 1917. Son of Ellen Schriebert (formerly Hunter), of Waitui, Inglewood, Taranaki. 8.

HUNTER, Rifleman, ROY CAMERON, 37066. 4th Bn 3rd NZ Rifle Brigade. Died of wounds 12 October 1917. Son of Mrs E.J. Hunter, of 148 Pittwater Rd, Manly, Sydney, Australia. 8.

HURLEY, Private, DANIEL, 41800. 1st Bn Wellington Regiment, NZEF. Killed in action 4 October 1917. Son of Mr and Mrs John Hurley, of 49 Main St, Palmerston

North. 7.

HUTCHINSON, Rifleman, ROBERT, 45600. 3rd Bn 3rd NZ Rifle Brigade. Killed in action 12 October 1917. Age 28. Son of Peter and Elizabeth Hutchinson, of Glen Oroua, Wellington, New Zealand. Native of Westmorland, England. 8.

INGRAM, Private, ERIC JAMES, 33548. 3rd Bn Wellington Regiment, NZEF. Killed in action 4 October 1917. Age 24. Son of Mary E. Cottrell, of 17 Park Rd, Grafton, Auckland. 7.

INGRAM, Serjeant, HERBERT, 24368. 2nd Bn Otago Regiment, NZEF. Killed in action 12 October 1917. Husband of Ellen Ingram, of 95 Ritchie St, Invercargill. 3.

INGRAM, Lance Corporal, RONALD WILLIAM, 25250. 1st Bn Otago Regiment, NZEF. Killed in action 12 October 1917. Age 30. Son of George Ronald and Charlotte Ingram, of Seville, Victoria, Australia. Native of Bendigo, Victoria. 4.

INGRAM, Private, WILLIAM RALSTON, 40328. 3rd Coy 1st Bn Auckland Regiment, NZEF. Killed in action 4 October 1917. Son of William and Annie Ingram, of Marohemo, Auckland. 1.

INWOOD, Lance Corporal, GODFREY ALAN, 12399. 4th Bn 3rd NZ Rifle Brigade. Killed in action 12 October 1917. Son of the late Mrs E. Inwood, of Westport, Greymouth. 8.

IRVIN, Rifleman, VICTOR CHRISTOPHER, 38837. J Coy 3rd Bn 3rd NZ Rifle Brigade. Killed in action 12 October 1917. Age 25. Son of Margaret A. Irvin, of Richardson Rd, Mount Albert, Auckland, and the late James Irvin. 8.

ISAAC, Second Lieutenant, HERBERT CYRIL, 12/2185. 1st Auckland Regiment, NZEF. 4 October 1917. 1.

JACKSON, Private, PERCIVAL HOUNSLOW, 33729. 3rd Bn Canterbury Regiment, NZEF. Killed in action 5 October 1917. Son of the late Richard and Letitia Jackson. Native of Masterton. 3.

JACKSON, Rifleman, ROYDEN GARSIDE, 46459. 1st Bn NZ Rifle Brigade. Killed in action 12 October 1917. Son of Mrs M.E. Jackson, of 21 St. George's Bay Rd, Parnell, Auckland. 8.

JACOBS, Private, WILLIAM NORLEY, 18807. 6th (Hauraki) Coy 1st Bn Auckland Regiment, NZEF. Killed in action 4 October 1917. Age 37. Son of Agnes Jacobs, of 99 Kilmore St, Christchurch, and the late William Norley Jacobs. 1.

JACOBSON, Lance Corporal, ERNEST RUEBEN, 30593. 3rd Bn Wellington Regiment, NZEF. Killed in action 4 October 1917. Age 33. Son of John Alfred and Caroline Charlotte Jacobson, of 43 Stanley St, Berhampore, Wellington. 6.

JAMES, Private, ERNEST, 39614. 1st Bn Otago Regiment, NZEF. Killed in action 12 October 1917. 4.

JAMIESON, Private, ERNEST HAROLD ALBERT, 42112. C Coy 1st Bn Auckland Regiment, NZEF. Killed in action 4 October 1917. Age 21. Son of John and Kate Jamieson, of Queen St, Thames. 1.

JANVIER, Private, ALBERT ROBERT, 28344. 2nd Bn Auckland Regiment, NZEF. Killed in action 4 October 1917. Brother of William Janvier. Staff Officer Railway Deviation Works, Marrangaroo, New South Wales, Australia. 1.

JAY, Lance Corporal, JOHN EDWARD, 6/4071. 2nd Bn Canterbury Regiment, NZEF. 12 October 1917. Age 32. Son of John Edward and Eliza Jay, of Wayland.

Looe, Cornwall; husband of Mabel Annie Jay, of Clifden Terrace, Liskeard, Cornwall, England. 2.

JELLEY, Private, CHARLES RAINTON, 22989. 10th Coy 2nd Bn Otago Regiment, NZEF. Killed in action 12 October 1917. Age 21. Son of Sarah Jelley, of 75 Sligo Terrace, Roslyn, Dunedin, and the late Albert Jelley. 4.

JENKINS, Private, JOSEPH NELSON, 40960. 1st Bn Otago Regiment, NZEF. Died of wounds, 12 October 1917. Son of Mr and Mrs John Jenkins, of Crown Terrace, Arrowtown, Invercargill. 4.

JENKINS, Private, THOMAS, 23557. 4th Coy 1st Bn Otago Regiment, NZEF. Died of wounds 16 October 1917. Age 35. Son of the late William and Mary Ann Jenkins. Native of Arrowtown, Invercargill. 4.

JENSON, Private, WILLIAM FREDERICK, 27906. 2nd Bn Canterbury Regiment, NZEF. Killed in action 12 October 1917. Age 20. Son of Edward and Ada Mary Jenson, of Whakatu, Hastings, Napier. Native of Woodville, Wellington. 3.

JESS, Corporal, THOMAS, 15307. 2nd Bn 3rd NZ Rifle Brigade. Killed in action 12 October 1917. Age 24. Son of John and Isabel Jess, of Rukuhia, Waikato. 7.

JOHANSON, Private, EMIL HENNING, 25255. J Coy 1st Bn Auckland Regiment, NZEF. Killed in action 4 October 1917. Age 23. Son of Caroline Johanson, of Hamua, Pahiatua, Wellington, and the late Emil Henning Johanson. 1.

JOHNSON, Corporal, CHARLES ARTHUR, 6/4276. 1st Bn Canterbury Regiment, NZEF. Killed in action 12 October 1917. Son of Mr and Mrs Peter Johnson, of 'Neensgarth', Temuka, South Canterbury. 2.

JOHNSTON, Corporal, ALBERT GEORGE, 32674. 1st Bn Otago Regiment, NZEF. Killed in action 12 October 1917. Son of Mr and Mrs G.P. Johnston, of Comley Bank, Gore, Southland, Invercargill. 3.

JOHNSTON, Corporal, CLIFFORD FREDERICK, 24/1095. 2nd Bn 3rd NZ Rifle Brigade. Killed in action 12 October 1917. Age 24. Son of Frederick and Mary Johnston, of 173 Huxley St, Sydenham, Christchurch. 8.

JOHNSTON, Lance Corporal, JOHN, 23186. 2nd Bn 3rd NZ Rifle Brigade. Killed in action 12 October 1917. Age 32. Son of James M. and Margaret Craig Johnston, of Homedale, Turriff, Scotland. 8.

JOHNSTON, Rifleman, JAMES STEWART, 25714. 2nd Bn 3rd NZ Rifle Brigade. 12 October 1917. 8.

JOHNSTON, Rifleman, MALCOLM ROBERT, 42113. 1st Bn 3rd NZ Rifle Brigade. Killed in action 12 October 1917. Son of Joseph and Agnes Mary Johnston, of Otorohanga, Hamilton. 8.

JOHNSTON, Corporal, PETER THOMAS, 24/199. 2nd Bn 3rd NZ Rifle Brigade. Killed in action 12 October 1917. Age 20. Son of Jessie Isabella Johnston, of McAndrew St, Otautau, Invercargill, and the late John Smith Johnston. 8.

JOLI, Rifleman, HENRY ALEXANDER, 47149. 3rd Bn 3rd NZ Rifle Brigade. Killed in action 12 October 1917. Age 28. Son of Peter Joseph and Ada Dalziel Joli, of Staveley, Christchurch. 8.

JONES, Private, ALEXANDER, 13/516. 2nd Bn Otago Regiment, NZEF. Killed in action 12 October 1917. Brother of Mrs Jean Primmer, of 32 Rosewame St, Spreydon, Christchurch. 4.

JONES, Private, ALLAN STUART, 26628. 3rd Bn Auckland Regiment, NZEF. Killed in action 18 October 1917. Son of Elizabeth Jones, of 36 Nicholson St, East Brunswick, Melbourne, Australia. 1.

JONES, Private, BERTIE ALMA, 38711. 3rd Bn Wellington Regiment, NZEF. Killed in action 4 October 1917. Age 30. Son of Alice Jones, of 8 Railway St, Newmarket, Auckland, and the late George Jones. 7.

JONES, Private, DAVID, 11677. 1st Bn Canterbury Regiment, NZEF. 12 October 1917. Age 28. Son of Richard and Jane Jones, of Dalfawr, Dolgelley, Wales. 3.

JONES, Corporal, FRED, 23/2016. 2nd Bn 3rd NZ Rifle Brigade. Killed in action 12 October 1917. Age 24. Son of Frances W. Henrietta Jones, of 1 Russell St, Marton, Wanganui. 8.

JONES, Private, FREDERICK GWYN, 23837. 1st Wellington Regiment, NZEF. 3 October 1917. 7.

JONES, Private, JAMES WILLIAM, 29788. 3rd Bn Otago Regiment, NZEF. Killed in action 17 October 1917. Age 20. Son of William and Alice Louisa Jones, of Kapuka, Southland, Invercargill, New Zealand. Native of Worcester, England. 4.

JONES, Private, LANCE HARRY, 40574. 2nd Bn Auckland Regiment, NZEF. Killed in action 4 October 1917. Son of Annie C. Jones, of 70 St. Hill St, Wanganui. 1.

JORDAN, Private, JOHN RAYMOND, 28151. 2nd Bn Wellington Regiment, NZEF. Killed in action 4 October 1917. Age 20. Son of William Henry and Ann Jordan, of 144 Leach St, New Plymouth. 7.

JORDAN, Corporal, SYDNEY CARL, 24/482. 2nd Bn 3rd NZ Rifle Brigade. Killed in action 12 October 1917. Son of Mr and Mrs James Jordan, of Tauranga, Thames. 8.

JOYNER, Private, ARTHUR, 38033. 1st Bn Wellington Regiment, NZEF. Killed in action 4 October 1917. Son of Mr and Mrs William Joyner, of 91 Molesworth St, Wellington. 7.

JULIAN, Private, MONTAGUE D'ARCY, 44384. 2nd Bn Canterbury Regiment, NZEF. Killed in action 12 October 1917. Son of Mr and Mrs Frank Julian, of Opunake, Taranaki. 3.

JURY, Private, ALFRED WILLIAM, 33383. 3rd Bn Wellington Regiment, NZEF. Killed in action 4 October 1917. Age 21. Son of Maurice Ingram Jury and Jane Jury, of Fenton St, Stratford, New Plymouth. 7.

KAVANAGH, Private, CHARLES, 14279. 1st Bn Otago Regiment, NZEF. Killed in action 12 October 1917. Brother of Mrs Magurk, of 6 St Mary St, Wellington. 4.

KAY, Private, JOHN, 33893. 2nd Bn Auckland Regiment, NZEF. Killed in action 4 October 1917. Son of the late John Kay. 1.

KEDDELL, Private, REGINALD AUBREY, 8/1763. 1st Bn Otago Regiment, NZEF. Killed in action 12 October 1917. Age 28. Son of Robina Bell Keddell, of 14 Lowe St, Invercargill, and the late Maj. Jackson Keddell. Also served at Gallipoli. Wounded at Armentieres, 1916. 4.

KEELE, Private, ALFRED WILLIAM, 8/2023. 1st Bn Otago Regiment, NZEF. Killed in action 12 October 1917. 4.

KEELEY, Rifleman, GEORGE CAMBRY, 39059. 1st Bn 3rd NZ Rifle Brigade. Killed in action 12 October 1917. Son of Charles and Maria Keeley, of Balclutha, Dunedin. 8.

KEIR, Captain, JOHN, M C, 30100. 1st Coy 1st Bn Wellington Regiment, NZEF. Killed in action 23 October 1917. Age 44. Husband of Mary F. Keir, of 7 Hay St, Seatoun, Wellington. Native of Dunedin. 6.

KELLEHER, Private, DENIS FRANCIS, 45521. 3rd Bn Auckland Regiment, NZEF.

Killed in action 17 October 1917. Son of Mrs T. Kelleher, of Musselburgh Rise, Dunedin. 1.

KELLY, Private, JOHN, 28157. 2nd Bn Wellington Regiment, NZEF. Killed in action 4 October 1917. Age 29. Son of Mr John and Mrs E. Kelly, of Wester Queensley House, Shettleston, Glasgow, Scotland. 7.

KELLY, Private, MARTIN, 28158. 1st Bn Wellington Regiment, NZEF. Killed in action 21 October 1917. Brother of D. Kelly, of Forty Mile Bush, Konini, Wellington. 7.

KELLY, Private, THOMAS BERTRAM, 14999. 2nd Bn Wellington Regiment, NZEF. Killed in action 4 October 1917. Age 21. Son of Rosa Phillis Kelly, of Buller St, New Plymouth. 7.

KEMP, Private, LIONEL GREGORY, 40335. 1st Bn Auckland Regiment, NZEF. Killed in action 4 October 1917. Husband of Alice Hilda Kemp, of 32 Pine St, Dominion Rd, Auckland. 1.

KEMP, Lance Corporal, RALPH MAINWARING, 25/395. 3rd Bn 3rd NZ Rifle Brigade. Killed in action 12 October 1917. Age 23. Son of Richard Kemp, of King Edward St, Papakura, Auckland, and the late Marian Kemp. 8.

KENCH, Private, ALEXANDER, 32681. D Coy 1st Bn Otago Regiment, NZEF. Killed in action 12 October 1917. Age 18. Son of James and Mary Ann Kench, of 18 Copeland St, Wanganui. 4.

KENNEDY, Private, JAMES, 35091. 3rd Bn Canterbury Regiment, NZEF. Killed in action 18 October 1917. Son of Mr and Mrs William Kennedy, of 17 Keith St, Wanganui. 3.

KERR, Private, WILLIAM, 39251. D Coy 1st Bn Otago Regiment, NZEF. Killed in action 12 October 1917. Age 39. Son of the late David and Jane Kerr, of Gimmerburn, Otago Central; husband of Janet Helen Kerr, of St Bathan's, Otago Central. 4.

KETTLE, Private, JOHN JAMES, 38716. E Coy 1st Bn Auckland Regiment, NZEF. Killed in action 4 October 1917. Age 31. Son of George William and Mary Kettle, of Otaika Rd, Whangarei. 1.

KEYMER, Rifleman, GEORGE EDWARD, 42123. 4th Bn 3rd NZ Rifle Brigade. Killed in action 12 October 1917. Age 23. Son of W. and M.E. Keymer, of 69 Wood St, Ponsonby, Auckland. 8.

KEYS, Private, GEORGE ERNEST, 41822. 3rd Bn Wellington Regiment, NZEF. Killed in action 4 October 1917. Son of Mr and Mrs Alfred Keys, of Wilson St, Upper Hutt, Wellington. 7.

KILGOUR, Corporal, JOHN DUNCAN, 241206. 2nd Bn 3rd NZ Rifle Brigade. Killed in action 12 October 1917. Age 22. Son of Emma Margaret Stokes (formerly Kilgour), of Paengaroa, Bay of Plenty, and the late James Kilgour. Native of Bulls, Wanganui. 8.

KILKENNY, Private, MICHAEL HAGEN, 24801. 2nd Coy NZ Machine Gun Corps. Died of wounds 12 October 1917. Son of Patrick and Margaret Kilkenny, of Taradale, Napier. 9.

KING, Private, ARTHUR WILLIAM, 2511769. 2nd Bn Auckland Regiment, NZEF. Killed in action 4 October 1917. Age 28. Son of Maria King, of 41 Browne St, Timaru, and the late W. King. Native of Temuka, South Canterbury. 1.

KING, Private, HENRY, 39254. 3rd Bn Otago Regiment, NZEF. Killed in action 4 October 1917. Son of Mr and Mrs Albert John King, of 390 Leith St, Dunedin. 4.

KING, Second Lieutenant, LANCEL LYTTON, 27696. 3rd Bn Wellington Regiment,

NZEF. Killed in action 4 October 1917. Age 28. Son of Margaret A. King, of 1 Ingram Rd, Remuera, Auckland. 6.

KING, Private, ROBERT JOSEPH, 28348. 1st Bn Auckland Regiment, NZEF. Killed in action 4 October 1917. Age 48. Son of Joseph and Jean King, of Te Pohue, Hawke's Bay; husband of Norah King. 1.

KING, Private, WILLIAM, 33560. 3rd Bn Wellington Regiment, NZEF. Killed in action 4 October 1917. Son of Mrs A.W. King, of Auckland. 7.

KININMONT, Private, WILLIAM NICOL, 36634. 10th Coy 1st Bn Otago Regiment, NZEF. Killed in action 12 October 1917. Age 22. Son of William and Mary Kininmont, of Inch-Holme, North Otago. 4.

KINLOCH, Private, GEORGE ALEXANDER, 39255. 1st Bn Otago Regiment, NZEF. Killed in action 12 October 1917. Age 33. Son of Alexander and Helen Kinloch, of 25 Franklin St, Gladstone, Dunedin. Native of Milton, Dunedin. 4.

KINZETT, Lance Corporal, INNESS, 2411410. 2nd Bn 3rd NZ Rifle Brigade. Killed in action 12 October 1917. Age 28. Son of Edward Robert and Zella Kinzett, of Glen Oroua, Wellington. 8.

KIRWAN, Private, JOHN, 13936. 1st Bn Otago Regiment, NZEF. Killed in action 12 October 1917. Son of Mr and Mrs John Kirwan, of 42 East Rd, Invercargill. 4.

KITCHING, Private, JOHN ARTHUR, 24181. 2nd Bn Canterbury Regiment, NZEF. Killed in action 12 October 1917. Age 43. Husband of Annie Kitching, of Flat Creek, Marlborough. 3.

KITTO, Private, JOHN FRANCIS, 15186. D Coy 2nd Bn Otago Regiment, NZEF. Killed in action 12 October 1917. Age 23. Son of John Francis and Mary Kitto, of 22 Jackson St, Kaikorai, Dunedin. 4.

KJOSS, Private, KARL, 23145. H Coy 2nd Bn Otago Regiment, NZEF. Killed in action 12 October 1917. Age 30. Son of Oluf Emil and Jorgine Kathrine Kjoss, of Norway. Native of Kristiansand, Norway. 4.

KLENNER, Private, JOHN, 10/3319. 1st Bn Wellington Regiment, NZEF. Killed in action 4 October 1917. Son of Victoria Butler (formerly Klenner), of Tariki, Stratford, New Plymouth. 7.

KNIGHT, Second Lieutenant, GEORGE BERNARD, 8/1532. 2nd Bn Otago Regiment, NZEF. Killed in action 12 October 1917. Age 24. Son of Herbert Douglas Knight and Ellen Knight, of Mokorua, Whakatane, Thames. Native of Dannevirke, Napier. Also served at Gallipoli. 3.

KNOWLES, Private, CLAUDE LEONARD, 6/2683. 1st Bn Canterbury Regiment, NZEF. Died of wounds 12 October 1917. Age 23. Son of the Rev. Walter Frank and Lizzie Knowles, of 'Knowlholm', 61 Esplanade, New Brighton, North Beach, Christchurch. Native of Prebbleton, Canterbury. 3.

KNOWLES, Private, FRANCIS WILLIAM, 48515. 2nd Bn Wellington Regiment, NZEF. Killed in action 4 October 1917. Age 29. Son of Francis and Elizabeth Knowles, of 40 King St, Newcastle, New South Wales, Australia. Native of Gisborne, New Zealand. 7.

KNUDSON, Private, CHARLES ROBERT, 13937. 1st Bn Otago Regiment, NZEF. Killed in action 12 October 1917. Son of Mr and Mrs Charles Knudson, of 277 Oxford St, South Dunedin. 4.

KORTEGAST, Private, HUGH SARSFIELD, 27657. No. 5 Coy NZ Machine Gun Corps. Killed in action 12 October 1917. Son of Mrs Sarah Kortegast, of Gibson's Quay, Hokitika, Greymouth. 9.

LALOLI, Lance Corporal, JOHN HENRY, 22630. 4th Bn 3rd NZ Rifle Brigade. Killed in action 12 October 1917. Age 22. Son of Francis and Mary Laloli, of Roxburgh, Otago. 8.

LAMB, Private, ALFRED JAMES, 29420. 1st Bn Wellington Regiment, NZEF. Killed in action 4 October 1917. Age 23. Son of Henry James and Mary Ann Lamb, of Houhora, North Auckland. 7.

LAMB, Private, ROBERT JAMES, 13940. 2nd Bn Otago Regiment, NZEF. Killed in action 12 October 1917. Age 26. Son of Robert and Alma G.F. Lamb, of Quarry Hills, Southland, Invercargill. 4.

LAMONT, Company Serjeant Major, WILLIAM ALFRED, 12/3381. 2nd Bn Auckland Regiment, NZEF. Killed in action 4 October 1917. Son of Mrs O.M. Lamont, of 54 Empire Rd, Epsom, Auckland. 1.

LANE, Private, THOMAS, 38966. 1st Bn Canterbury Regiment, NZEF. Killed in action 12 October 1917. Age 30. Son of Andrew and Julia Lane, of Carraganes, Kingwilliamstown, Co Cork, Ireland. 3.

LANG, Private, ANDREW, 23397. 2nd Bn Auckland Regiment, NZEF. Killed in action 4 October 1917. Age 29. Son of James and Elizabeth Lang, of Waimangaroa, Greymouth. 1.

LANGDON, Private, ROBERT WILFRED, 44492. 3rd Bn Wellington Regiment, NZEF. Killed in action 4 October 1917. Age 33. Son of Margaret A. Langdon, of Tinui, Wairarapa, Wellington, and the late Jarnes S. Langdon. 7.

LANGFORD, Corporal, ALEXANDER JOSEPH, 10041. 2nd Bn Auckland Regiment, NZEF. Killed in action 4 October 1917. Age 23. Son of Francis and Mary Langford, of South Hillend, Southland. 1.

LARGE, Private, HERBERT, 29034. 15th Coy 3rd Bn Auckland Regiment, NZEF. Killed in action 4 October 1917. Age 24. Son of Mary Ann Large, of 72 Wyon St, Linwood, Christchurch. 1.

LASH, Private, HAROLD SAMWAYS, 42809. 2nd Bn Canterbury Regiment, NZEF. Killed in action 12 October 1917. Brother of Hubert D. Lash, of Nelson St, Hamilton East, Waikato. 3.

LAURENCE, Private, PETER, 32520. 1st Bn Auckland Regiment, NZEF. Killed in action 4 October 1917. Father of Audrey E. Laurence, of 43 Burwood Crescent, Remuera, Auckland. 1.

LAW, Private, WILLIAM, 36338. 3rd Bn Canterbury Regiment, NZEF. Killed in action 4 October 1917. Son of Robert and Annie Law, of 28 Cowlishaw St, Avonside, Christchurch. 3.

LEAROYD, Private, HYDE KELSO, 16042. No. 2 Coy NZ Machine Gun Corps. Killed in action 4 October 1917. Brother of William Kelso Learoyd, of Rotorua, Hamilton. 9.

LEATHER, Private, GEORGE ALFRED, 30822. 15th Coy 2nd Bn Auckland Regiment, NZEF. Killed in action 4 October 1917. Age 43. Son of the late W. and Mary Leather; husband of Alice Mary Leather, of 5 Shaw Rd, Newbury, England. 1.

LEATT, Private, JAMES, 12/2011. 1st Bn Auckland Regiment, NZEF. 4 October 1917. Age 33. Son of George Gore Leatt, and Sarah Ellen Leatt, of 43 Pendle St, Skipton, Yorks, England. 1.

LECKNER, Private, THEODORE ERNEST, 6/3069. 1st Bn Canterbury Regiment, NZEF. Killed in action 12 October 1917. Age 28. Son of Alfred and Annie Leckner, of Wellington; husband of Vivienne Dallimore (formerly Leckner), of Dargaville,

Auckland. 3.

LEECE, Private, CHARLES, 46195. 2nd Bn Canterbury Regiment, NZEF. Killed in action 12 October 1917. Son of Mrs W.J. Staines (formerly Leece), of Masterton. 3.

LEHNDORF, Private, ARTHUR RUBEN, 39833. 3rd Bn Wellington Regiment, NZEF. Killed in action 4 October 1917. Son of Mr and Mrs August Frederick Lehndorf, of Grey St, Waitara, New Plymouth. 7.

LEITCH, Private, CHARLES, 39582. 3rd Bn Otago Regiment, NZEF. Died of wounds 12 October 1917. Son of Mr and Mrs John Graham Leitch, of Arawai, Southland, Invercargill. 4.

LESLIE, Private, JAMES, 27533. 1st Bn Otago Regiment, NZEF. Died of wounds 12 October 1917. Age 25. Son of John Robert and Margaret Cockburn Leslie, of 94 Albany St, Dunedin, New Zealand. Native of Scotland. 4.

LESLIE, Rifleman, JAMES FRANCIS, 44645. J Coy 2nd Bn 3rd NZ Rifle Brigade. Killed in action 12 October 1917. Age 30. Son of William Day Leslie and Cecelia Leslie, of Kaeo, North Auckland. 8.

LESLIE, Rifleman, JOHN GEORGE, 44646. 2nd Bn 3rd NZ Rifle Brigade. Killed in action 12 October 1917. Age 47. Son of William Day Leslie and Cecelia Leslie; husband of Olive Leslie, of 84 Nelson St, Auckland. Native of Kaeo, North Auckland. 8.

LETFORD, Private, FRANCIS EDWARD, 38046. 1st Bn Canterbury Regiment, NZEF. Killed in action 12 October 1917. Age 20. Son of the late William and Eliza Letford, of Otaki, Wellington. 3.

LEVY, Serjeant, EDWARD TED, 36749. H Coy 4th Bn 3rd NZ Rifle Brigade. Killed in action 12 October 1917. Age 27. Son of Abraham and Frances Levy, of Wellington. 7.

LEWIS, Rifleman, DAVID MORGAN, 24/1917. 2nd Bn 3rd NZ Rifle Brigade. 12 October 1917. Age 45. Son of David Lewis; husband of Jane Dorothea Cornell (formerly Lewis), of 234 Boulevard, Scarsdale, New York, U.S.A. 8.

LEYDEN, Private, JAMES FRANCIS, 15194. 2nd Bn Otago Regiment, NZEF. 12 October 1917. 4.

LEWIS, Private, GEORGE FORRESTER, 24026. No. 2 Coy NZ Machine Gun Corps. Killed in action 2 October 1917. Husband of Kate Marion Lewis, of 111 Green Lane Rd, Remuera, Auckland. 9.

LILLE, Private, JOHN, 27529. 1st Bn Otago Regiment, NZEF. Killed in action 12 October 1917. Son of Mr and Mrs George Lilley, of Awarua Plains, Southland, Invercargill. 4.

LILLEY, Private, CHARLES DONALD, 46958. 2nd Bn Canterbury Regiment, NZEF. Killed in action 12 October 1917. Age 22. Son of Walter Donald and Mary Lilley, of 58 Gibbon St, Sydenham, Christchurch. 3.

LILLO, Private, HENRY GEORGE, 45101. 1st Bn Otago Regiment, NZEF. Died of wounds 12 October 1917. Age 31. Son of George and Jane Lillo, of 55 Trehurst St, Clapton Park, London, England. 4.

LIMBRICK, Serjeant, EDWARD LOOSEMORE, 30242. 3rd Bn Otago Regiment, NZEF. Killed in action 4 October 1917. Age 23. Son of Edward and Hilda Limbrick, of Meeanee, Hawke's Bay, Napier. 3.

LINDSAY, Rifleman, ALEXANDER MILNE, 39835. 3rd Bn 3rd NZ Rifle Brigade. 12 October 1917. Age 31. Son of William and Margaret Gordon Lindsay, of 9 Gladstone Place, Aberdeen, Scotland. 8.

LINTON, Private, JOHN KEDDIE, 32686. 2nd Bn Otago Regiment, NZEF. Killed in action 12 October 1917. Age 24. Son of Mrs Margaret Linton, of 'The Oaks', Benhill Wood Rd, Sutton, Surrey, England, and the late Archibald Linton. Received Diploma at the East of Scotland College of Agriculture; went to New Zealand in 1913. 4.

LIVERMORE, Private, PERCY STAFFORD, II/592. 1st Bn Otago Regiment, NZEF. Killed in action 12 October 1917. Son of Mr and Mrs E. Livermore, of 'Puriri', 84A Grafton Rd, Auckland. 4.

LIVINGSTONE, Corporal, ALEXANDER, 34475. 3rd Bn Auckland Regiment, NZEF. 4 October 1917. 1.

LLOYD, Private, EDWARD GEORGE ALBERT, 34100. 10th Coy 3rd Bn Otago Regiment, NZEF. Killed in action 12 October 1917. Age 24. Son of Thomas and Mary Ann Lloyd, of Pakipaki, Hawke's Bay, Napier. Native of Hastings, Hawke's Bay. 4.

LOFTS, Rifleman, JOSEPH, 38914. 4th Bn 3rd NZ Rifle Brigade. 12 October 1917. Age 34. Son of Philip and Harriet Lofts, of 9 Parnell Rd, Roman Rd, Bow. London, England. 8.

LOGAN, Private, JAMES ROBERT, 40224. 2nd Bn Canterbury Regiment, NZEF. Killed in action 12 October 1917. Age 26. Son of James and Mary Ethel Logan, of 168 Waimea St, Nelson. 3.

LONG, Rifleman, JOSEPH LAWRENCE, 14187. 4th Bn 3rd NZ Rifle Brigade. Killed in action 12 October 1917. Husband of Alice Long, of Mount Albert Rd, Onehunga, Auckland. 8.

LOOMES, Private, WILLIAM GEORGE, 6/2194. 1st Bn Canterbury Regiment, NZEF. Killed in action 12 October 1917. Age 42. Son of Rose Loomes, of Fairlie, South Canterbury, and the late Charles Loomes. 3.

LORD, Serjeant, ERIC JOHN, 28590. 3rd Coy 3rd Bn Auckland Regiment, NZEF. Killed in action 4 October 1917. Age 28. Son of John Maurice and Mary Blanche Lord, of 206 Greenlane Rd, Epsom, Auckland. Native of Wade, Auckland. 7.

LORD, Private, SIDNEY WALTER, 33564. 1st Bn Wellington Regiment, NZEF. Killed in action 17 October 1917. Son of Samuel Joseph and Elizabeth Lord, of Howick, Auckland. 7.

LOVE, Private, CECIL, 38721. 3rd Bn Wellington Regiment, NZEF. Killed in action 4 October 1917. Husband of Selina Love, of Auckland. 7.

LOW, Rifleman, ALEXANDER JAMES, 38187. 4th Bn 3rd NZ Rifle Brigade. Killed in action 12 October 1917. Son of Ellen Low, of 83 Shakespeare Rd, Napier. 8.

LUKER, Private, ERIC, 32193. 3rd Bn Canterbury Regiment, NZEF. 5 October 1917. Age 23. Son of Henry and Mary Luker, of 8 Green's Lane, Wroughton, Swindon, England. 3.

LYFORD, Private, GEORGE HERBERT, 29428. 1st Bn Wellington Regiment, NZEF. Killed in action 4 October 1917. Son of Mr and Mrs George Lyford, of Pirongia, Hamilton. 7.

LYON, Rifleman, GEORGE ERNEST, 24/2029. 4th Bn 3rd NZ Rifle Brigade. Killed in action 12 October 1917. Son of Mary Elizabeth Lyon, of 502 George St, Dunedin. 8.

MACDONALD, Rifleman, ALEXANDER, 31878. 3rd Bn 3rd NZ Rifle Brigade. Killed in action 12 October 1917. Brother of Mrs Catherine Hall, of Moutoa, Manawatu, Wellington. 8.

MACDONALD, Private, ALEXANDER, 28626. 1st Bn Wellington Regiment, NZEF. Killed in action 21 October 1917. Son of Sarah Macdonald, of Raumai, Ashhurst, Wellington. 7.

MACDONALD, Rifleman, NEIL, 26/1658. 4th Bn 3rd NZ Rifle Brigade. Killed in action 12 October 1917. Son of Mr and Mrs Neil Macdonald, of Union Line, Wanganui. 8.

MacGREGOR, Corporal, DONALD BRUCE, 22194. 1st Bn Otago Regiment, NZEF. Killed in action 12 October 1917. Son of Mr and Mrs John MacGregor, of 72 Ellis Rd East, Invercargill. 3.

MACHU, Private, NORMAN JOSEPH, 40824. 3rd Bn Canterbury Regiment, NZEF. Killed in action 15 October 1917. Son of Mr and Mrs Henry Louis Joseph Machu, of 370 Tinakori Rd, Wellington. 3.

MacINDOE, Private, GEORGE, 29053. 3rd Bn Otago Regiment, NZEF. Killed in action 4 October 1917. Age 26. Son of George Dobbie MacIndoe and Jane, his wife, of 115 Ness St, Invercargill, New Zealand. Native of London, England. 4.

MACKENZIE, Rifleman, ALLAN NEIL DAVID, 26752. G Coy 4th Bn 3rd NZ Rifle Brigade. Killed in action 12 October 1917. Age 21. Son of the late Rev. Patrick Kennedy Mackenzie and Ethel Maud May Mackenzie, of Winchester St, Lyttelton, New Zealand. Native of Coatbridge, Scotland. Senior National Scholarship, New Zealand, and highest pass in Greek for NZ in 1916. (MA, London.) 8.

MACKINTOSH, Private, ROBERT MACGREGOR, 29274. C Coy 3rd Bn Canterbury Regiment, NZEF. Killed in action 4 October 1917. Age 27. Son of Jane MacKintosh, of 28 Clarence Rd, Lower Riccarton, Christchurch, New Zealand, and the late James MacKintosh. Native of Aberdeen, Scotland. 3.

MACKY, Second Lieutenant, THOMAS ROY BAYNTUN, 25/73. 1st Bn Otago Regiment, NZEF. Killed in action 11 October 1917. Age 31. Son of Thomas and Elizabeth Stuart Macky, of 36 Cheltenham Terrace, Devonport, Auckland. 3.

MACLEAN, Private, JAMES, 48249. 2nd Bn Canterbury Regiment, NZEF. Killed in action 12 October 1917. Husband of Mrs A. Maclean, of 118 Ghuznee St, Wellington. 3.

MACLEAN, Serjeant, KENRICK CHARLES, 20927. 3rd Bn Auckland Regiment, NZEF. Killed in action 4 October 1917. Age 25. Son of Charles and Isabella Maclean, of Selwyn Rd, Kohimarama, Auckland. 1.

MACLEOD-SMITH, Rifleman, NORMAN, 29584. 4th Bn 3rd NZ Rifle Brigade. Killed in action 12 October 1917. Son of Mr and Mrs James Thomas Macleod-Smith, of Cashel St, Christchurch. 8.

MAGUIRE, Private, JOHN, 32777. 3rd Bn Otago Regiment, NZEF. 4 October 1917. Age 33. Son of Patrick and Catherine Lilley Maguire, of Eastern Hotel, Duke St, Glasgow, Scotland. 4.

MAHAN, Major, ADAM GEORGE, 13/2001. 1st Bn Auckland Regiment, NZEF. Killed in action 4 October 1917. Husband of Mrs A.G. Mahan. of Oamaru. 1.

MAHONEY, Private, GORDON RICHARD, 36464. 3rd Bn Auckland Regiment, NZEF. Killed in action 4 October 1917. Son of Mr and Mrs Richard Mahoney, of Washdyke, South Canterbury. 1.

MAHONEY, Corporal, JOHN JAMES, 34524. 1st Bn Canterbury Regiment, NZEF. Killed in action 12 October 1917. Son of Mary Mahoney, of 9 Earn St, Invercargill, and the late Tom Mahoney. 2.

MAINE, Serjeant, WILLIAM FREDERICK, 35119. 16th (Waikato) Coy. 3rd Bn

Auckland Regiment, NZEF. Killed in action 4 October 1917. Age 23. Son of William and Louisa Jane Maine, of Cameron St, Whangarei, North Auckland. 1.

MAINMAN, Private, EDWIN ROWLAND, 46055. 2nd Bn Canterbury Regiment, NZEF. Killed in action, 12 October 1917. Age 32. Son of Thomas and Sarah Mainman, of 'Birchwood', Knaresborough, England; husband of Pearl Mainman, of 'Wendron', Ayers St, Rangiora, Canterbury, New Zealand. 3.

MAKER, Private, WILLIAM JOHN, G/1332. No. 1 Coy NZ Machine Gun Corps. Killed in action 4 October 1917. Age 28. Son of William and Margaret Maker, of Barr St, Balclutha, Dunedin. 9.

MANHIRE, Private, ERNEST ARTHUR DANESBURY, 40825. 3rd Bn Canterbury Regiment, NZEF. Killed in action 4 October 1917. Age 30. Son of William Henry and Lucy Manhire, of Hornby, Christchurch, New Zealand; husband of Alice B. Manhire, of Perth-Freemantle Rd, Claremont, Western Australia. 3.

MANN, Rifleman, ERNEST, 42682. 2nd Bn 3rd NZ Rifle Brigade. Killed in action 12 October 1917. Age 27. Son of Herbert and Elizabeth Ann Mann, of 1 Lowe St, Avenal, Invercargill. Native of Southland. 8.

MANNING, Serjeant, PATRICK, 23/1726. 2nd Bn Canterbury Regiment, NZEF. Killed in action 12 October 1917. Brother of Mrs Mary Carey, of Colenso St, Sumner, Christchurch. 2.

MANSELL, Rifleman, FRANCIS JOSEPH, 45709. H Coy 3rd Bn 3rd NZ Rifle Brigade. Killed in action 12 October 1917. Age 21. Son of Alfred John and Elizabeth Mansell, of Epuni Hamlet, Lower Hutt, Wellington. 8.

MANSON, Rifleman, STANLEY ROY, 24/2031. D Coy 2nd Bn 3rd NZ Rifle Brigade. Killed in action 12 October 1917. Age 28. Son of the late George and Marian Manson. Native of Wanganui. 8

MARRIS, Lance Corporal, ROBERT CHARLES, 30606. 17th Coy 3rd Bn Wellington Regiment, NZEF. Killed in action 4 October 1917. Age 21. Son of Helen Marris, of 53 Baker St, Parkside, Dunedin, and the late Robert Dudding Marris. Native of Auckland. Employed in Government Census Offices. 6.

MARSDEN, Second Lieutenant, JOSEPH STANLEY, 18580. 3rd Bn Wellington Regiment, NZEF. Killed in action 4 October 1917. Age 24. Son of Arthur and Bessie Marsden, of Petone, Wellington; husband of Vera Marsden, of 139 Upland Rd, Kelburn, Wellington. 6.

MARSH, Private, JOHN EDWARD CALEB, 24202. No. 1 Coy NZ Machine Gun Corps. Killed in action 12 October 1917. Age 21. Son of Thomas and Annie Louisa Marsh, of Inglewood, Taranaki. Native of Le Bon's Bay, Christchurch. 9.

MARSHALL, Private, ADAM, 26288. 1st Bn Canterbury Regiment, NZEF. 12 October 1917. 3.

MARSON, Private, RICHARD, 49423. 2nd Bn Otago Regiment, NZEF. Killed in action 12 October 1917. Age 33. Son of George and Alice Marson, of 12 Hensley St, Invercargill. Native of Drummond, Southland, Invercargill. 4.

MARTIN, Private, CHARLES FREDERICK, 39850. 3rd Bn Wellington Regiment, NZEF. Killed in action 4 October 1917. Son of Mrs E.K. Martin, of 15 Ivy Rd, Cricklewood, London, England. 7.

MARTIN, Private, PETER JOSEPH, 29905. No. 2 Coy NZ Machine Gun Corps. Killed in action 12 October 1917. Husband of Mrs F. Martin, of Hokitika, Greymouth. 9.

MARTIN, Private, ROBERT WITHERALL, 6/1929. 13th Coy 1st Bn Canterbury

Regiment, NZEF. Killed in action 12 October 1917. Age 38. Son of Matthew and Ann Martin. St. Johnston, Co Donegal, Ireland. 3.

MASON, Private, JAMES FARQUARSON, 38052. 1st Bn Wellington Regiment, NZEF. Killed in action 21 October 1917. Husband of Annie Agnes Mason, of Wellington. 7.

MATHESON, Private, ANGUS, 44132. 1st Bn Canterbury Regiment, NZEF. Killed in action 12 October 1917. Age 31. Son of the late John and Annie Matheson, of Blairford, Avoch, Ross-shire, Scotland. 3.

MATHESON, Rifleman, JAMES WEIR, 36874. 2nd Bn 3rd NZ Rifle Brigade. Killed in action 12 October 1917. Age 25. Son of John and Margaret Nicholson Matheson, of 5 Princes St, Invercargill. Native of Kennington, Southland, Invercargill. 8.

MATHEWS, Lance Serjeant, JOHN PATRICK, IO/3646. 3rd Bn Wellington Regiment, NZEF. Killed in action 4 October 1917. Son of Mr and Mrs George Mathews, of Nelson. 6.

MATHEWSON, Corporal, JAMES LAWRENCE, 17/119. 1st Bn Otago Regiment, NZEF. Killed in action 12 October 1917. Age 43. Native of Hyde, Otago. Son of the late Laurence and Johanna Mathewson, of Otago; husband of Effie Mary Forster Mathewson (née Morgan), of 60 Grosvenor St, Kensington, Dunedin. Left New Zealand in 1914 as a member of the Veterinary Corps. Also served in Egypt. 3.

MATTSON, Private, LUDWIG, 24205. 1st Bn Canterbury Regiment, NZEF. Killed in action 12 October 1917. Brother of Mr K.A. Mattson, of Tammerfors, Finland. 3.

MAWHINNEY, Private, ALLEN, 40978. 2nd Bn Otago Regiment, NZEF. Killed in action 12 October 1917. Age 25. Son of Wilson and Bethia Mawhinney, of Ranfurly, Otago. 4.

MAWLEY, Lieutenant, GERALD, 26/35. 4th Bn 3rd NZ Rifle Brigade. Killed in action 12 October 1917. Age 30. Son of Septimus and Emma Mawley, of Ditton, Masterton, Wellington; husband of Elsa Mawley, of Lansdowne, Masterton. 7.

MAY, Private, FREDERICK CHARLES, 10/3948. 17th Coy 1st Bn Wellington Regiment, NZEF. Killed in action 4 October 1917. Age 25. Son of Henry and Elizabeth Ann May, of Raetihi Rd, Ohakune, Wanganui. Native of Maharahara, Napier. 7.

McADAM, Private, GEORGE, 44006. 2nd Bn Canterbury Regiment, NZEF. 12 October 1917. 3.

McBRIDE, Private, OLIVER, 9/315. 2nd Bn Otago Regiment, NZEF. Killed in action 12 October 1917. Son of Andrew and Mary McBride, of Nightcaps, Otago. 4.

McCABE, Private, BERNARD ALBERT, 33923. 3rd Bn Auckland Regiment, NZEF. Killed in action 18 October 1917. Son of Mrs Agnes McCabe, of 132 Victoria St, Auckland. 1.

McCALL, Lance Serjeant, HUGH WILLIAM, 8/1776. 1st Bn Otago Regiment, NZEF. Killed in action 12 October 1917. Age 26. Son of John and Marion McCall, of Scandrett St, Invercargill. Also served at Gallipoli. Native of Eastern Bush, Invercargill. 3.

McCAMMON, Private, FORBES JAMES, 30825. 1st Bn Auckland Regiment, NZEF. Killed in action 4 October 1917. Son of Mrs S. Hall (formerly McCammon), of Swanson, Auckland. 1.

McCAW, Private, WILLIAM ARMSTRONG, 3/602. NZ Medical Corps. Killed in action 12 October 1917. Son of Mr and Mrs William Armstrong McCaw, of 177 Leet St, Invercargill. 9.

McCLYMONT, Private, CHARLES ROBERT, 30446. North Auckland Coy 3rd Bn Auckland Regiment, NZEF. Killed in action 4 October 1917. Age 22. Son of the late

Gilbert and Johann Margarett McClymont. Native of Woodville, Wellington. 1.

McCONNELL, Private, JAMES, 12/2050. 2nd Bn Otago Regiment, NZEF. 12 October 1917. Age 28. Son of David McConnell and Elizabeth McClean, his wife, of Ballybim, Manorcunningham, Co Donegal, Ireland. 4.

McCONNELL, Corporal, ROBERT JAMES PATRICK, 29049. 2nd Bn 3rd NZ Rifle Brigade. Killed in action 12 October 1917. Son of Ellen McConnell, of Christchurch. 8.

McCORLEY, Serjeant, JOHN, 29696. 1st Bn Otago Regiment, NZEF. Killed in action 12 October 1917. Brother of Margaret McCorley, of 245 Cashel St, Christchurch. 3.

McCRACKEN, Lance Corporal, JAMES, 21058. 3rd Bn 3rd NZ Rifle Brigade. Killed in action 12 October 1917. Age 28. Son of David and Ellen Jane McCracken, of Te Puke, Thames. 8.

McCREA, Private, ROBERT, 27330. 1st Bn Canterbury Regiment, NZEF. Killed in action 12 October 1917. Age 27. Son of Joseph and Fanny McCrea, of Gorticross, Drumshoe, Londonderry, Ireland. 3.

McCREADY, Private, WILLIAM LYLE, 41246. 1st Bn Auckland Regiment, NZEF. Killed in action 4 October 1917. Age 26. Son of James and Mary Jane McCready, of Whakatane, Bay of Plenty. 1.

McCULLOCH, Rifleman, DAVID, 48737. 3rd Bn 3rd NZ Rifle Brigade. Killed in action 12 October 1917. Age 40. Son of the late Samuel and Helen McCulloch, of 15 Carr St, North East Valley, Dunedin. Native of Waimate South, Canterbury. 8.

McCULLOUGH, Private, FRANCIS PURVIS, 40041. 2nd Bn Otago Regiment, NZEF. Killed in action 12 October 1917. Age 19. Son of William Francis and Alice McCullough, of East Rd, Stratford, New Plymouth. Native of Le Bon's Bay, Christchurch. 4.

McDONALD, Private, HECTOR SIDNEY, 33416. 2nd Bn Wellington Regiment, NZEF. Killed in action 4 October 1917. Age 24. Son of John and Sarah McDonald, of 7 Frankville Terrace, Wellington. 7.

McDOUGALL, Private, ALEXANDER, 32457. 1st Bn Canterbury Regiment, NZEF. Killed in action 12 October 1917. Age 34. Son of Alexander and Letitie McDougall, of 159 Salisbury St, Christchurch. Native of Kaiapoi. 3.

McFARLAND, Corporal, THOMAS NIGEL, 8/252. No. 1 Coy NZ Machine Gun Corps. Killed in action 12 October 1917. Son of Mr and Mrs Charles William McFarland, of Auckland. 9.

McFARLANE, Private, STANLEY NORMAN, 27331. J Coy 1st Bn Canterbury Regiment, NZEF. Killed in action 12 October 1917. Age 21. Son of the late Robert and Sarah McFarlane, of Christchurch. 3.

McGEE, Private, WILLIAM, 29176. No. 2 Coy 3rd Bn Canterbury Regiment, NZEF. Killed in action 4 October 1917. Age 26. Son of Thomas and Kathrine McGee; husband of Margaret Marsden (formerly McGee), of William St, Ashburton. Native of Winslow, Christchurch. 3.

McGOWAN, Private, W J, 30834. 2nd Bn Auckland Regiment, NZEF. Killed in action 21 October 1917. Age 25. Son of Marianne McGowan, of 34A Antrim Rd, Belfast, Ireland, and the late George McGowan. 1.

McHALE, Private, WILLIAM HAROLD, 37851. 1st Bn Wellington Regiment, NZEF. Killed in action 3 October 1917. Age 33. Son of James Wentworth McHale and Emily Rosina McHale, of Tokoroa, Putaruru, Hamilton. 7.

McHARDIE, Private, RAYMOND SHIRLEY, 37934. 1st Bn Otago Regiment, NZEF. Killed in action 12 October 1917. Son of Florence Grace McHardie, of 23 Heads Rd, Wanganui. 4.

McILROY, Lieutenant, GEORGE THOMAS, 2431 1. G Coy 1st Bn 3rd NZ Rifle Brigade. Killed in action 12 October 1917. Age 22. Son of William John and Mary Ann Laura McIlroy, of 108 Rossall St, Christchurch. Native of Kumara, Greymouth. 7.

McILROY, Corporal, ARTHUR HAROLD, 17807. H Coy 4th Bn 3rd NZ Rifle Brigade. Killed in action 12 October 1917. Age 24. Son of William John and Mary Ann Laura McIlroy, of 108 Rossall St, Christchurch. Native of Kumara, Greymouth. 8.

McINTOSH, Rifleman, JOHN, 23/511. B Coy 1st Bn 3rd NZ Rifle Brigade. Killed in action 12 October 1917. Age 29. Son of Mary McIntosh, of 32 Brown St, Dunedin, and the late James McIntosh. 8.

McINTOSH, Private, JOHN, 27553. 2nd Bn Otago Regiment, NZEF. Killed in action 12 October 1917. Son of Grace Sophia McIntosh, of 375 George St, Dunedin, and the late J.C. McIntosh. 4.

McINTYRE, Private, ARCHIBALD, 38567. No. 1 Coy NZ Machine Gun Corps. Killed in action 12 October 1917. Son of Mary McIntyre, of 39 Grange St, Dunedin. 9.

McINTYRE, Lieutenant, PETER, 6/684. No. 2 Coy NZ Machine Gun Corps. Killed in action 12 October 1917. Age 40. Son of Peter and Jean McIntyre, of 215 York Place, Dunedin. Native of Anderson's Bay, Dunedin. 9.

McKAY, Lance Corporal, CHARLES DONALD, 36473. G Coy 3rd Bn Wellington Regiment, NZEF. Killed in action 4 October 1917. Age 31. Son of the late John and Mary McKay; husband of Charlotte McKay, of 70 Chancellor St, Shirley, Christchurch. 6.

McKAY, Private, JOHN ALEXANDER, 24455. 3rd Bn Canterbury Regiment, NZEF. Killed in action 4 October 1917. Brother of the late George M. McKay, of Roxburgh, Otago. 3.

McKELVY, Private, JOHN GEORGE, 29930. 3rd Bn Canterbury Regiment, NZEF. Killed in action 4 October 1917. Son of Mrs A. Leonard (formerly McKelvy), of Wyndham, Southland. 3.

McKENNA, Rifleman, ALBERT EDWARD, 46891. 2nd Bn 3rd NZ Rifle Brigade. Killed in action 12 October 1917. Age 35. Son of Peter James and Selina Mary McKenna, of Hastings St, Nelson. Native of Westport, Greymouth. 8.

McKENNA, Serjeant, ISADORE, 24/1142. 3rd Bn Otago Regiment, NZEF. Killed in action 4 October 1917. Age 27. Only son of Owen and Francis McKenna, of Leith Valley, Dunedin. 3.

McKENZIE, Private, EDWARD WALKER, 11918. 1st Bn Wellington Regiment, NZEF. Killed in action 22 October 1917. Son of Mr and Mrs Alexander McKenzie, of Mangaweka, Wanganui. 7.

McKENZIE, Private, GORDON DACHER, 7/1498. 1st Bn Otago Regiment, NZEF. Killed in action 12 October 1917. Age 20. Son of John and Annie McKenzie, of Avon Rd, Clifton, Southland, Invercargill. Also served at Gallipoli. 4.

McKENZIE, Rifleman, JAMES, 32880. 4th Bn 3rd NZ Rifle Brigade. Killed in action 11 October 1917. Son of Mr and Mrs David McKenzie, of Lumsden, Invercargill. 8.

McKENZIE, Lance Corporal, WILLIAM, 6/3805. 2nd Bn Canterbury Regiment, NZEF. Killed in action 12 October 1917. Son of Mr and Mrs William McKenzie, of Rotowaro, Huntly, Hamilton. 2.

McKENZIE, Rifleman, WILLIAM ALEXANDER, 45225. 2nd Bn 3rd NZ Rifle Brigade. Killed in action 12 October 1917. Age 23. Son of the late William and Catherine McKenzie, of Poolburn, Dunedin. 8.

McKENZIE, Private, WILLIAM LOUIS, 44619. 3rd Bn Wellington Regiment, NZEF. Killed in action 4 October 1917. Age 32. Son of Jessie McKenzie, of Killinchy, Canterbury, and the late Samuel McKenzie. Native of Dunsandel, Christchurch. 7.

McKENZIE, Rifleman, WILLIAM THOMAS CHARLES, 27098. C Coy 2nd Bn 3rd NZ Rifle Brigade. Killed in action 12 October 1917. Age 21. Son of Margaret R. McKenzie, of 14 Avonhead Rd, Riccarton, Christchurch. Native of Waikaia, Invercargill. 8.

McKEOWN, Private, CHARLES JOSEPH, 30621. 3rd Bn Canterbury Regiment, NZEF. 18 October 1917. Age 27. Son of Felix McKeown, of 18 Herbert St, Camlough, Co Antrim, Ireland, and the late Mary McKeown. 3.

McKINSTRY, Private, JAMES LAURENCE, 18838. A Coy 1st Bn Auckland Regiment, NZEF. Killed in action 4 October 1917. Age 28. Son of James and Margaret McKinstry, of Hunua Rd, Papakura, Auckland. 1.

McKONE, Private, PATRICK, 42552. 3rd Bn Otago Regiment, NZEF. Killed in action 4 October 1917. Son of Michael McKone, of Torridge St, Oamaru. 4.

McKOY, Rifleman, GODFREY GERALD, 23022. 1st Bn 3rd NZ Rifle Brigade. Killed in action 12 October 1917. Son of Mary Ann McKoy, of New Plymouth, Taranaki. 8.

McLAREN, Private, ALEXANDER, 27566. 1st Bn Otago Regiment, NZEF. Killed in action 12 October 1917. Age 22. Son of James McLaren, of 16 Baldwin St, North East Valley, Dunedin, and the late Sarah Jane McLaren. 4.

McLAUGHLAN, Serjeant, FRANCIS, 10/3966. 3rd Bn Wellington Regiment, NZEF. Killed in action 4 October 1917. Son of Mr and Mrs P. McLaughlan, of Main St, Taihape, Wellington. 6.

McLAUGHLIN, Private, EDWARD, 39548. 3rd Bn Wellington Regiment, NZEF. Killed in action 4 October 1917. Age 20. Son of James and Annie McLaughlin, of Rangataua, Wanganui. 7.

McLEAN, Rifleman, JOHN WILSON, 24/1437. 2nd Bn 3rd NZ Rifle Brigade. Killed in action 12 October 1917. Son of Mrs E. McLean, of Leithfield, Christchurch. 8.

McLEAN, Private, OWEN ANGUS, 38432. 2nd Bn Auckland Regiment, NZEF. Killed in action 4 October 1917. Age 28. Son of Mr and Mrs Neil McLean. Native of Whangarei. 1.

McLEAN, Serjeant, WILFRED ERNEST, 23/514. 1st Bn 3rd NZ Rifle Brigade. Killed in action 12 October 1917. Age 27. Son of James John Hamilton McLean and Elspeth Mary McLean, of Brookyale, Ohai, Invercargill. Also served in Egypt. 7.

McLEOD, Corporal, JOHN WILLIS, 11159. D Coy 2nd Bn Otago Regiment, NZEF. Killed in action 12 October 1917. Age 31. Son of John Willis McLeod and Mary his wife, of 11 Princes St, Invercargill. 3.

McMANUS, Private, JOHN BERNARD, 44591. 2nd Bn Canterbury Regiment, NZEF. Died of wounds 12 October 1917. Son of Mr and Mrs William A. McManus, of High St, Leeston, Christchurch. 3.

McMILLAN, Private, HECTOR NORMAN, 14021. 1st Bn Otago Regiment, NZEF. Killed in action 12 October 1917. Son of Mr and Mrs Donald McMillan, of Raes Junction, Otago. 4.

McMURRICH, Rifleman, DUNCAN, 20211. 3rd Bn 3rd NZ Rifle Brigade. Killed in action 12 October 1917. Age 33. Son of Margaret McMurrich, of Naughton

Terrace, Kilbirnie, Wellington. 8.

McNEIL, Rifleman, JOHN, 26/193. 4th Bn 3rd NZ Rifle Brigade. Killed in action 12 October 1917. Son of Mr and Mrs Archibald McNeil, of Benhar, Dunedin. 8.

McNICOL, Private, ALEXANDER, 51223. 2nd Bn Canterbury Regiment, NZEF. Killed in action 12 October 1917. Son of Margaret McNicol, of Ross, Westland, Greymouth. 3.

McNIECE, Private, JOHN ALEXANDER, 45107. 3rd Bn Otago Regiment, NZEF. Died of wounds 15 October 1917. Age 30. Son of John and Esther McNiece, of Ballymatoskerty, Toome, Co Antrim. Ireland. 4.

McPHEE, Private, JOHN, M M, 12240. 1st Bn Wellington Regiment, NZEF. Killed in action 9 October 1917. Age 21. Son of James and Ellen McPhee, of Rakauroa, Gisborne. 7.

McROBERTS, Second Lieutenant, EVAN OSWALD, 22550. 15th (North Auckland) Coy 1st Bn Auckland Regiment, NZEF. Killed in action 4 October 1917. Age 33. Son of James and Mary McRoberts, of Auckland; husband of Sarah Isabel McRoberts, of 'Ranui', Hillsborough Rd, Onehunga. Native of Tauranga. Silver Medal Royal Humane Society. 1.

McWATT, Rifleman, WILLIAM, 32883. 3rd Bn 3rd NZ Rifle Brigade. Killed in action 12 October 1917. Son of Mr and Mrs James McWatt, of Ayr St, Invercargill. 8.

MEAD, Lance Corporal, ERNEST WILLIAM LOUDEN, 15004. C Coy 2nd Bn Canterbury Regiment, NZEF. Died of wounds 12 October 1917. Age 24. Son of William and Alice Mary Mead, of Motupiko, Nelson. 2.

MEANEY, Private, ANDREW WILLIAM, 46371. A Coy 1st Bn Auckland Regiment, NZEF. Killed in action 22 October 1917. Age 25. Son of Andrew and Barbara Meaney, of Custom St, Auckland. Native of Waiwera Hot Springs, North Auckland. 1.

MEDDINGS, Major, WALTER HARRY, 48142. 2nd Bn Canterbury Regiment, NZEF. Killed in action 11 October 1917. Age 46. Husband of Jessie Meddings, of 16 Holly Rd, Christchurch. Was a member of the New Zealand Staff Corps. 2.

MEDWELL, Private, FREDERICK DANIEL, 21294. 1st Bn Auckland Regiment, NZEF. Killed in action 4 October 1917. Age 26. Son of Daniel and Elizabeth Medwell, of Richardson Rd, Mount Albert, Auckland, New Zealand. Native of Brisbane, Australia. 1.

MEE, Private, ALEXANDER, 42532. 2nd Bn Otago Regiment, NZEF. Killed in action 12 October 1917. Age 31. Son of the late Samuel and Margaret Mee, of Kuri Bush, Otago; husband of Jessie Mee, of Brighton, Otago. 4.

MELLON, Private, OWEN, 6/1621. 1st Bn Canterbury Regiment, NZEF. 2 October 1917. 3.

METTAM, Rifleman, THOMAS HENRY, 33913. 2nd Bn 3rd NZ Rifle Brigade. Killed in action 12 October 1917. Age 31. Son of John Tunnard Mettam and Lavinia Mettam, of Swanson, Auckland. 8.

MIDDLETON, Private, JOSEPH GEORGE, 41594. 1st Bn Otago Regiment, NZEF. Killed in action 3 October 1917. Brother of Albert Edward Middleton, of Waipiro Bay, Gisborne. 4.

MIDFORD, Private, WILLIAM GEORGE, 14289. 1st Bn Auckland Regiment, NZEF. Killed in action 4 October 1917. Brother of Henry Blackett Midford, of Taumarunui, Hamilton. 1.

MILBURN, Serjeant, CHARLES LOMBARD, 25/782. 3rd Bn 3rd NZ Rifle Brigade. Killed in action 12 October 1917. Son of the late James Milburn, of Auckland. 7.

MILLAR, Second Lieutenant, JOHN, 18018. 4th Bn 3rd NZ Rifle Brigade. Killed in action 12 October 1917. Age 22. Son of Annie Cleland Millar, of 73 Bowmont St, Invercargill, and the late John Millar. 7.

MILLAR, Rifleman, JAMES SCRYMGEOUR, 39271. D Coy 1st Bn 3rd NZ Rifle Brigade. Killed in action 12 October 1917. Age 21. Son of Margaret Millar, of Ranfurly, Dunedin, and the late James Millar. Native of Kokonga, Dunedin. 8.

MILLAR, Serjeant, WILLIAM, 81443. 1st Bn Otago Regiment, NZEF. Killed in action 12 October 1917. Son of Mr and Mrs Alex. Millar, of Puketiro, Catlins Branch, Otago. 3.

MILLER, Private, EDWARD DONALD, 38299. 2nd Bn Auckland Regiment, NZEF. Killed in action 4 October 1917. Son of Mr and Mrs Edward Miller, of Belfast, Christchurch; husband of Mrs L.R. Ward (formerly Miller), of Kaiapoi, Christchurch. 2.

MILLER, Private, ERNEST JOHN, 14728. 1st Bn Otago Regiment, NZEF. Killed in action 12 October 1917. Age 22. Son of John Young Miller and Maria his wife, of Vincent Rd, Mount Albert, Auckland. 4.

MILLER, Private, JOHN ALEX, 8/3009. 4th Coy. 1st Bn Otago Regiment, NZEF. Killed in action 12 October 1917. Age 22. Son of Mr and Mrs John Miller, of Station Rd, Green Island, Dunedin. 4.

MILLER, Private, PETER WILLIAM, 9/1068. 1st Bn Otago Regiment, NZEF. Killed in action 12 October 1917. Son of Emma Miller, of Purakanui, Otago. 6.

MILLINGTON, Corporal, WILLIAM BERTIE, 28627. 9th Coy 3rd Bn Wellington Regiment, NZEF. Killed in action 4 October 1917. Age 26. Son of Louisa Lavinia Millington, of 347 The Terrace, Wellington, and the late Sidney George Millington. 6.

MILNE, Private, EDWARD DUFFY, 33013. 2nd Bn Otago Regiment, NZEF. Killed in action 12 October 1917. Son of Ellen Milne, of Cape Wanbrow, Oamaru. 6.

MILNE, Private, FRANCIS, 45886. 3rd Bn Wellington Regiment, NZEF. Killed in action 4 October 1917. Age 41. Son of James and Christian Milne, of Raes Junction, Tuapeka, Otago, New Zealand. Native of Aberdeenshire, Scotland. A Presbyterian Missionary. 7.

MINOGUE, Private, ANTHONY, 27540. 2nd Bn Otago Regiment, NZEF. Killed in action 12 October 1917. Brother of John Minogue, of 5 Gordon St, Invercargill. 6.

MIRK, Private, JAMES, 37844. 2nd Bn Otago Regiment, NZEF. Killed in action 12 October 1917. Husband of Priscilla Mirk, of Palmerston North, Wellington. 6.

MITCHELL, Private, HERBERT WALTER ARTHUR, 23/2039. Hawke's Bay Coy 3rd Bn Wellington Regiment, NZEF. Killed in action 4 October 1917. Age 25. Son of Arthur Alexander and Emma Mitchell, of Otaki Railway, Wellington. 7.

MOFFATT, Private, ALFRED, 11312. D Coy 3rd Bn Otago Regiment, NZEF. Killed in action 3 October 1917. Age 22. Son of John Seaton Moffatt and Isabella, his wife, of 'Fairview', Roberton Rd, Avondale, Auckland. Native of Wharehine, Auckland. Previously served at Awanui Wireless Station as a Territorial. 6.

MOIR, Private, JOHN BUCHAN, 29832. 2nd Bn Otago Regiment, NZEF. Killed in action 12 October 1917. Age 22. Son of Margaret Moir, of Port Chalmers, Dunedin, and the late John Moir. 6.

MOJE, Private, GEORGE HENRY, 32202. 12th (Nelson) Coy 2nd Bn Canterbury Regiment, NZEF. Killed in action 12 October 1917. Age 20. Son of Henry Albert and Jane Elizabeth Moje, of Kopuaranga, Wellington. 3.

MONK, Private, FRANK LYLE, 3/2582. NZ Medical Corps. Killed in action 12

October 1917. Age 28. Son of William John Monk, of Auckland. 9.

MONKMAN, Corporal, ALFRED JAMES, M M, 24/1124. 2nd Bn 3rd NZ Rifle Brigade. Killed in action 12 October 1917. Age 25. Son of James Henry and Katie Monkman, of 38 Brookfield St, Hamilton East. 8.

MOODY, Private, DAVID STANLEY, 32693. 3rd Bn Wellington Regiment, NZEF. Killed in action 4 October 1917. Age 23. Son of James and Annie Moody, of 16 Cumnor Terrace, Radley, Woolston, Christchurch. Late of NZ Railways and Mercantile Marine. 7.

MOORE, Lance Corporal, ASHLEY CHARLES, 51660. C Coy 3rd Bn Canterbury Regiment, NZEF. Killed in action 12 October 1917. Age 21. Son of Agnes Moore, of 'Wharepuni', 1156 Milton St, Nelson, and the late James F. Moore. 2.

MOREY, Private, FREDERICK, 2/1633A. 1st Bn Canterbury Regiment, NZEF. Killed in action 12 October 1917. Son of Elizabeth O'Connor (formerly Morey), of Costerville, Rakaia, New Plymouth. 3.

MORGAN, Lance Corporal, HARRY CROSS, IO/3037. 1st Bn Wellington Regiment, NZEF. 4 October 1917. Age 37. Son of David and Mary Morgan. 6.

MORGAN, Rifleman, JOHN EDWARD, 22348. 1st Bn 3rd NZ Rifle Brigade. Killed in action 12 October 1917. Age 22. Son of John Gavin Morgan and Mary Jane Morgan, of 7 Main Rd, North East Valley, Dunedin. Native of Ranfurly, Dunedin. 8.

MORGAN, Rifleman, STEPHEN, 25/446. 3rd Bn 3rd NZ Rifle Brigade. Killed in action 12 October 1917. Age 25. Son of Richard George and Elizabeth Morgan, of 803 Cook St, Hastings, Napier. Native of Eketahuna, Wellington. 8.

MORGAN, Corporal, WILLIAM ALFRED REGINALD, 3/140A. NZ Medical Corps. Killed in action 12 October 1917. Son of Mr and Mrs Alfred Morgan, of Avondale, Auckland. 9.

MORIARTY, Private, JOHN, 47679. C Coy. 2nd Bn Canterbury Regiment, NZEF. Killed in action 12 October 1917. Age 26. Son of Timothy and Johanna Moriarty, of Stillwater, Westland. 3.

MORRIS, Private, JOHN, 32692. 2nd Bn Otago Regiment, NZEF. Killed in action 12 October 1917. Brother of Robert Morris, of Meadow St, Mornington, Dunedin. 6.

MORRISON, Private, MURDOCH, 41601. 1st Bn Otago Regiment, NZEF. Killed in action 4 October 1917. Son of Mrs H. Morrison, of Orawai, Southland, Invercargill. 6.

MORROW, Private, JOHN, 20386. 2nd Bn Wellington Regiment, NZEF. Killed in action 4 October 1917. Age 30. Son of Richard and Sarah Ann Morrow, of 305 Devon St West, New Plymouth. Native of Rahotu, Taranaki. 7.

MORTON, Private, JAMES, 42542. 1st Bn Otago Regiment, NZEF. Killed in action 12 October 1917. Son of Mr and Mrs Adam Morton, of Mount Cargill, Dunedin. 6.

MOSTYN, Private, GEORGE, 8/1807. 1st Bn Otago Regiment, NZEF. Killed in action 12 October 1917. Son of Mr and Mrs Isaac Mostyn, of Manildra, New South Wales, Australia. 6.

MOYNIHAN, Private, MICHAEL ALEXANDER, 42545. 3rd Bn Otago Regiment, NZEF. Killed in action 17 October 1917. Age 25. Son of William and Susan Moynihan, of Ngapuna, Otago Central. Native of Middlemarch, Otago Central. 6.

MUIR, Rifleman, DAVID, 45714. 2nd Bn 3rd NZ Rifle Brigade. Killed in action 12 October 1917. Age 42. Son of John and Elizabeth Muir, of Karitane, Dunedin. 8.

MULLEY, Rifleman, ROBERT, 29935. 4th Bn 3rd NZ Rifle Brigade. Killed in action 12 October 1917. Son of Mr and Mrs Robert Mulley, of Lower Kangaroo Creek, Clarence River, New South Wales, Australia. 8.

MUMFORD, Rifleman, HENRY EDWIN, 44005. 4th Bn 3rd NZ Rifle Brigade. Killed in action 12 October 1917. Brother of Robert Samuel Mumford, of 35 Lytton St, Sydenham, Christchurch. 8.

MUNRO, Private, ALEXANDER, 8/3959. 3rd Bn Otago Regiment, NZEF. Killed in action 12 October 1917. Age 19. Son of Lachlan and Kate Munro, of Toiro, Otago. 6.

MURFITT, Corporal, STANLEY DAVID, 30257. 10th Coy 3rd Bn Otago Regiment, NZEF. Killed in action 4 October 1917. Son of Nellie Murfitt, of King St, Hastings, Hawke's Bay, Napier. 3.

MURLAND, Private, WILLIAM, 12/2406. 1st Bn Auckland Regiment, NZEF. Died of wounds 4 October 1917. Age 31. Son of John and Sarah Murland, of Waitekauri, Thames. 2.

MURPHY, Private, JAMES PATRICK, 45892. 2nd Bn Wellington Regiment, NZEF. Killed in action 22 October 1917. Son of Mary Murphy, of 127 Brougham St, Wellington. 7.

MURPHY, Private, STANLEY, 28761. 15th (North Auckland) Coy 2nd Bn Auckland Regiment, NZEF. Killed in action 4 October 1917. Age 23. Son of James and Margaret Murphy, of 7 Selbourne St, Grey Lynn, Auckland. 2.

NANKERVIS, Private, WILLIAM, M M, 27139. A Coy 1st Bn Auckland Regiment, NZEF. Killed in action 22 October 1917. Age 42. Son of Henry Casley Nankervis and Jane Nankervis; husband of Maud Evelyn Nankervis, of 265 Ponsonby Rd, Auckland. Native of Auckland. 2.

NEAL, Serjeant, ERNEST, 23/1762. 2nd Bn Wellington Regiment, NZEF. Killed in action 4 October 1917. Son of Mariane Ellen Neal, of Birkenhead, Auckland: husband of Ruby Maud Neal, of Papakura, Auckland. 6.

NEAVE, Rifleman, SIMON HENRY, 41001. 1st Bn 3rd NZ Rifle Brigade. Killed in action 12 October 1917. Age 28. Son of James Sampson Neave and Ada Neave, of 19 Goodall St, Caversham, Dunedin. Native of Invercargill. 8.

NEILSON, Corporal, ERNEST, 6/3411. 1st Bn Canterbury Regiment, NZEF. Killed in action 12 October 1917. Son of Mr and Mrs John Neilson, of Rocky Crossing, Albany, Western Australia. 2.

NELSON, Rifleman, DAVID, 18695. 1st Bn 3rd NZ Rifle Brigade. Killed in action 12 October 1917. Son of Mr and Mrs George Nelson, of Nen St, Oamaru. 8.

NELSON, Serjeant, WILLIAM HENRY, 27184. 3rd Bn Otago Regiment, NZEF. Killed in action 4 October 1917. Age 24. Son of James and Jane Nelson, of Owaka, Otago. 3.

NEVILLE, Private, PATRICK, 41927. 3rd Bn Canterbury Regiment, NZEF. Killed in action 4 October 1917. Age 24. Son of Mary Cecilia Neville, of 19 Onslow Rd, Epsom Auckland, and the late Patrick Neville. 3.

NEWLANDS, Lance Serjeant, JAMES ERNEST, 29937. 3rd Bn Otago Regiment, NZEF. Killed in action 16 October 1917. Husband of Mrs J. Newlands, of 3 MacAndrew Rd, Dunedin. 3.

NEWLOVE, Private, EDWIN, 40234. 2nd Bn Canterbury Regiment, NZEF. Killed in action 12 October 1917. Son of Mary Ann Newlove, of Takaka, Nelson. 3.

NEWLOVE, Private, LEONARD CHARLES, 33755. 3rd Bn Auckland Regiment, NZEF. Killed in action 4 October 1917. Son of Mary Ann Newlove, of Takaka, Nelson. 2.

NEWLOVE, Private, LESLIE MALCOLM, 31530. 2nd Bn Canterbury Regiment, NZEF. Killed in action 12 October 1917. Husband of Maud Newlove, of Takaka, Nelson. 3.

NEWPORT, Private, NELSON, 6/3114. 2nd Bn Canterbury Regiment, NZEF. Killed in action 1–2 October 1917. Son of Mr and Mrs George Newport, of Haven Rd, Nelson. 3.

NEWTON, Serjeant, GEORGE, 151171. 13th Coy 2nd Bn Canterbury Regiment, NZEF. Killed in action 12 October 1917. Age 25. Son of George William and Catherine Newton, of 3 Broomhedge St, Wellington. 2.

NIAS, Lance Corporal, GEORGE WILLIAM, 30631. 3rd Bn Wellington Regiment, NZEF. Killed in action 4 October 1917. Age 38. Son of George Elmes Nias and Sarah his wife, of 46 Sussex St, Wellington. Native of Nelson. Served in the South African Campaign. 6.

NICHOLL, Serjeant, JOSEPH ALBERT, 24/2548. 3rd Bn Wellington Regiment, NZEF. Killed in action 4 October 1917. Age 28. Son of Samuel and Eliza Ann Nicholl, of Spreydon, Christchurch, New Zealand; husband of Dora Lily Nicholl, of 406 Morgan Lane, Broken Hill, New South Wales, Australia. 6.

NICHOLLS, Private, OSCAR ALVA, 23084. 2nd Bn Canterbury Regiment, NZEF. Killed in action 12 October 1917. Son of Mrs Agnes Nicholls, of Longford, Tasmania. 3.

NICKLIN, Private, ALFRED, 24/1765. 2nd Bn Wellington Regiment, NZEF. Killed in action 5 October 1917. Age 31. Son of Agnes Nicklin, of Walsall, England, and the late Alfred Nicklin. 7.

NIELD, Private, CYRIL WHITEHURST, 29461. Hawke's Bay Coy 1st Bn Wellington Regiment, NZEF. Killed in action 4 October 1917. Age 22. Son of Jesse and Emily Maud Nield, of Corbett St, Paeroa, Thames. 7.

NOBLETT, Lance Corporal, JOHN, 29059. 3rd Bn Auckland Regiment, NZEF. 15 October 1917. Age 25. Son of Mrs F.J. Noblett, of 3 Malvern Rd, Bootle, Liverpool, England. Native of Newtownbarry, Co Wexford, Ireland. 1.

NORDSTROM, Private, ALFRED WILLIAM, 24214. 1st Bn Canterbury Regiment, NZEF. Killed in action 12 October 1917. Age 34. Son of Alfred and Annie Nordstrom. Native of Ashburton, Canterbury. 3.

NORMAN, Private, GEORGE, 8/2092. 1st Bn Otago Regiment, NZEF. 12 October 1917. 6.

NORRIS, Rifleman, HERBERT WILLIAM, 41004. 4th Bn 3rd NZ Rifle Brigade. Killed in action 12 October 1917. Brother of Harry Joseph Norris, of Bluff, Invercargill. 8.

NORTHOVER, Lance Corporal, LANCELOT WILLIAM, IO/3355. 7th Coy 1st Bn Wellington Regiment, NZEF. Killed in action 22 October 1917. Age 24. Son of William and Catherine Northover, of 19 Bay St, Petone, Wellington. 6.

NORTON, Rifleman, ALEXANDER, 21073. 4th Bn 3rd NZ Rifle Brigade. Killed in action 12 October 1917. Son of Mr and Mrs Charles Norton, of Taumarunui, Hamilton. 8.

O'BRIEN, Rifleman, ANDREW JOSEPH, 25/667. D Coy 3rd Bn 3rd NZ Rifle Brigade. Killed in action 12 October 1917. Age 35. Son of Jeremiah and Annie O'Brien, of Slope Point, Southland. Native of Waikawa, Invercargill. 9.

O'BRIEN, Private, JOHN, 39300. D Coy 2nd Bn Otago Regiment, NZEF. Killed in action 12 October 1917. Age 22. Son of Norah O'Brien, of 359 Cargill Rd, South Dunedin. 6.

O'BRIEN, Private, JOHN, 25573. 2nd Bn Wellington Regiment, NZEF. Killed in action 4 October 1917. Son of Mr and Mrs Patrick O'Brien, of 406 Eastbourne St, Hastings, Napier. 7.

O'BRIEN, Rifleman, JAMES PATRICK, 41869. 2nd Bn 3rd NZ Rifle Brigade. Killed in action 12 October 1917. Brother of Mrs A.K. Ward, of Pomahaka, Dunedin. 9.

O'BRIEN, Private, WILLIAM THOMAS, 53259. D Coy 1st Bn Otago Regiment, NZEF. Killed in action 12 October 1917. Age 24. Son of Morgan and Catherine O'Brien, of Makarewa, Southland, Invercargill. Native of Orawai, Southland. 6.

O'CALLAGHAN, Captain, LESLIE GEORGE, 24291. 1st Bn Canterbury Regiment, NZEF. Killed in action 12 October 1917. Age 38. Son of Arthur Pyne O'Callaghan and Florence O'Callaghan, of 16 Craigie St, Timaru; husband of Julia Marie O'Callaghan, of Hadlow, Timaru. Native of The Springs, Lincoln, Canterbury. 2.

O'CONNOR, Rifleman, DAVID, 47176. 4th Bn 3rd NZ Rifle Brigade. 12 October 1917. Age 27. Son of Daniel and Mary O'Connor (née Murphy), of Glenseagh, Kiskeam, Banteer, Co Cork, Ireland. 9.

O'DONOGHUE, Private, DANIEL, 16786. 3rd Bn Canterbury Regiment, NZEF. Killed in action 4 October 1917. Son of Mrs M. O'Donoghue, of 103 Shakespeare Rd, Napier. 3.

O'DRISCOLL, Rifleman, CORNELIUS, M M, 26/1019. 4th Bn 3rd NZ Rifle Brigade. 12 October 1917. 9.

O'GORMAN, Private, JOHN, 24274. 1st Bn Otago Regiment, NZEF. Killed in action 12 October 1917. Son of Thomas and Bridget O'Gorman, of 12 Lewisville Terrace, Tinakori Rd, Wellington. 6.

O'GORMAN, Private, THOMAS, 30396. 3rd Bn Wellington Regiment, NZEF. Killed in action 4–6 October 1917. Son of Thomas and Bridget O'Gorman, of 12 Lewisville Terrace, Tinakori Rd, Wellington. 7.

O'ROURKE, Private, STEPHEN WILLIAM, G/1343. 1st Bn Otago Regiment, NZEF. Killed in action 12 October 1917. Son of Mr and Mrs Michael O'Rourke, of Gore, Southland, Invercargill. 6.

OKEY, Rifleman, JOSEPH THOMAS, 27132. 2nd Bn 3rd NZ Rifle Brigade. Killed in action 12 October 1917. Son of Jane Okey, of Preston Rd, Greymouth. 9.

OLDFIELD, Rifleman, FREDERICK WILLIAM, 40715. 2nd Bn 3rd NZ Rifle Brigade. Killed in action 12 October 1917. Age 21. Son of Sarah Oldfield, of Temuka, Timaru, and the late Henry Oldfield. 9.

OLDS, Rifleman, HAROLD, 46478. 3rd Bn 3rd NZ Rifle Brigade. 12 October 1917. Age 31. Son of Harold and Mary E.G. Olds, of Little Bargus, Perranwell Station, Cornwall, England. 9.

OLSEN, Private, RICHARD BARNEY, 48258. 2nd Bn Canterbury Regiment, NZEF. Killed in action 12 October 1917. Son of Mr and Mrs O. Olsen, of Hastwells, Eketahuna, Wellington. 3.

OLSON, Rifleman, NORMAN SELBY, 41871. G Coy 4th Bn 3rd NZ Rifle Brigade. Killed in action 12 October 1917. Age 29. Son of Cart Magnus Olson and Ingere Olson, of Masterton. Native of Petone, Wellington. 9.

ORR, Private, JOHN WILLIAM, 26966. 2nd (Waikato) Coy 2nd Bn Auckland Regiment, NZEF. Killed in action 4 October 1917. Age 30. Son of Matilda Orr, of Main Rd, Maheno, Oamaru, and the late John Orr. 2.

ORR, Private, LESLIE, 25298. 1st Bn Otago Regiment, NZEF. Killed in action 12 October 1917. Son of Mr and Mrs Archibald Orr, of 1728 Davie St, Victoria, British

Columbia, Canada. 6.

OSBORNE, Private, CHARLES PATRICK, 42174. 2nd Bn Wellington Regiment, NZEF. Killed in action 4 October 1917. Age 29. Son of Thomas and Cathrine Osborne, of Newstead, Hamilton, New Zealand. Native of Forest Gate, London, England. 7.

OSBORNE, Private, JOHN, 12/2427. 1st Bn Auckland Regiment, NZEF. Killed in action 4 October 1917. Son of Mr and Mrs G.E. Osborne, of Hinuera, Waikato. 2.

OXLEY, Private, WILLIAM FRANK, 29849. 1st Bn Otago Regiment, NZEF. Killed in action 12 October 1917. Age 20. Son of William and Mary Oxley, of 28 James St, North East Valley, Dunedin, New Zealand. Native of Birmingham, England. 6.

PADDEN, Private, PATRICK, 45903. 1st Bn Wellington Regiment, NZEF. Killed in action 4 October 1917. Son of Mr and Mrs James Padden, of Waikanae, Wellington. 7.

PAGE, Private, JOHN ROY, 42818. 2nd Bn Canterbury Regiment, NZEF. Killed in action 12 October 1917. Age 33. Son of James and Adeline Page, of Waitapu, Takaka, Nelson. 3.

PAGET, Private, SAMUEL FRANCIS, 10/3694. 2nd Bn Wellington Regiment, NZEF. Killed in action 4 October 1917. Age 24. Son of Samuel Francis Thomas and Nielsine Paget, of Takaperu Rd, Waipukurau, Napier. 7.

PAGET, Private, TRAVIS EDWARD, 8/2375. 2nd Bn Otago Regiment, NZEF. Killed in action 12 October 1917. Son of Mr and Mrs Edwin Paget, of Rangiriri, Waikato. 6.

PAIGE, Private, CHARLES HENRY, 44782. 1st Bn Auckland Regiment, NZEF. Killed in action 4 October 1917. 2.

PAISLEY, Corporal, ROBERT, 813931. 2nd Bn Otago Regiment, NZEF. Killed in action 12 October 1917. Son of Mr and Mrs Robert Paisley, of 552 Cumberland St, Dunedin. 3.

PALMER, Private, JAMES WILLIAM, 22281. 2nd Bn Otago Regiment, NZEF. Killed in action 12 October 1917. 6.

PANNELL, Private, EDGAR DOUGLAS, 32463. 1st Bn Canterbury Regiment, NZEF. Killed in action 12 October 1917. Son of Harry and Annie Pannell, of 98 Kerr's Rd, Christchurch. 3.

PARDOE, Serjeant, HAROLD, 12/832. 2nd Bn Auckland Regiment, NZEF. Killed in action 4 October 1917. 1.

PARKER, Private, WILLIAM, 38740. 6th (Hauraki) Coy 2nd Bn Auckland Regiment, NZEF. Killed in action 4 October 1917. Age 24. Son of John and Marian Parker, of 1 Waterview Rd, Devonport, Auckland. 2.

PARKER, Lance Corporal, WALTER JOHN, 32715. 3rd Bn Otago Regiment, NZEF. Killed in action 4 October 1917. Son of Mrs W. Parker, of 341 Cumberland St, Dunedin. 4.

PARKINSON, Rifleman, LIONEL EUSTACE, 24/1158. 2nd Bn 3rd NZ Rifle Brigade. Killed in action 12 October 1917. Age 20. Son of Edmund Albert and Mary Ann Parkinson, of 180 Balmoral Rd, Mount Eden, Auckland. 9.

PARKMAN, Private, WILLIAM, 46072. 3rd Bn Canterbury Regiment, NZEF. Killed in action 5 October 1917. Husband of Lilian May Parkman, of Gisborne. 3.

PARLETT, Private, LOUIS, 41011. 3rd Bn Otago Regiment, NZEF. Killed in action 4 October 1917. 6.

PARMENTER, Private, JACK, 33941. 3rd Bn Wellington Regiment, NZEF. Killed in action 15 October 1917. Age 24. Son of Charles and Mary Parmenter, of 7 Union St,

Newmarket Auckland. Native of Riverton, Invercargill. 7.

PARNHAM, Private, ERIC JAMES, 29625. No. 5 Coy NZ Machine Gun Corps. Killed in action 4 October 1917. Son of Mr and Mrs Herbert Parnham, of North Brighton, Christchurch. 9.

PARR, Driver, ELLIS ALEXANDER, M M, 1312887. NZ Field Artillery. Killed in action 30 October 1917. Age 26. Son of Ann Stuart Parr, of 6 Union St, Petone, Wellington, and the late Thomas Edgar Parr. Native of Martinborough, Featherston. 1.

PARR, Lance Serjeant, THOMAS ALBERT, 10/2730. 1st Bn Wellington Regiment, NZEF. Killed in action 4 October 1917. Age 27. Son of James and Caroline Parr, of Waotu, Putaruru, Hamilton. 6.

PARRY, Captain, ERNEST CHARLES, 12/2904. 16th (Waikato) Coy 1st Bn Auckland Regiment, NZEF. Killed in action 6 October 1917. Age 31. Husband of Mary Okaro Parry, of Miller's Avenue, Paeroa, Thames. Native of Paeroa. 1.

PARSLOW, Private, HARRY ROBERTSON, 30072. 2nd Bn Otago Regiment, NZEF. Killed in action 12 October 1917. Age 20. Son of Harry and Louisa Parslow, of 14 Beach St, Port Chalmers, Dunedin. 6.

PARSONS, Rifleman, JOSEPH ARCHIBALD, 25/903. 3rd Bn 3rd NZ Rifle Brigade. Killed in action 12 October 1917. Age 33. Son of William F. and Mary Parsons, of Tapuhi, Hukerenui, North Auckland. 9.

PARTRIDGE, Private, JOHN, 18573. 3rd Bn Auckland Regiment, NZEF. Killed in action 3 October 1917. 2.

PATERSON, Private, WILLIAM, 42568. 2nd Bn Otago Regiment, NZEF. 12 October 1917. Age 39. Son of Mary Paterson, of 199 Hamilton Rd, Cambuslang, Scotland. 6.

PATTON, Rifleman, WILLIAM CHARLES, 25/1198. 3rd Bn 3rd NZ Rifle Brigade. Killed in action 12 October 1917. Son of John Patton, of Piopio, Te Kuiti, Hamilton. 9.

PAUL, Second Lieutenant, SYDNEY VICTOR, 10/2274. 1st Bn Wellington Regiment, NZEF. Killed in action 23 October 1917. Age 23. Son of Alice Paul, of New Plymouth. 6.

PAULSON, Corporal, BERTIE, M M, 24/1776. 2nd Bn Otago Regiment, NZEF. Killed in action 12 October 1917. Age 24. Son of Alfred and Mary Paulson, of Gisborne. 4.

PAUWELS, Serjeant, LOUIS CHARLES, 24/1165. 2nd Bn 3rd NZ Rifle Brigade. Killed in action 12 October 1917. 7.

PAYNE, Rifleman, WALTER, 48840. 2nd Bn 3rd NZ Rifle Brigade. Killed in action 12 October 1917. Husband of Bertha Payne, of Sydenham, Christchurch. 9.

PAYTON, Private, CHARLES, 28367. 1st Bn Auckland Regiment, NZEF. Killed in action 4 October 1917. Age 23. Son of Charles and Annie Elizabeth Payton, of Broad Arrow Rd, Dumbleton, Hurstville, Sydney, New South Wales, Australia. Native of England. 2.

PEARCE, Serjeant, ARTHUR HAMBLEY, 10/2500. B Coy 1st Bn Wellington Regiment, NZEF. Killed in action 23 October 1917. Age 27. Son of Emily Hambley Pearce, of 101 Bumley Terrace, Dominion Rd, Auckland. Native of Whangarei, Auckland. 6.

PEARCE, Rifleman, JOHN WILLIAM, 25/349. D Coy 3rd Bn 3rd NZ Rifle Brigade. Killed in action 12 October 1917. Age 33. Son of Thomas and Sarah Pearce, of 123 Main Rd, Wadestown, Wellington. Native of Christchurch. 9.

PEARCE, Rifleman, LESLIE GORDON, 17816. H Coy 4th Bn 3rd NZ Rifle Brigade. Killed in action 12 October 1917. Age 23. Son of Ann Pearce, of Fitzgerald, Tasmania, and the late John Clyne Pearce. Native of Ballarat, Victoria, Australia. 9.

PEARCE, Private, WILLIAM, 5/894. No. 3 Coy NZ Machine Gun Corps. Killed in action 12 October 1917. Age 29. Son of Mary Ann Pearce, of 78 Munro St, Seatoun, Wellington, and the late Alexander Pearce. Native of Thames. 9.

PELL, Private, ALFRED JAMES THOMAS, 27954. 2nd Bn Canterbury Regiment, NZEF. Killed in action 12 October 1917. Son of Robert Thomas and Elizabeth Pell, of Wellington. 3.

PENNY, Lance Corporal, WALTER BLAYMIRES, 10/4487. 2nd Bn Wellington Regiment, NZEF. Killed in action 4 October 1917. Son of Mr and Mrs Edward Henry Penny, of Blenheim. 6.

PEPPERELL, Corporal, FRANK, 14320. E Coy 1st Bn Auckland Regiment, NZEF. Killed in action 4 October 1917. Age 23. Son of William Francis and Elizabeth Pepperell, of Lichfield, Waikato. 1.

PERFECT, Private, ERNEST, 32781. 2nd Bn Otago Regiment, NZEF. Killed in action 12 October 1917. Age 25. Son of the late George and Jane Perfect. Native of Woodville, Wellington. 6.

PERI, Private, HUGHIE, 13798. 1st Bn Otago Regiment, NZEF. Killed in action 12 October 1917. Brother of Kera Peri, of Purangi, Taranaki. 6.

PERRIN, Private, JOHN HAROLD, 31702. 2nd Bn Auckland Regiment, NZEF. Killed in action 4 October 1917. Age 34. Son of William and Elizabeth Perrin, of Onehunga, Auckland; husband of Catherine Ann Perrin, of Komokoriki, Ahuroa, Auckland. 2.

PERRY, Private, DAVID, 48261. 2nd Bn Canterbury Regiment, NZEF. Killed in action 12 October 1917. Age 27. Son of John and Ellen Perry, of Fitzherbert Avenue, Wanganui. 3.

PERRY, Private, ERNEST WALTER, 29190. 1st Bn Canterbury Regiment, NZEF. Killed in action 12 October 1917. Son of Mr and Mrs John Perry, of Victoria St, Eaglehawk, Victoria, Australia. 3.

PETERS, Private, WILLIAM JAMES, 39638. 3rd Bn Otago Regiment, NZEF. Killed in action 4 October 1917. Son of Mr and Mrs James Peters of Waverley St, Waipawa, Napier. 6.

PETERSEN, Private, JOHN, 6/4125. 2nd Bn Canterbury Regiment, NZEF. Killed in action 12 October 1917. Age 29. Son of Niels F. and Katarine U. Petersen, of Smedegade, 27 Middelfurt, Denmark. 3.

PETERSEN, Private, TIMIS FRED, 38065. 3rd Bn Wellington Regiment, NZEF. Killed in action 4 October 1917. Son of Mr and Mrs Hemming Petersen, of Pleckville, Eketahuna, Wellington. 7.

PETERSON, Private, ALEXANDER HENDERSON, 32718. ID Coy 1st Bn Otago Regiment, NZEF. Killed in action 1 October 1917. Age 33. Son of Andrew Bruce and Catherine Peterson, of 18 Bridgman St, Kensington, Dunedin. 6.

PHILIPPS, Rifleman, FREDERICK EMERSON, 46486. 1st Bn 3rd NZ Rifle Brigade. Killed in action 12 October 1917. Son of Frederick Robert and Flora Martha Philipps, of Kohukohu, Auckland. 9.

PICKERING, Rifleman, GEORGE, 38307. 2nd Bn 3rd NZ Rifle Brigade. Killed in action 12 October 1917. Age 35. Son of William and Jennet Pickering, of Claremont, Timaru. Native of Hororata, Christchurch. 9.

PILCHER, Serjeant, WILLIAM THOMAS, 25/231. No. 1 Coy 3rd Bn Canterbury Regiment, NZEF. Killed in action 4 October 1917. Age 26. Son of William Edward Pilcher, of Raumati, Hawke's Bay, New Zealand, and the late Mary Pilcher. Native of Ladysmith, South Africa. 2.

PIPER, Private, MICHAEL, 8/1314. 4th Coy 1st Bn Otago Regiment, NZEF. Killed in action 12 October 1917. Age 25. Son of Alice Gillespie (formerly Piper), of Culverden, North Canterbury. Previously wounded at Gallipoli. 6.

PLUCK, Corporal, JOHN THOMAS, 7/2126. 2nd Bn Canterbury Regiment, NZEF. Died of wounds 12 October 1917. Age 24. Son of Charles Pluck, of Rakaia, Canterbury, and the late Caroline Mary Ann Pluck. 2.

PLUNKETT, Private, JOHN, 22088. 2nd Bn Otago Regiment, NZEF. Killed in action 12 October 1917. Age 30. Son of Margaret Plunkett, of 130 Melbourne St, South Dunedin, and the late James Plunkett. 6.

POLASCHEK, Private, WILLIAM, 14144. G Coy 1st Bn Canterbury Regiment, NZEF. Killed in action 12 October 1917. Age 36. Brother of Joseph Polaschek, of 14 Byron St, Sydenham, Christchurch. Native of Temuka, Canterbury. 3.

POLL, Serjeant, ARTHUR LANGLEY, 25139. 2nd Bn 3rd NZ Rifle Brigade. Killed in action 12 October 1917. Son of Frederick Poll, of London, England; husband of Jessie Poll, of Christchurch, New Zealand. 7.

POLLARD, Private, NORMAN ALFRED, 10/3982. 3rd Bn Wellington Regiment, NZEF. Killed in action 4 October 1917. Son of Mr and Mrs William Joseph Pollard, of Eltham, Taranaki. 7.

POMEROY, Private, SAMUEL, 22091. 2nd Bn Otago Regiment, NZEF. Killed in action 12 October 1917. Age 28. Husband of Ethel Jessie Pomeroy, of 100 Kilbirnie Crescent, Kilbirnie, Wellington. Native of Invercargill. 6.

POOL, Rifleman, CHARLES, 241559. 2nd Bn 3rd NZ Rifle Brigade. Killed in action 12 October 1917. Son of Ellen Pool, of Dillmanstown, Westland. 9.

POOLE, Corporal, ALBERT WILLIAM GRESHAM, 10/3058. No. 1 Coy 1st Bn Wellington Regiment, NZEF. Killed in action 4 October 1917. Age 23. Son of Albert William and Hannah Maria Poole, of Te Aroha, Auckland. 6.

POOLE, Private, EDWARD ARTHUR, 39308. 2nd Bn Otago Regiment, NZEF. Killed in action 12 October 1917. Age 23. Son of Margaret M. Poole, of Isla Bank, Southland, Invercargill, and the late Edward Samuel Poole. 6.

POPE, Private, EDWARD THOMAS, 42395. 1st Bn Auckland Regiment, NZEF. Killed in action 4 October 1917. Age 26. Son of Charles and Aloe Pope, of Mangatawhiri, Pokeno, Auckland. 2.

PORTEOUS, Private, WILLIAM NESBIT, 29857. 1st Bn Otago Regiment, NZEF. 12 October 1917. Age 26. Son of Mr and Mrs James Porteous, of Nisbet Place, Roslin, Midlothian, Scotland. 6.

POSHA, Rifleman, ANTON, 231562. 1st Bn 3rd NZ Rifle Brigade. Killed in action 12 October 1917. 9.

POTROZ, Rifleman, BERNARD, 30402. H Coy 4th Bn 3rd NZ Rifle Brigade. Killed in action 12 October 1917. Age 24. Son of Thomas and Mary Potroz, of Kaimata, Taranaki. 9.

POTTS, Rifleman, JAMES WILLIAM, 26/1023. 4th Bn 3rd NZ Rifle Brigade. Killed in action 12 October 1917. Age 21. Son of James and Philippa Ports, of 102 Tainui St, Greymouth. 9.

POWELL, Private, JAMES, 47682. 2nd Bn Canterbury Regiment, NZEF. Killed in action 12 October 1917. Age 30. Son of Thomas and Agnes Powell, of Oxford, Canterbury. 3.

POWELL, Private, THOMAS HENRY, 33603. 3rd Bn Wellington Regiment, NZEF. Killed in action 4 October 1917. Age 26. Son of Thomas Isaac and Hannah Matilda Powell, of Te Hana, Auckland. 7.

POWER, Private, EDMOND MARK, 30001. 2nd Bn Otago Regiment, NZEF. Killed in action 12 October 1917. Age 26. Son of Edmond and Mary Power, of Hauraki St, Birkenhead, Auckland. 6.

POWER, Private, THOMAS EDWARD, IO/3984. 1st Bn Wellington Regiment, NZEF. Killed in action 4 October 1917. Son of Patrick and Alice Power, of Franklin Rd, Woodville, Wellington. 7.

PREEN, Rifleman, ERNEST GEORGE, IG/221. 3rd Bn 3rd NZ Rifle Brigade. Killed in action 12 October 1917. Age 44. Son of George Preen and the late Constance Preen; husband of Helen Preen, of 4 High St, Timaru. 9.

PROFFITT, Lieutenant, WILLIAM REYNOLDS, 24/548. No. 3 Coy NZ Machine Gun Corps. Killed in action 4 October 1917. Age 31. Son of Sarah Ann Proffitt, of 46 Wellesley Rd, Napier, and the late William Proffitt. Also served in Samoa. 9.

PULLAR, Private, EDWARD WILLIAM, M M, 32724. 1st Bn Otago Regiment, NZEF. Killed in action 12 October 1917. Age 25. Son of William and Marion Alice Pullar, of Tussock Creek, Southland, Invercargill. 6.

PURCELL, Lance Corporal, ARTHUR ROBERT, 15962. 1st Bn 3rd NZ Rifle Brigade. Killed in action 12 October 1917. Husband of Florence Emily May (formerly Purcell), of Auckland. 8.

QUIN, Private, THOMAS, 13983. 1st Bn Otago Regiment, NZEF. Killed in action 12 October 1917. Age 39. Son of John and Mary Quin, of Hampden, Otago. 6.

QUINN, Rifleman, MICHAEL CONWAY, 41109. 4th Bn 3rd NZ Rifle Brigade. Killed in action 12 October 1917. Age 29. Son of James and Mary Conway Quinn, of Mill St, Tullow, Co Carlow, Ireland. 9.

RADCLIFFE, Private, PERCY NOEL, 34143. 2nd Bn Canterbury Regiment, NZEF. Killed in action 12 October 1917. Age 32. Son of Frances Emily Rosa Radcliffe, of Ngaio, Wellington, and the late James Radcliffe. 3.

RADFORD, Lance Corporal, LESTER ROYAL, 36487. 3rd Bn Wellington Regiment, NZEF. Killed in action 4 October 1917. Son of Mr and Mrs Walter Edmund Radford, of 'Karetu', Seaward Valley, Kaikoura, Christchurch. 6.

RADFORD, Private, WILLIAM, 42396. 3rd Bn Auckland Regiment, NZEF. Killed in action 18 October 1917. Age 37. Son of Charles and Martha Radford; husband of Mary Jane Eade (formerly Radford), of Muritai Rd, Takapuna, Auckland, New Zealand. Native of Hulme, Manchester, England. Formerly Tpr (1243) British S. African Police. 2.

RAMSAY, Private, JOHN, 45129. 2nd Bn Otago Regiment, NZEF. Killed in action 12 October 1917. 6.

REDSTONE, Private, BERNARD EDWIN, 41891. 3rd Bn Wellington Regiment, NZEF. Killed in action 4 October 1917. Son of Mr and Mrs John Robert Redstone, of Gisborne. 7.

REECE, Private, ARTHUR, 44868. 1st (Hawke's Bay) Coy 2nd Bn Wellington Regiment, NZEF. Killed in action 4 October 1917. Age 22. Son of Edwin and Lucy

Reece, of Opotiki, Thames. 7.

REID, Private, ALEXANDER, 42397. A Coy 1st Bn Auckland Regiment, NZEF. 4 October 1917. Age 36. Son of the late Serjt. L. Reid (RMLI, Woolwich). 2.

REID, Private, GAVIN, 39893. 3rd Bn Wellington Regiment, NZEF. Killed in action 4 October 1917. Age 32. Son of Hugh Andrew Reid and Elizabeth Reid, of Middleton, Milnathort, Kinrossshire, Scotland. 7.

RHODES, Private, WALTER JAMES, 40365. 1st Bn Auckland Regiment, NZEF. Killed in action 4 October 1917. Son of Mrs S. Rhodes, of Whitianga, Auckland. 2.

RICE, Private, HARKNESS HENRY, 39317. 2nd Bn Otago Regiment, NZEF. Killed in action 12 October 1917. Age 37. Son of John Harkness Rice and Emily, his wife, of Tataraimaka, Taranaki. 6.

RICE, Lance Corporal, JOSEPH, 23432. 1st Bn Auckland Regiment, NZEF. Killed in action 4 October 1917. Son of Michael and Elizabeth Rice, of Opua, Bay of Islands. 1.

RICHARDSON, Private, MICHAEL, 38794. 1st Bn Wellington Regiment, NZEF. 4 October 1917. Age 42. Father of John Richardson, of 2 Ashton St, Poplar, London, England. 7.

RIDDLE, Private, GEORGE, 22285. 2nd Bn Otago Regiment, NZEF. Killed in action 12 October 1917. Husband of Lavinia Riddle, of 50 Maclaggan St, Dunedin. 6.

RIDLEY, Rifleman, JOHN WILLIAM LAWRENCE, 29083. B Coy 1st Bn 3rd NZ Rifle Brigade. Killed in action 12 October 1917. Age 28. Only son of Jane Ridley, of 10 Medway St, North Richmond, Christchurch, and the late William Laurence Ridley. Native of Christchurch. 9.

RILEY, Lance Corporal, SINCLAIR MALCOLM, 814485. 2nd Bn Otago Regiment, NZEF. Killed in action 12 October 1917. Step-brother of William Kingston, of 121 Molle St, Hobart, Tasmania. 4.

RIVETT, Rifleman, GEORGE, 41885. 4th Bn 3rd NZ Rifle Brigade. 12 October 1917. Age 25. Son of Edward and Mary Rivett, of 9 Pratt Rd, Rushden, Northants, England. 9.

ROBB, Private, WILLIAM JAMES, 21737. 2nd Bn Canterbury Regiment, NZEF. Killed in action 12 October 1917. Son of Letitia Robb, of Doyleston, Canterbury. 3.

ROBERTS, Private, ANDREW CLARK, 29866. 2nd Bn Otago Regiment, NZEF. Killed in action 13 October 1917. 6.

ROBERTSON, Rifleman, THOMAS, 18709. 1st Bn 3rd NZ Rifle Brigade. Killed in action 12 October 1917. Age 21. Son of Jane Robertson, of Muir St, Te Hapara, Gisborne, and the late John Robertson. Native of Ettrick, Dunedin. 9.

ROBINSON, Private, FRANK DUNCAN, 33951. 3rd Bn Auckland Regiment, NZEF. 4 October 1917. Age 38. Son of James William Robinson, of 106 Hither Green Lane, Lewisham, London, England; husband of Jane Robinson. 2.

ROBINSON, Private, RALPH EDWARD, 29301. 2nd Bn Canterbury Regiment, NZEF. Killed in action 12 October 1917. 3.

RODGER, Lance Corporal, ANDREW, 8/2796. 1st Bn Otago Regiment, NZEF. Killed in action 12 October 1917. Age 26. Son of Hugh and Euphemia Rodger, of Lynn Craig, Dalry, Ayrshire, Scotland. 4.

RODGERS, Corporal, HARRY, 24/1798. 2nd Bn Wellington Regiment, NZEF. Killed in action 4 October 1917. Husband of Mrs Nan Rodgers, of 14 Estuary Rd, Redcliffs, Christchurch. 6.

RODGERS, Private, SAMUEL CECIL, 45127. 14th Coy 3rd Bn Otago Regiment,

NZEF. Killed in action 15 October 1917. Age 21. Son of John Thomas and Sarah Rodgers, of Tuapeka Mouth, Otago. Native of Waimate, South Canterbury. 6.

ROGERS, Rifleman, GORDON GLADSTONE, 23440. 2nd Bn 3rd NZ Rifle Brigade, Killed in action 12 October 1917. Son of Amelia Rogers, of Maungaturoto, Auckland. 9.

ROGERS, Private, GEORGE HENRY, 38750. 1st Bn Wellington Regiment, NZEF. Killed in action 3 October 1917. Son of Mrs M. Rogers, of Leigh, North Auckland. 7.

ROSE, Second Lieutenant, EVELYN JACK, 25147. 6th (Hauraki) Coy 1st Bn Auckland Regiment, NZEF. Killed in action 4 October 1917. Age 23. Son of Robert Griffiths Rose and Bessie Rose, of 15 Gladwin Rd, Onehunga, Auckland. 1.

ROSE, Private, WILLIAM AUSTIN, 51070. 3rd Bn Wellington Regiment, NZEF. Killed in action 13 October 1917. Age 23. Son of James and Rosetta Rose, of Salisbury St, Levin, Wellington. 7.

ROSE, Private, WILLIAM MCILWRAITH, 26920. 6th (Hauraki) Coy 2nd Bn Auckland Regiment, NZEF. Killed in action 4 October 1917. Age 29. Son of Catherine Louisa Rose, of 24 Grange Rd, Mount Eden, Auckland, and the late Francis Rose. Native of Tirau, Waikato. 2.

ROSE, Corporal, WILLIAM RICHARD, 13097. D Coy 3rd Bn 3rd NZ Rifle Brigade. Killed in action 12 October 1917. Age 27. Son of Norah Rose, of Bluff, Invercargill, and the late C. Rose. 8.

ROSS, Private, ALFRED WILLIAM, 14868. 2nd Bn Wellington Regiment, NZEF. Died of wounds 3–4 October 1917. 7.

ROSS, Rifleman, CHARLES, 49006. 3rd Bn 3rd NZ Rifle Brigade. Killed in action 12 October 1917. Brother of Mr Toni Ross, of Murchison, Nelson. 9.

ROSS, Private, SILVESTER MORALEE, 37864. 2nd Bn Canterbury Regiment, NZEF. Killed in action 12 October 1917. Son of Mrs F.L.J. Ross, of 97 Coromandel St, Newtown, Wellington. 3.

ROSS, Rifleman, WALLACE ALEX, 40717. 2nd Bn 3rd NZ Rifle Brigade. Killed in action 12 October 1917. Husband of Grace Ross, of East St, Ashburton, Christchurch. 9.

ROSSITER, Rifleman, HENRY, 41362. 4th Bn 3rd NZ Rifle Brigade. Killed in action 12 October 1917. Age 28. Son of Edward and Emma Rossiter, of 20 Christian St, Dannevirke, Napier. Native of Oxford, Christchurch. 9.

ROUD, Private, WALTER, 44021. 3rd Bn Canterbury Regiment, NZEF. Killed in action 5 October 1917. Age 27. Husband of Catherine Roud, of 822 Colombo St, Christchurch. 3.

ROWE, Private, JAMES COLEMAN, 18858. 2nd Bn Auckland Regiment, NZEF. Killed in action 5 October 1917. Age 20. Son of James Rowe, of Ward St, Pukekohe, Auckland, and the late Blanch Rowe. Native of Auckland. 2.

ROWE, Private, WILLIAM CHARLES, 45918. 3rd Bn Wellington Regiment, NZEF. Killed in action 4 October 1917. Son of Charles Rowe, of Lower Matakana, Auckland. 7.

RUDDICK, Private, FREDERICK, 37869. 2nd Bn Otago Regiment, NZEF. Killed in action 12 October 1917. Age 33. Son of William Ruddick, of Woodville, Wellington, and the late Sarah Ruddick. Native of Clive, Hawke's Bay, Napier. 6.

RUDKIN, Rifleman, GERARD NOEL, 23256. D Coy 4th Bn 3rd NZ Rifle Brigade. Killed in action 12 October 1917. Age 33. Son of the late George Robert and Amy Jane Rudkin, of Kumara, Greymouth. 9.

RULE, Lieutenant, WILLIAM BRAMWELL, 39722. 1st Bn 3rd NZ Rifle Brigade. Killed in action 12 October 1917. Son of the Rev. Francis Rule, of 45 Richmond Terrace, Christchurch. 7.

RUSCOE, Rifleman, HUGH GRANVILLE, 13808. 2nd Bn 3rd NZ Rifle Brigade. Killed in action 12 October 1917. Age 17. Son of Herbert and Isabella Ruscoe, of 37 Adelaide Rd, Wellington. 9.

RUSSELL, Rifleman, REGINALD STEPHEN, 25949. 3rd Bn 3rd NZ Rifle Brigade. Killed in action 12 October 1917. Husband of Mrs Louise Russell, of Auckland. 9.

RYAN, Lance Corporal, ARNOLD EDWIN, 26179. 4th Bn 3rd NZ Rifle Brigade. Killed in action 12 October 1917. Son of Mrs Elizabeth Ryan, of Weber, Napier. 8.

RYAN, Private, JOHN, 42580. 3rd Bn Otago Regiment, NZEF. Killed in action 4 October 1917. Age 34. Son of John and Catherine Ryan, of 220 Oxford St, South Dunedin. 6.

RYBURN, Second Lieutenant, ERIC MIDDLETON, 811625. 2nd Bn Otago Regiment, NZEF. Killed in action 12 October 1917. Age 21. Son of the Rev. Robert Middleton Ryburn and Anna Jane, his wife, of 88 Flocton St, Christchurch. Native of Gisborne. 3.

SABIN, Private, JOHN NORTHEY, 14871. 1st Bn Wellington Regiment, NZEF. Killed in action 21 October 1917. Age 24. Son of Arthur and Elizabeth Sabin, of 11 Edwardes St, Napier. Native of Makotuku, Napier. 7.

SALISBURY, Private, GEORGE HENRY, 41631. 3rd Bn Otago Regiment, NZEF. Killed in action 17 October 1917. Son of the late John and Mary Salisbury. 6.

SALLY, Private, JOHN, 10/3078. 1st Bn Wellington Regiment, NZEF. Killed in action 4 October 1917. Brother of Arthur Sally, of Pemau, Gulf of Riga, Russia. 7.

SANDERS, Lance Corporal, HUGH, 6/3454. 2nd Bn Canterbury Regiment, NZEF. Killed in action 12 October 1917. Age 27. Son of James and Charlotte A. Sanders, of Goring St, Opotiki, Bay of Plenty. 2.

SANDERSON, Private, WILLIAM, 24063. 15th (North Auckland) Coy 2nd Bn Auckland Regiment, NZEF. Killed in action 4 October 1917. Age 32. Son of Eliza Jane Sanderson, of 8 Kelly St, Eden Vale Rd, Mount Eden, Auckland, and the late Benjamin Sanderson. Native of Okupu, Great Barrier Island. 2.

SANDIFORTH, Private, FRED, 23259. 1st Bn Canterbury Regiment, NZEF. Killed in action 12 October 1917. 3.

SANG, Lance Corporal, RICHARD CLAUDE, 11346. No. 4 Coy NZ Machine Gun Corps. Killed in action 13 October 1917. Son of Mr and Mrs William Sang, of Ribble St, Oamaru. 9.

SAUNDERS, Private, JOHN LEO, 36843. No. 4 Coy 2nd Bn Otago Regiment, NZEF. Killed in action 12 October 1917. Age 24. Son of Timothy and Kathleen Saunders, of Greymouth, New Zealand; husband of Mary Saunders, of 17 Spring St, Melbourne, Australia. 6.

SCHUMACHER, Private, GEORGE JAMES, 32472. 1st Bn Canterbury Regiment, NZEF. Killed in action 12 October 1917. Age 26. Son of Emily Kezia Schumacher, of 54 Blenheim Rd, Riccarton, Christchurch. Native of Canterbury. 3.

SCOLTOCK, Private, WILLIAM, 32391. 3rd Bn Canterbury Regiment, NZEF. Killed in action 4 October 1917. Son of Mr and Mrs Charles Scoltock, of Lincoln, Canterbury. 3.

SEATON, Private, JOHN FINLAY, 40647. 3rd Bn Auckland Regiment, NZEF. Killed in action 4 October 1917. Son of Mr and Mrs James Seaton, of 'Dalzien', Papakura, Auckland. 2.

SEATON, Private, WILLIAM HAIGH, 12/4085. 1st Bn Auckland Regiment, NZEF. Killed in action 4 October 1917. Age 27. Son of Kemp and Jane Seaton, of King Edward Avenue, Bayswater, Auckland, New Zealand. Native of Grimsby, England. 2

SEYMOUR, Private, FELIX, 38228. A Coy 1st Bn Wellington Regiment, NZEF. Killed in action 4 October 1917. Age 27. Son of Joseph William and Ellen Seymour, of 20 Bridge St, Port Ahuriri, Napier. 7.

SHAKESHAFT, Corporal, ALFRED, 10/1649. 1st Bn Wellington Regiment, NZEF. Killed in action 24 October 1917. Age 27. Son of Edmund Shakeshaft, of 12 Wright St, Widnes, England, and the late Janet Shakeshaft. 6.

SHAND, Private, ALEXANDER, 3/2496. NZ Medical Corps. Killed in action 12 October 1917. Age 30. Son of John Shand, of Craigellachie, Scotland; husband of Florence Shand, of Green Island, Dunedin, New Zealand. 9.

SHARMAN, Private, JOHN, 46618. 3rd Bn Canterbury Regiment, NZEF. Killed in action 16 October 1917. 3.

SHEARY, Sapper, JOHN EDWARD, 4/2135. NZ Engineers. Killed in action 12 October 1917. Son of Mr and Mrs James Sheary, of Richmond, Nelson. 1.

SHEDDAN, Private, ALEXANDER, 46792. 1st Bn Otago Regiment, NZEF. Killed in action 12 October 1917. Brother of Miss F. Sheddan, of Tapanui, Otago. 6.

SHEEHAN, Private, FREDERICK, 8/2129. 1st Bn Otago Regiment, NZEF. Killed in action 12 October 1917. Son of Mary Sheehan, of 24 Conference St, Christchurch. 6.

SHELDON, Private, GEORGE, 30003. 2nd Bn Otago Regiment, NZEF. Killed in action 12 October 1917. Son of Mrs K. Sheldon, of Stout St, Westport, Greymouth. 6.

SHEPHERD, Private, BENJAMIN ALEXANDER, 34738. 3rd Bn Canterbury Regiment, NZEF. Killed in action 4 October 1917. Brother of Mrs C. Wilson, of 105 Aldwins Rd, Linwood, Christchurch. 3.

SHERWOOD, Private, SIDNEY HERBERT, 33456. 2nd Bn Wellington Regiment, NZEF. Killed in action 4 October 1917. Son of Mr and Mrs Herbert Sherwood, of King St, Pahiatua, Wellington. 7.

SHIELDS, Private, THOMAS, 45145. 2nd Bn Otago Regiment, NZEF. 12 October 1917. Age 48. Son of James and Margaret Shields, of Donacloney, Co Down, Ireland. 6.

SHIRLEY, Private, WILLIAM, 32245. 3rd Bn Canterbury Regiment, NZEF. Killed in action 20 October 1917. Son of Mrs J. Shirley, of Pahiatua, Wellington; husband of Isabel Gertrude Shirley, of Argyle St, Hawera. 3.

SHORE, Private, NORMAN, 39640. F Coy 3rd Bn Canterbury Regiment, NZEF. Killed in action 12 October 1917. Age 21. Son of Herbert and Sarah Jane Shore, of 4 Brewster St, Napier. 3.

SIMM, Rifleman, JAMES CRAIG, 39713. A Coy 3rd Bn 3rd NZ Rifle Brigade. Killed in action 12 October 1917. Age 42. Son of Marion Simm, of Wellington, New Zealand, and the late William Simm. Native of Glasgow, Scotland. 9.

SIMPSON, Private, FREDERICK LEONARD, 36494. 3rd Bn Auckland Regiment, NZEF. Killed in action 4 October 1917. Son of Mr and Mrs Frederick Simpson, of Lincoln, Canterbury. 2.

SIMS, Rifleman, ROBERT JOHN, 40725. D Coy 2nd Bn 3rd NZ Rifle Brigade. Killed in action 12 October 1917. Age 21. Son of John and Annie Sims, of Fairlie, Timaru. 9.

SINCLAIR, Serjeant, WALTER GRAHAM, M M, 812134. 1st Bn Otago Regiment, NZEF. Killed in action 12 October 1917. Son of Mr and Mrs Robert Paterson Sinclair, of Browns, Southland, Invercargill. 3.

SLADE, Private, FRANK, 26928. 1st Bn Auckland Regiment, NZEF. Killed in action 3 October 1917. Son of Thomas and Fannie Slade, of Manurewa, Auckland. 2.

SLATTERY, Private, JOHN PATRICK, 22410. 1st Bn Canterbury Regiment, NZEF. Killed in action 12 October 1917. Brother of Mrs Nora Godkin, of Wellington. 3.

SLAYMAKER, Lance Corporal, CHARLES, 25769. 2nd Bn 3rd NZ Rifle Brigade. 12 October 1917. Age 35. Son of Thomas Slaymaker, of 111 High St, Merton, London, England. 8.

SLY, Private, ERNEST LAWRENCE, 47003. 3rd Bn Wellington Regiment, NZEF. Killed in action 4 October 1917. Brother of Mr O.D. Sly, of Jubilee Rd, Ellerslie, Auckland. 7.

SMALL, Lance Corporal, FREDERICK WILLIAM, 38986. 2nd (South Canterbury) Coy 3rd Bn Canterbury Regiment, NZEF. Killed in action 4 October 1917. Age 21. Son of James and Ellen Small. Native of Ashburton. 2.

SMART, Rifleman, WILLIAM, 25/1813. 3rd Bn 3rd NZ Rifle Brigade. Killed in action 12 October 1917. 9.

SMITH, Rifleman, ALBERT, 22378. 3rd Bn 3rd NZ Rifle Brigade. Killed in action 12 October 1917. Son of Mr and Mrs Edward Smith, of 26 Hawke St, New Brighton, Christchurch. 9.

SMITH, Lieutenant, ALBERT DAVID, 14716. 1st Bn 3rd NZ Rifle Brigade. Killed in action 12 October 1917. Age 23. Son of Robert Young Smith and Mary Ann Smith, of 180 High St, Waimate, South Canterbury. 7.

SMITH, Second Lieutenant, ALEXANDER LAING, 24412. 1st Bn Otago Regiment, NZEF. Killed in action 12 October 1917. Son of Mr and Mrs J. Smith, of 'Netherby', Abbotsford, Otago. 3.

SMITH, Rifleman, CROSBIE, 14156. 4th Bn 3rd NZ Rifle Brigade. Killed in action 12 October 1917. Son of Mary Germaine Smith, of Devonport, Auckland, and the late Edward Smith. 9.

SMITH, Private, EDWARD PERCY, 27971. 3rd Bn Canterbury Regiment, NZEF. Died of wounds 6 October 1917. Age 23. Son of Harry and Harriett Smith, of 78 Washington Avenue, Brooklyn, Wellington, New Zealand. Native of Nottingham, England. 3.

SMITH, Second Lieutenant, ERIC SUMMERS, 29702. C Coy 3rd Bn 3rd NZ Rifle Brigade. Killed in action 12 October 1917. Age 22. Son of Frederick and Lucy Helen Smith, of Mornington, Dunedin. 7.

SPENCE, Rifleman, JOHN ROBERT, 39343. 4th Bn 3rd NZ Rifle Brigade. 12 October 1917. Age 27. Son of Robert A. Spence and Mary C. Spence, of Makerhouse, Dounby, Orkney, Scotland. 9.

SPENCE, Second Lieutenant, ROBERT, 24413. 3rd Bn 3rd NZ Rifle Brigade. Killed in action 12 October 1917. Age 38. Son of David and Bridget Spence, of 8 Woodville St, St Albans, Christchurch. 7.

SPRATT, Private, HENRY, 27614. 4th Coy 2nd Bn Otago Regiment, NZEF. Killed in action 12 October 1917. Age 24. Son of Patrick Spratt, of Sutton, Otago Central. 6.

SQUIRE, Rifleman, ERNEST GEORGE, 41936. 2nd Bn 3rd NZ Rifle Brigade. 12 October 1917. Age 23. Son of Sydney and Jessie Squire, of 24 Bradiford, Barnstaple, Devon, England. 9.

STANDEN, Private, SYDNEY, 42228. 1st Bn Wellington Regiment, NZEF. Killed in action 22 October 1917. Age 29. Son of Samuel and Ellen Elizabeth Standen, of Turama Road, Royal Oak, Auckland. Native of Palmerston North. 7.

STAUB, Rifleman, WILLIAM ROBSON, 39907. 3rd Bn 3rd NZ Rifle Brigade. Killed in action 12 October 1917. Age 20. Son of Jacob Alfred and Elizabeth Louise Staub, of Fortunatus St, Connaught Terrace, Brooklyn, Wellington. 9.

STEEDS, Private, PAUL MEREDITH, 12/4095. 2nd Bn Canterbury Regiment, NZEF. Died of wounds 12 October 1917. Age 23. Son of Edwin Playster Steeds and Marian Steeds, of 2 Marina Court, Bexhill-on-Sea, England. 3.

STENSON, Private, NORMAN RALPH, 10179. 1st Bn Canterbury Regiment, NZEF. Killed in action 12 October 1917. Age 22. Son of Edward Frederick and Flora Maude Stenson, of 39 Voelas Rd, Lyttelton. 3.

STEPHEN, Corporal, EDWARD ARTHUR, 4/480. Div Sig Coy NZ Engineers. Killed in action 12 October 1917. Age 24. Son of Alured Gibson Stephen and Eliza Stephen, of 'Orawaiti', Westport, Greymouth. Also served at Gallipoli. 1.

STEVENS, Rifleman, JOSEPH CLARENCE, 44318. 3rd Bn 3rd NZ Rifle Brigade. Killed in action 12 October 1917. Husband of Lucy May Griffen (formerly Stevens), of 461 Palmerston Rd, Gisborne. 9.

STEVENSON, Rifleman, JAMES, 45774. 2nd Bn 3rd NZ Rifle Brigade. Killed in action 12 October 1917. Brother of John Stevenson, of Hokitika, Greymouth. 9.

STEWART, Second Lieutenant, HARRY, 18429. 1st Bn 3rd NZ Rifle Brigade. Killed in action 12 October 1917. Age 37. Son of the late Joseph and Anne Stewart; husband of Nancy Rhoda Stewart, of 85 Rongotai Terrace, Wellington. Native of Govan, Glasgow, Scotland. Served in the South African Campaign. 7.

STEWART, Private, HAROLD STEPHEN DOUGLAS, 37886. 2nd Bn Otago Regiment, NZEF. Killed in action 12 October 1917. Age 21. Son of Jane Elizabeth Rhoda Maud Shalders (formerly Stewart), of Ridgelands, Feilding, Wellington, and the late John Stephen Stewart. 6.

STEWART, Private, JAMES ROY CAMPBELL, 41421. F Coy 3rd Bn Otago Regiment, NZEF. Killed in action 12 October 1917. Age 19. Son of Dugald and Jemima Flora Stewart, of Pahiatua St, Palmerston North, Wellington. 6.

STIRLING, Private, JACK, 25124. No. 3 Coy NZ Machine Gun Corps. Killed in action 4 October 1917. Age 23. Son of Richard Stirling, of Fitzroy House, Wakefield St, Auckland, New Zealand. Native of Colac, Australia. 9.

STOCKHAM, Private, THOMAS WILLIAM, 30658. 3rd Bn Wellington Regiment, NZEF. Killed in action 4 October 1917. Son of Mr and Mrs William Thomas Stockham, of Claude St, St Helier's Bay, Auckland. 7.

STOKES, Private, CLAUDE HAMILTON, 32080. 1st Bn Auckland Regiment, NZEF. Killed in action 5 October 1917. Age 21. Only son of Fredick and Matilda Stokes, of 'Claudeville', Cameron St, Onehunga. 2.

STONEHAM, Corporal, ERIC ARTHUR, 36840. 3rd Bn Otago Regiment, NZEF. Killed in action 4 October 1917. Age 20. Son of Arthur and Mary Ellen Stoneham, of 3 Dornett St, Gisborne. Native of Dunedin. 4.

STRACHAN, Rifleman, GEORGE, 29947. 2nd Bn 3rd NZ Rifle Brigade. Killed in action 12 October 1917. Son of Mr and Mrs Andrew Strachan, of Gore, Invercargill. 9.

STRACK, Second Lieutenant, KARL JUSTUS, 10/2822. 3rd Bn Wellington Regiment, NZEF. Killed in action 4 October 1917. Age 23. Son of Conrad Antony Strack and Clara Emily, his wife, of 10 Falcon St, Roslyn, Dunedin. Native of Hawera, New

Plymouth. 6.

STRATTON, Lance Corporal, WILLIAM JAMES, 15794. 2nd Bn Wellington Regiment, NZEF. Killed in action 4 October 1917. Age 25. Son of George John and Cathrine Sarah Stratton, of Weraroa Rd, Levin, Wellington. 6.

STRINGFELLOW, Private, GEORGE, 41169. 3rd Bn Wellington Regiment, NZEF. Died of wounds 5 October 1917. Age 22. Son of James and Rosina Stringfellow, of 14 Collins St, Addington, Christchurch. Native of Canterbury. 7.

STROUD, Rifleman, WILLIS ROBERT, 46497. 1st Bn 3rd NZ Rifle Brigade. Killed in action 12 October 1917. Age 34. Son of Frederick William and Mary Jane Stroud, of 15 Victoria Crescent, High Park, Ryde, Isle of Wight, England. 9.

STRUTHERS, Private, JAMES REID, 3/1552. NZ Medical Corps. Killed in action 12 October 1917. Husband of Maud Isabella Ellwood (formerly Struthers), of Seacliff, Dunedin. 9.

STUMBLES, Private, ALBERT, 28227. 2nd Bn Wellington Regiment, NZEF. Killed in action 4 October 1917. Son of Mr and Mrs John Stumbles, of Pleasant Point, Timaru. 7.

STURGES, Private, ALFRED, 28601. 3rd Bn Canterbury Regiment, NZEF. Killed in action 5 October 1917. Son of Margaret Sturges, of 3 Wairere Rd, Remuera, Auckland. 3.

SULLIVAN, Rifleman, JACK, 18714. 1st Bn 3rd NZ Rifle Brigade. Killed in action 12 October 1917. Age 22. Son of Patrick Dillon O'sullivan and Mary Sullivan, of Taradale, Hawke's Bay. 9.

SUTHERLAND, Private, CLAIR NELSON, 41118. No. 1 Coy NZ Machine Gun Corps. Killed in action 12 October 1917. Age 21. Son of the Rev. Robert Rose McKay Sutherland and Catherine Juliet Sutherland, of 21 Sheen St, Dunedin. 9.

SUTHERLAND, Private, FRANCIS NICOLL, 8/2827. 1st Bn Otago Regiment, NZEF. Killed in action 1 October 1917. Son of Mrs Catherine Sutherland, of 161 Sprey St, Invercargill. 6.

SUTHERLAND, Private, ROBERT, 26331. 2nd Bn Canterbury Regiment, NZEF. Killed in action 12 October 1917. Age 24. Son of John and Elizabeth Sutherland, of White Cliffs, Canterbury. Native of Glentunnel, Christchurch. 3.

SUTHERLAND, Rifleman, WILLIAM ROBERT, 34166. 3rd Bn 3rd NZ Rifle Brigade. Killed in action 12 October 1917. Son of Mary Dowie (formerly Sutherland), of Palmerston, Otago. 9.

SUTTON, Private, JOHN STAINTON, 23/612. 2nd Bn Otago Regiment, NZEF. Killed in action 10 October 1917. Age 41. Son of John Bennworth Sutton and Margaret (his wife), of Centre Bush, Southland Invercargill. Native of Garryowen, Southland. Served in the South African Campaign. 6.

SUTTON, Rifleman, WILLIAM, 41957. 4th Bn 3rd NZ Rifle Brigade. Killed in action 12 October 1917. 9.

SWENSON, Corporal, JOHN CORNELIUS, 23/2097. E Coy 2nd Bn 3rd NZ Rifle Brigade. Killed in action 12 October 1917. Age 26. Son of Martin and Annie Swenson, of Taihape, Wanganui. 8.

SYLVESTER, Private, WILLIAM ANDREW, 13481. 3rd Bn Wellington Regiment, NZEF. Killed in action 4 October 1917. Age 19. Son of the late Arthur and Charlotte Sylvester, of Taunton, Somerset, England. 7

SYME, Private, CHARLES, 42218. 1st Bn Auckland Regiment, NZEF. Killed in action 20 October 1917. Husband of Kathleen Eleen Bradly (formerly Syme), of Dargaville, Auckland. 2.

SYMOND, Private, ROBERT, 40083. No. 2 Coy 3rd Bn Canterbury Regiment, NZEF. Killed in action 5 October 1917. Husband of Eva Symonds, of 2 Morris St, Marton, Wellington. 3.

TALBOT, Second Lieutenant, ARTHUR, 14037. 2nd Bn Canterbury Regiment, NZEF. Killed in action 12 October 1917. Age 41. Son of John and Emily Talbot, of Temuka; husband of Olivia Anne Talbot, of 55A Evans St, Timaru. 2.

TANSLEY, Private, FRANK, 26333. 2nd Bn Otago Regiment, NZEF. Killed in action 12 October 1917. Son of Annie Tansley, of 107 Dale End, Birmingham, England. 6.

TARBARD, Private, GEORGE, 27983. 1st Bn Canterbury Regiment, NZEF. 2 October 1917. Age 27. Son of the late Alfred and Catherine Tarbard. 3.

TARRANT, Rifleman, CHARLES RICHARD, 17835. 2nd Bn 3rd NZ Rifle Brigade. Killed in action 12 October 1917. Age 25. Son of Kate Tarrant, of 255 Princes St, Hawera, New Plymouth. 9.

TARRANT, Private, HERBERT, 11978. 2nd Bn Canterbury Regiment, NZEF. 12 October 1917. Age 33. Son of Henry and Elizabeth Tarrant. 3.

TATTERSALL, Rifleman, ALBERT, 20262. 4th Bn 3rd NZ Rifle Brigade. Killed in action 12 October 1917. 9.

TATTERSALL, Rifleman, WILLIAM JOSEPH, 38769. 2nd Bn 3rd NZ Rifle Brigade. Killed in action 12 October 1917. Son of William and Elizabeth Tattersall, of 62 Paices Avenue, Dominion Rd, Auckland. 9.

TAVINOR, Private, HENRY GEORGE, 40395. E Coy 1st Bn Auckland Regiment, NZEF. Killed in action 4 October 1917. Age 28. Son of Hannah Tavinor, of Puwera, Whangarei, and the late Albert Tavinor. 2.

TAYLOR, Private, CLAUDE EDWARD, 33477. 3rd Bn Wellington Regiment, NZEF. Killed in action 4 October 1917. Son of Mrs Till Taylor, of 427 Gill St East, New Plymouth. 7.

TAYLOR, Private, EDGAR, 22134. No. 5 Coy NZ Machine Gun Corps. Killed in action 12 October 1917. Age 21. Son of William and Rachel Taylor, of Otara, Invercargill. 9.

TAYLOR, Private, GEORGE, 24/301. 3rd Bn Otago Regiment, NZEF. Killed in action 16 October 1917. Age 25. Son of John and Margaret Taylor, of Fitzroy; husband of Louisa M. Taylor, of Richmond St, Fitzroy, New Plymouth. 6.

TAYLOR, Private, ORTON CECIL, 34172. 3rd Bn Wellington Regiment, NZEF. Killed in action 4 October 1917. Age 26. Son of Isaac Edward and Mary Elizabeth Taylor, of 'Burnside', Frasertown, Hawke's Bay, Napier. 7.

TELFER, Private, DAVID, 36694. D Coy 3rd Bn Otago Regiment, NZEF. Killed in action 4 October 1917. Age 21. Son of William and Emily Telfer, of Mataura, Southland, Invercargill. 6.

TERRY, Serjeant, FRANK, 12/2131. 2nd Bn Auckland Regiment, NZEF. Killed in action 4 October 1917. 1.

TERRY, Private, PERCY EDWARD, 44536. B Coy 2nd Bn Wellington Regiment, NZEF. Killed in action 4 October 1917. Age 21. Son of Albert and Edith Terry, of Nireaha, Eketahuna, Wellington. Enlisted at Pahiatua. 7.

THAYER, Lance Corporal, HENRY ROBERT, 42425. 1st Bn Auckland Regiment, NZEF. Killed in action 4 October 1917. Age 29. Son of Robert Jones Thayer and Elizabeth Esther Thayer, of 177 Hastings St, Napier. 1.

THOMAS, Private, GEOFFREY HAMLIN, 21117. 3rd Bn Auckland Regiment, NZEF. Killed in action 12 October 1917. Son of Mr and Mrs Howard James Thomas, of 'Wenvoe', Whawharua, Otorohanga, Hamilton. 2.

THOMPSON, Corporal, HERBERT, 32798. 3rd Bn 3rd NZ Rifle Brigade. Killed in action 12 October 1917. Age 27. Son of John and Elizabeth Thompson, of 6 Mary Hill Terrace, Mornington, Dunedin. 8.

THOMPSON, Private, HENRY VNATT, 23/1216. 3rd Bn Wellington Regiment, NZEF. Killed in action 20 October 1917. Son of Mr and Mrs James Henry Thompson, of 56 Hankey St, Wellington. 7.

THOMPSON, Private, JAMES, 13131. No. 2 Coy NZ Machine Gun Corps. Killed in action 12 October 1917. Age 25. Husband of Lulu Thompson, of 34 Helen St, South Dunedin. 9.

THOMSON, Private, FRASER JOHN, 39643. 10th Coy 2nd Bn Otago Regiment, NZEF. Killed in action 12 October 1917. Age 21. Son of John and Janet Cameron Thomson, of 7 Matthew St, Dannevirke, Napier. 6.

THOMSON, Serjeant, STANLEY BOWIE, 23/1305. 1st Bn 3rd NZ Rifle Brigade. Killed in action 12 October 1917. Grandson of Emma Harriet Bowie, of 117 Sherbourne St, St Albans, Christchurch. 7.

THORBURN, Private, JOHN, 42594. D Coy 1st Bn Otago Regiment, NZEF. Killed in action 12 October 1917. Son of the late William and Margaret Thorburn, of Waikouaiti, Dunedin; husband of Margaret A. Thorburn, of 35 Nen St, Oamaru. 6.

THORPE, Private, ARTHUR, 8/2161. 10th Coy 1st Bn Otago Regiment, NZEF. 12 October 1917. Age 26. Son of Mr and Mrs Arthur Thorpe, of Yorkshire, England; husband of Mrs E. Mona Thorpe. 6.

TODD, Lance Corporal, HARRY PACKER, 31376. 1st Bn Wellington Regiment, NZEF. Killed in action 21 October 1917. Son of Mr and Mrs David George Todd, of Waite St, Featherston, Wellington. 6.

TOMLINSON, Private, JAMES DANIEL BPANLEY, 31553. 1st Bn Canterbury Regiment, NZEF. Killed in action 12 October 1917. Brother of C.R.F. Tomlinson, of Waimea West, Nelson. 3.

TOMPSETT, Second Lieutenant, NORMAN, 12/2495. 2nd Bn Otago Regiment, NZEF. 12 October 1917. Age 23. Son of Benjamin Tompsett, of 'Castlemaine', Hollington Park, St Leonards-on-Sea, England. 3.

TOOMEY, Private, NICHOLAS EDWARD JOHN, 40393. 3rd Bn Auckland Regiment, NZEF. Killed in action 19 October 1917. Age 22. Son of Edward and Mary Toomey, of Waihi, Thames. 2.

TOSSWILL, Private, WILLIAM WYNDHAM, 12514. 1st Bn Wellington Regiment, NZEF. Killed in action 4 October 1917. Son of Mr and Mrs William Tosswill, of Albany, Auckland. 7.

TOWNSEND, Lance Corporal, SAMUEL HAYDON, 15047. 13th Coy 2nd Bn Canterbury Regiment, NZEF. Killed in action 12 October 1917. Age 39. Son of Priscilla Alice Townsend, of 67 Elizabeth St, Lower Riccarton, Christchurch, New Zealand, and the late Samuel Haydon Townsend. Native of Boxmoor, Herts, England. 2.

TRAILL, Private, JAMES HENRY, 15260. D Coy 2nd Bn Otago Regiment, NZEF. Killed in action 12 October 1917. Age 22. Son of Sarah O'Donnell (formerly Traill), of 152 Dundas St, Dunedin, and the late Mr J.A. Traill. 6.

TROTT, Private, ALFRED, 37891. 2nd Bn Canterbury Regiment, NZEF. Killed in action 12 October 1917. Age 31. Son of Alfred Trott, of 126A Roman Rd, East Ham,

London, England; husband of Beatrice Elizabeth Fowler (formerly Trott), of 190 School Rd, Yardley Wood, Moseley, Birmingham, England. 3.

TUCKER, Rifleman, ERIC CLAUDE, 14886. D Coy 2nd Bn 3rd NZ Rifle Brigade. Killed in action 12 October 1917. Age 28. Son of Sarah Ann Tucker, of West Clive, Napier, and the late Joseph Tucker. 9.

TULLOCH, Private, JOHN ALEXANDER, 45153. 1st Bn Otago Regiment, NZEF. Killed in action 12 October 1917. Brother of Mr W.R.G. Tulloch, of Omeo, Victoria, Australia. 6.

TULLOCH, Private, JOHN CHRISTOPHER, 34754. 1st (Canterbury) Coy 3rd Bn Canterbury Regiment, NZEF. Killed in action 4 October 1917. Son of John and Agnes Tulloch, of New Zealand. 3.

TURNER, Major, WILLIAM WILSON, 23469. 2nd Bn Otago Regiment, NZEF. Killed in action 12 October 1917. Husband of Ann Turner, of Leamington, Cambridge, Waikato, Hamilton. 3.

TWEED, Rifleman, JOHN ORR, 42726. 3rd Bn 3rd NZ Rifle Brigade. Killed in action 12 October 1917. Age 25. Son of Andrew and Margaret Tweed, of Lovell's Flat, Dunedin. 9.

TWISLETON, Corporal, RONALD BURNSALL, 7/2323. 3rd Bn Wellington Regiment, NZEF. Killed in action 4 October 1917. Age 22. Son of Frederick Fiennes Twisleton and Rachel, his wife, of Ashhurst, Wellington. 6.

TYRIE, Rifleman, ALEXANDER MCNAUGHT, 12/1815. 2nd Bn 3rd NZ Rifle Brigade. 12 October 1917. Age 29. Brother of James Tyrie, of 187 High St, Ayr, Scotland. 9.

URE, Corporal, WILLIAM HENRY, 28242. 3rd Bn Wellington Regiment, NZEF. Killed in action 4 October 1917. Son of Mr and Mrs William H. Ure, of Waipiata, Central Otago. 6.

URWIN, Lance Serjeant, FREDERICK CHARLES, 18508. 3rd Bn 3rd NZ Rifle Brigade. Killed in action 12 October 1917. Son of Mr and Mrs Frank Victor Urwin, of Waihopo, North Auckland. 7.

VALLENDER, Private, WALTER, 40090. 2nd Bn Otago Regiment, NZEF. Killed in action 12 October 1917. Age 23. Son of Evan and Susan Vallender, of Rongotea, Feilding, Wellington. 6.

VARNEY, Rifleman, ALFRED CHARLES, 13145. 3rd Bn 3rd NZ Rifle Brigade. Killed in action 12 October 1917. Son of Mrs E. Varney, of 28 Hanover St, Dunedin; husband of Violet Varney, of 27 Harrow St, Dunedin. 9.

VARNEY, Serjeant, ALFRED JAMES FRANCIS, 6/3190. No. 1 Coy 1st Bn Canterbury Regiment, NZEF. Killed in action 12 October 1917. Age 29. Son of Alfred Francis and Phillis Barbara Varney, of 76 London St, Lyttelton, Christchurch. 2.

VAUGHAN, Corporal, OSWALD DE WITT, 11/833. 3rd Bn Wellington Regiment, NZEF. Killed in action 4 October 1917. Age 41. Youngest Son of Mrs E.J. Vaughan, of Rhydd Gardens, Hanley Castle, Worcester, England, and the late Rev. Charles Vaughan. 6.

VAUGHAN, Second Lieutenant, ROBERT PATRICK, 18021. 2nd Bn 3rd NZ Rifle Brigade. Killed in action 12 October 1917. Husband of Lilian Maud Wall (formerly Vaughan), of Railway Rd, Hastings, Napier. 7.

VAVASOUR, Second Lieutenant, GEORGE MARMADUKE, 33106. 2nd Bn 3rd NZ

Rifle Brigade. Killed in action 12 October 1917. Age 26. Son of Henry Dunstan Vavasour and Bertha Eleanor Vavasour, of Ugbrooke Station, Blenheim. Native of Marlborough. 7.

VERCOE, Private, ERIC HENRY, 11558. 1st Bn Auckland Regiment, NZEF. Killed in action 4 October 1917. Son of Mr and Mrs Joseph Lawry Vercoe, of Rangiuru, Te Puke, Thames. 2.

VIALL, Rifleman, SAMUEL ROLAND, 46500. 3rd Bn 3rd NZ Rifle Brigade. Killed in action 12 October 1917. Age 26. Son of Samuel and Edith Mary Viall, of Warkworth, Auckland. 9.

VIEIRA, Rifleman, MANUEL, 26720. 2nd Bn 3rd NZ Rifle Brigade. Killed in action 12 October 1917. Age 22. Son of Manuel and Annie Vieira, of Puketui, Thames. 9.

VINCENT, Lance Corporal, STANLEY VICTOR CARTHEW, 28927. C Coy 2nd Bn Canterbury Regiment, NZEF. Killed in action 12 October 1917. Age 20. Son of Alfred and Eliza Vincent, of 70 Wilson St, Timaru. 2.

WAINE, Private, FREDERICK JOHN WILLIAM, 34757. 2nd Bn Canterbury Regiment, NZEF. Killed in action 12 October 1917. Age 22. Son of Frederick Thomas and Sarah Emily Waine, of 18 Fyfe St, Christchurch. 3.

WALDEN, Private, FREDERICK JAMES, 32265. 1st Bn Otago Regiment, NZEF. Killed in action 12 October 1917. Age 21. Son of Frederick and Susannah Walden, of 808 Lawrence St, Hastings, Hawke's Bay, Napier. 6.

WALDING, Private, ARTHUR, 12/273. 1st Bn Auckland Regiment, NZEF. Killed in action 22 October 1917. Age 23. Son of John and Eliza Walding, of Driving Creek, Coromandel, Auckland. 2.

WALE, Private, ROY ALLAN, 33482. 17th Coy 3rd Bn Wellington Regiment, NZEF. Killed in action 4 October 1917. Age 33. Native of Wellington. Son of the late John Wood Wale and Matilda Alice Wale. 7.

WALLACE, Serjeant, GEORGE, 8/3108. 1st Bn Otago Regiment, NZEF. Killed in action 12 October 1917. Age 28. Son of Jane Wallace, of Selbourne St, Mataura, Southland, Invercargill, and the late William Wallace. 3.

WALLACE, Private, HAROLD JOHN, 36375. 3rd Bn Canterbury Regiment, NZEF. Killed in action 5 October 1917. Age 21. Son of George John and Emma Eliza Wallace, of Timaru. 3.

WALLACE, Rifleman, KENNETH JAMES, 15315. E Coy 2nd Bn 3rd NZ Rifle Brigade. Killed in action 12 October 1917. Age 19. Son of Mary Anne Wallace, of Pukeroro, Hamilton, and the late James Joiner Wallace. 9.

WALLIS, Private, CHARLES, 44040. 1st (Canterbury) Coy 3rd Bn Canterbury Regiment, NZEF. Killed in action 18 October 1917. Age 41. Son of George and Amy Emma Wallis, of Governor's Bay, Canterbury; husband of Lizzie Mary Wallis, of 140 Pages Rd, Christchurch. 3.

WALLIS, Lance Corporal, EDWARD THOMAS BOYES, G/1755. 1st Bn Canterbury Regiment, NZEF. Killed in action 12 October 1917. Son of Mr and Mrs Arnold Philip Wallis, of Kent St, Carterton, Wellington. 2.

WALLIS, Lance Corporal, FRANK DOCKERY, 12/3858. 1st Bn Auckland Regiment, NZEF. Killed in action 23 October 1917. Age 30. Son of Philip and Minnie Wallis, of Short St, Masterton, Wellington. 1.

WALSH, Private, DAVID JAMES, 9/1619. 2nd Bn Otago Regiment, NZEF. Killed in action 12 October 1917. Age 21. Son of John and May Walsh, of Mangapapa,

Gisbome. 6.

WALSH, Private, THOMAS JAMES, 51669. 3rd Bn Canterbury Regiment, NZEF. Killed in action 16 October 1917. Brother of John Walsh, of 3 Lorne St, South Dunedin. 3.

WARD, Private, ANDREW HANNAH, 33046. 1st Bn Otago Regiment, NZEF. Killed in action 12 October 1917. Age 20. Son of Thomas Ward, of Fairfax, Southland, Invercargill, and the late Margaret Ward. Native of Riverton, Invercargill. 6.

WARD, Private, CHARLES RICHARD, 33483. 3rd Bn Wellington Regiment, NZEF. Killed in action 4 October 1917. Age 21. Son of George and Isabella Ward, of James St, Inglewood, Taranaki. 7.

WARD, Private, GEORGE HENRY, 36704. 3rd Bn Wellington Regiment, NZEF. Killed in action 4 October 1917. Age 21. Only son of Henry William and Agnes Thomson Ward, of 15 Millward St, Wanganui East. Native of Dunedin. 7.

WARD, Private, JOHN FRANCIS, 28836. 1st Bn Auckland Regiment, NZEF. Killed in action 4 October 1917. Son of Mr and Mrs John Ward, of Papatoetoe, Auckland. 2.

WARD, Private, ROLAND ALFRED, 24086. 1st Bn Auckland Regiment, NZEF. Killed in action 4 October 1917. Son of Edith Annie Ward, of Remuera, Auckland. 2.

WARD, Lance Corporal, WILLIAM RUEBEN, 10982. 4th Bn 3rd NZ Rifle Brigade. Killed in action 12 October 1917. Son of Mr and Mrs W.H. Ward, of 34 Station Place, Glenhuntly, Victoria, Australia. 8.

WARDROP, Lance Corporal, WILLIAM WEBB, 34957. 4th Coy 3rd Bn Otago Regiment, NZEF. Killed in action 4 October 1917. Age 24. Son of Robert Service Wardrop and Charlotte, his wife, of Dunedin, New Zealand. Native of Melbourne, Australia. 4.

WARDS, Private, ROBERT, 39368. 2nd Bn Otago Regiment, NZEF. Killed in action 12 October 1917. Age 30. Son of David Fubister Wards and Catherine, his wife, of Tuturau, Mataura, Invercargill. 6.

WARNER, Private, HARRY, 45938. 1st Bn Wellington Regiment, NZEF. Killed in action 4 October 1917. Son of Kate Elizabeth Warner, of 9 Holloway Rd, Wellington. 7.

WARRINGTON, Serjeant, HENRY FRANK, 10/2788. 3rd Bn Auckland Regiment, NZEF. Killed in action 4 October 1917. Age 23. Son of Annie Eliza Warrington, of Opotiki, Bay of Plenty, and the late Henry Warrington. Also served at Gallipoli. 1.

WASLEY, Lance Corporal, ALBERT SAMUEL, 23460. 1st Bn Auckland Regiment, NZEF. Killed in action 4 October 1917. Son of Mr and Mrs Edwin Wasley, of Auckland. 1.

WATERS, Private, CECIL, 22386. 1st Bn Otago Regiment, NZEF. Killed in action 1 October 1917. 6.

WATKINSON, Lance Corporal, PERCY, 11140. 2nd Bn Canterbury Regiment, NZEF. Killed in action 12 October 1917. Age 27. Son of Joseph and Sarah Ann Watkinson, of 18 Sherwood Rd, Mount Eden, Auckland. 2.

WATSON, Second Lieutenant, NORMAN FORRESTER, 9/96. 1st Bn Otago Regiment, NZEF. Killed in action 12 October 1917. Age 30. Son of John and Helen Watson, of 'Bellvue', Port Chalmers, Dunedin. Also served at Gallipoli. 3.

WATSON, Private, ROBERT, 51204. 1st Bn Canterbury Regiment, NZEF. Died of wounds 12 October 1917. Age 29. Son of Robert and Flora Ann Cameron Grant Watson, of 5 Horne St, Wellington. 3.

WATSON, Private, ROSEWALL JAMES, 8/2493. 4th Coy 2nd Bn Otago Regiment, NZEF. Killed in action 12 October 1917. Age 22. Son of Robert Harry and Mary Elizabeth Watson, of 53 Douglas St, St. Kilda, Dunedin. Native of Oamaru. Also served at Gallipoli. 6.

WATSON, Private, THOMAS, 45158. 1st Bn Otago Regiment, NZEF. Killed in action 12 October 1917. Age 50. Son of Thomas and Eleanor Watson. Native of Invercargill. 6.

WATTS, Lance Serjeant, FREDERICK JAMES, 15056. 2nd Bn Canterbury Regiment, NZEF. Killed in action 12 October 1917. Husband of Mrs R.W. Watts, of Parnell, Auckland. 2.

WATTS, Rifleman, WILLIAM JAMES, 25657. C Coy 2nd Bn 3rd NZ Rifle Brigade. Killed in action 12 October 1917. Age 22. Son of John and Theresa Watts, of 9 Kennedy Rd, Napier. 9.

WAY, Rifleman, PEARCE HARMAN, 48119. 2nd Bn 3rd NZ Rifle Brigade. Killed in action 12 October 1917. Age 29. Son of George Edward and Emma Kate Way, of 20 Helmore's Rd, Fendalton, Christchurch. 9.

WEBB, Rifleman, GEORGE, 31914. 3rd Bn 3rd NZ Rifle Brigade. Killed in action 12 October 1917. Age 27. Son of George and Ellen Webb Native of Hamua, Wellington. 9.

WEBB, Private, THOMAS CHARLES, 39920. 3rd Bn Wellington Regiment, NZEF. Killed in action 4 October 1917. Son of Mr and Mrs Thomas Charles Webb, of 276 Cuba St, Wellington. 7.

WEENINK, Rifleman, HENRY WILLIAM, 41202. B Coy 1st Bn 3rd NZ Rifle Brigade. Killed in action 12 October 1917. Age 32. Son of Harry and Elizabeth Weenink, of Karoro, Greymouth. 9.

WEIR, Private, JOHN GEORGE HENRY, 32407. 3rd Bn Canterbury Regiment, NZEF. Killed in action 4 October 1917. Brother of M.J.R. Weir, of 30 Marlborough St, Riccarton, Christchurch. 3.

WELLINGS, Private, WILLIAM, 11751. 1st Bn Canterbury Regiment, NZEF. Killed in action 12 October 1917. Age 31. Husband of Jane Wellings, of 20 Olliviers Rd, Christchurch, New Zealand. Native of Warrington, England. 3.

WELLS, Private, HARRY, 24495. 1st Bn Auckland Regiment, NZEF. Killed in action 4 October 1917. Son of Mr and Mrs John Wells, of Kaingaroa North, Auckland. 2.

WELLS, Private, HENRY CHARLES, 41687. 1st Bn Otago Regiment, NZEF. Killed in action 12 October 1917. Age 23. Son of Charles and Mary Wells, of Warea, Taranaki. 6.

WELSH, Rifleman, JOHN, 21923. 2nd Bn 3rd NZ Rifle Brigade. Killed in action 12 October 1917. Husband of Mary Matilda Welsh, of 306 Hazeldean Rd, Sydenham, Christchurch. 9.

WEST, Corporal, HERBERT JAMES, 14893. 1st Bn Auckland Regiment, NZEF. Killed in action 4 October 1917. Son of Mr and Mrs Frank Northey West, of 41 New North Rd, Kingsland, Auckland. 1.

WESTENRA, Private, FREDERICK ALAN, 32481. No. 1 Coy 3rd Bn Canterbury Regiment, NZEF. Killed in action 16 October 1917. Age 38. Son of Arthur Henry and Julia Westenra, of Akaroa, Canterbury. 3.

WHEARTY, Rifleman, PATRICK, 13159. 1st Bn 3rd NZ Rifle Brigade. Killed in action 12 October 1917. Son of Mr and Mrs Patrick Whearty, of Long Beach, Ashburton, Christchurch. 9.

WHEELER, Rifleman, CHARLES DAVID, 40734. 2nd Bn 3rd NZ Rifle Brigade. Killed in action 12 October 1917. Son of Phoebe Wheeler, of 37 Stafford St, Timaru. 9.

WHELHAM, Private, ASHLEY ROY, 26353. C Coy 2nd Bn Otago Regiment, NZEF. Killed in action 12 October 1917. Age 23. Son of Arthur and Mary Whelham, of Takaka, Nelson. 6.

WHITAKER, Rifleman, FRANK SILK, 2511840. 3rd Bn 3rd NZ Rifle Brigade. Killed in action 12 October 1917. Husband of Agnes Harriet Whitaker, of Selwyn St, Onehunga, Auckland. 9.

WHITE, Private, DONALD, 53297. 2nd Bn Otago Regiment, NZEF. Killed in action 12 October 1917. Son of Mr and Mrs Adam White, of Wild Bush, Riverton, Southland, Invercargill. 6.

WHITE, Private, ERIC RAYMOND, 40404. 1st Bn Auckland Regiment, NZEF. Killed in action 4 October 1917. Age 21. Son of Albert and Ethel White, of 1 William St, Devonport, Auckland. 2.

WHITE, Private, GEORGE DALY, 10/2358. 1st Coy NZ Machine Gun Corps. Killed in action 4 October 1917. Son of Mr and Mrs Thomas White, of 7 Buchanan St, Timaru. 9.

WHITE, Second Lieutenant, KENNETH ROBERT, 14726. 1st Bn Auckland Regiment, NZEF. Killed in action 4 October 1917. Son of David and Catherine Ann White, of 61 Calliope Rd, Devonport, Auckland. 1.

WHITE, Lance Corporal, NORMAN CHARLES, 7/2578. 1st Bn Wellington Regiment, NZEF. Killed in action 4 October 1917. Age 27. Son of William and Mary White, of Otane, Hawke's Bay, Napier. 6.

WHITE, Corporal, RALPH, 14518. 2nd Bn Auckland Regiment, NZEF. Killed in action 4 October 1917. Age 36. Son of Robert and Janet White, of 5 Belmont Terrace, Kirkintilloch, Scotland. Served in the South African Campaign with 2nd Bn Scots Guards. 1.

WHITEHORN, Private, WALTER KNYVETT, 51584. 3rd Bn Auckland Regiment, NZEF. Died of wounds 15 October 1917. Son of Mary B. Whitehorn, of Otaki, Wellington. 2.

WHITFIELD, Private, PERCY PRESTON, 44614. 3rd Bn Canterbury Regiment, NZEF. 9 October 1917. Age 38. Son of Francis and Annie Whitfield, of Bentham, Lancaster, England. 3.

WHITING, Private, ALFRED, 42251. 1st Bn Auckland Regiment, NZEF. Killed in action 22 October 1917. Son of Mr and Mrs Joseph Whiting, of Bunnythorpe, Palmerston North. 2.

WHITWELL, Private, BEAUMONT, 47491. 1st Bn Wellington Regiment, NZEF. Killed in action 4 October 1917. Husband of Mrs L.M. Whitwell, of Eastbourne, Wellington. 7.

WHYTE, Private, ROBERT HOLMES, 14174. 1st Bn Canterbury Regiment, NZEF. Killed in action 12 October 1917. Age 22. Son of James Heron Whyte and Ann, his wife, of 15 Clyde St, Timaru. 3.

WILD, Private, HARVEY, 24259. No. 2 Coy 1st Bn Canterbury Regiment, NZEF. Killed in action 12 October 1917. Age 27. Son of the late William and Charlotte Wild. Native of Waimate, Timaru. 3.

WILDEY, Lance Corporal, MILTON, 813114. 1st Bn Otago Regiment, NZEF. Killed in action 12 October 1917. 4.

WILKIE, Private, DAVID HOWARD, 10/3429. 2nd Bn Wellington Regiment, NZEF.

Killed in action 4 October 1917. Son of Emma Wilkie, of 21 Elizabeth St, Wellington. 7.

WILLIAMS, Corporal, LAURY SALTER, D C M, 25765. 2nd Bn 3rd NZ Rifle Brigade. Killed in action 12 October 1917. Son of the late T.R. Williams, of Russell, Auckland. 8.

WILLIAMS, Rifleman, WILLIAM HENRY, 42441. 3rd Bn 3rd NZ Rifle Brigade. Killed in action 12 October 1917. Age 27. Son of James and Amelia Williams, of 77 Orakei Rd, Remuera, Auckland; husband of Grace Williams. 9.

WILLIAMSON, Lance Corporal, FRANCIS, 23/1876. 10th Coy 2nd Bn Otago Regiment, NZEF. Killed in action 12 October 1917. Age 32. Son of Harry and Elizabeth Williamson, of Townsend St, Mortlake, Victoria; Australia. 4.

WILLS, Lance Corporal, LESLIE JAMES, 30415. 3rd Bn Wellington Regiment, NZEF. Killed in action 4 October 1917. Son of Mr and Mrs J.D. Wills, of Lake Rd, Hawera, New Plymouth. 6.

WILLSTEED, Lance Corporal, CHARLES EDGAR, 34766. No. 1 Coy 3rd Bn Canterbury Regiment, NZEF. Killed in action 4 October 1917. Son of the late W.S. Willsteed, of Christchurch. 2.

WILSON, Private, ALBERT JERVIS, 32491. 1st Bn Canterbury Regiment, NZEF. Killed in action 12 October 1917. Son of Mr and Mrs J. Wilson, of 51 Sherbourne St, St Albans, Christchurch. 3.

WILSON, Private, HENRY, 34953. 3rd Bn Otago Regiment, NZEF. Killed in action 4 October 1917. Brother of Andrew Wilson, of Shag Point, Otago. 6.

WILSON, Private, HUGH, 36714. 3rd Bn Wellington Regiment, NZEF. Killed in action 4 October 1917. Age 37. Son of John and Isabella Wilson, of Scotland; husband of Janet Wilson, of Stirling, Otago, New Zealand. Native of Bowmore, Isle of Islay, Scotland. 7.

WILSON, Private, HARRY WILLIAM, 25763. No. 4 Coy NZ Machine Gun Corps. Killed in action 4–5 October 1917. Age 21. Son of James Edward and Margaret Wilson, of Clevedon, Auckland. 9.

WILSON, Private, JOHN, 29893. 1st Bn Otago Regiment, NZEF. Killed in action 12 October 1917. Son of Mr and Mrs G. Wilson, of 'Woodside', Mabel Bush, Southland, Invercargill. 6.

WILSON, Private, JOSEPH ADDISON YOUNG, 8/2764. 1st Bn Otago Regiment, NZEF. Killed in action 12 October 1917. Son of Mr and Mrs Henry Peter Wilson, of Abbotsford, Green Island, Dunedin. 6.

WILSON, Private, MICHAEL, 40416. 2nd Bn Wellington Regiment, NZEF. Killed in action 4 October 1917. Son of Alice Wilson, of 15 Wanganui Avenue, Ponsonby, Auckland. 7.

WILSON, Private, ROBERT ALEXANDER, 15277. 2nd Bn Otago Regiment, NZEF. Died of wounds 12 October 1917. Son of Mrs A. Wilson, of Omarama, Otago. 6.

WINTER, Private, WILLIAM, 45291. 1st Bn Canterbury Regiment, NZEF. Killed in action 12 October 1917. Son of Mr and Mrs J. Winter, of Waenga, Otago Central. 3.

WINTER-EVANS, Lieutenant Colonel, ALFRED, D S 0, 26/11. 3rd Bn 3rd NZ Rifle Brigade. Killed in action 12 October 1917. 7.

WISHART, Lance Corporal, JAMES SMAIL, 27636. 2nd Bn Otago Regiment, NZEF. Killed in action 12 October 1917. Age 25. Son of David and Mary Ann Wishart, of Ryal Bush, Southland, Invercargill. 4.

WOOD, Corporal, EDWARD HENRY, 12/3516. 2nd Bn Auckland Regiment, NZEF.

12 October 1917. Age 33. Son of Mr and Mrs E.H. Wood, of 23 Melbourne Rd, Leyton, London, England. 1.

WOODALL, Private, ANDREW DAVID, 40426. 1st Bn Auckland Regiment, NZEF. Killed in action 22 October 1917. Son of Mr and Mrs Alfred Oliver Woodall, of 15 Cheltenham Terrace, Devonport, Auckland. 2.

WOODS, Private, REUBEN, 16034. 3rd Bn Auckland Regiment, NZEF. Killed in action 4 October 1917. Son of Mr and Mrs William Thomas Woods, of 'Willowbank', East Tamaki Auckland. 2.

WORNER, Serjeant, ALEXANDER, 14725. 12th (Nelson) Coy 2nd Bn Canterbury Regiment, NZEF. Killed in action 12 October 1917. Age 27. Husband of Elizabeth Jane Worner, of Dunbeath St, Blenheim. 2.

WORNER, Corporal, GEORGE WILLIAM, 31758. 2nd Bn Auckland Regiment, NZEF. Killed in action 4 October 1917. Son of Mrs F.M.C. Smith (formerly Worner), of 123 Ilam Rd, Fendalton, Christchurch. 1.

WRIGHT, Rifleman, FREDRICK BALLINTINE, 23/1248. 3rd Bn 3rd NZ Rifle Brigade. Killed in action 12 October 1917. Age 24. Son of Thomas John and Annie Wright, of Collingwood, Nelson; husband of Frances E.S. McConnachie (formerly Wright), of 8 Rankeilor St, South Dunedin. 9.

WRIGHT, Private, SEPTIMUS EVELYN, 32489. 1st Bn Canterbury Regiment, NZEF. Killed in action 2 October 1917. Age 44. Son of Fortunatus Evelyn Wright and Ellen Wright; husband of Grace Ida Beryl Wright, of 'Lethan', Wanganui. Native of Christchurch. 3.

YOUNG, Private, DAVID, 22150. 2nd Bn Otago Regiment, NZEF. Killed in action 12 October 1917. Son of Alexander Young, of Main Rd, Green Island, Dunedin. 6.

YOUNG, Private, JOHN, 22151. 2nd Bn Otago Regiment, NZEF. Killed in action 12 October 1917. Age 33. Son of William Young, of 9 Cranley St, Tainui, Dunedin and the late Jessie Young. 6.

YOUNG, Private, ROBERT, 39385. 13th Coy 2nd Bn Otago Regiment, NZEF. Killed in action 12 October 1917. Age 28. Son of the late John Rose Smith Young and Margaret Young. Native of Arthurton, Otago. 6.

YOUNG, Rifleman, WILLIAM EDWARD, 20593. 3rd Bn 3rd NZ Rifle Brigade. Killed in action 12 October 1917. Brother of Samuel H. Young, of Bulls, Wanganui. 9.

YOUNG, Rifleman, WILLIAM SCOTT, 15318. 1st Bn 3rd NZ Rifle Brigade. Killed in action 12 October 1917. Son of Elizabeth Emma Readford (formerly Young), of 33 Ardmore Rd, Herne Bay, Auckland. 9.

SELECT BIBLIOGRAPHY

Primary Material

Three main centres provided primary source material for this study of Passchendaele: the Alexander Turnbull Library in Wellington, the National Archives, also in Wellington, and the Kippenberger Military Archive and Research Library at Waiouru. Of these centres, the records held by the Alexander Turnbull Library proved the most useful. A search using their Tapuhi computer programme revealed over 190 separate records of Passchendaele in the Manuscripts and Records Section, while much useful information also surfaced in the Oral History Centre. The staff of both these sections of the Alexander Turnbull Library could not be more helpful in the assistance they provide researchers, and the library is a 'must' for those working in any field of New Zealand history.

Secondary Material

C.E.W. Bean, The Official History of Australia in the War of 1914–1918. Volume IV The AIF in France: 1917, Angus and Robertson, Sydney, 1933.

N. Boyack, Behind the Lines. The Lives of New Zealand Soldiers in the First World War, Allen & Unwin and Port Nicholson Press, Wellington, 1989.

O. Burton, The Silent Division. New Zealanders at the Front:1914–1919, Angus and Robertson, Sydney, 1935.

A.D. Carbery, The New Zealand Medical Service in the Great War 1914–18, Whitcombe and Tombs, Auckland, 1924.

N. Cave, Ypres. Passchendaele. The Fight for the Village, Leo Cooper, London, 1997.

G. Chapman, Vain Glory, Cassell and Company, London, 1937.

Brig. Sir J. Edmonds, History of the Great War. Military Operations

France and Belgium 1917 Volume II 7th June–10th November. Messines and Third Ypres (Passchendaele), HMSO, London, 1948.

J. Keegan, The First World War, Hutchinson, London, 1998.

Peter H. Liddle, (ed.) Passchendaele in Perspective. The Third Battle of Ypres, Leo Cooper, London, 1997.

C. McCarthy, The Third Ypres Passchendaele. The Day-by-Day Account, Arms & Armour Press, London, 1995.

L. Macdonald, They Called it Passchendaele, Penguin Books, London, 1993.

R. Prior and T. Wilson, Passchendaele. The Untold Story, Yale University Press, London.

C. Pugsley, On the Fringe of Hell, Hodder and Stoughton, Auckland, 1991.

G. Serle, John Monash, Melbourne University Press, Melbourne, 1982.

H. Stewart, The New Zealand Division 1916–1919, Whitcombe and Tombs, Auckland, 1921.

H. Strachan, (ed.) The Oxford Illustrated History of the First World War, Oxford University Press, Oxford, 1998.

J. Terraine, The Western Front 1914–18, Arrow Books, London, 1964.

J. Terraine, The Road to Passchendaele, Leo Cooper, London, 1977.

T. Travers, The Killing Ground. The British Army, the Western Front and the Emergence of Modern Warfare, 1900–1918, Allen & Unwin, London, 1987.

D. Winter, Haig's Command. A Reassessment, Viking, London, 1991.

J. Winter and B. Baggett, 1914–18. The Great War and the Shaping of the 20th Century, BBC Books, London, 1996.

L. Wolff, In Flanders Fields. The 1917 Campaign, Longman, Green and Co., London, 1958.

INDEX